TO BE AN IMMIGRANT

TO BE AN IMMIGRANT

Kay Deaux

Russell Sage Foundation
New York

The Russell Sage Foundation

The Russell Sage Foundation, one of the oldest of America's general purpose foundations, was established in 1907 by Mrs. Margaret Olivia Sage for "the improvement of social and living conditions in the United States." The Foundation seeks to fulfill this mandate by fostering the development and dissemination of knowledge about the country's political, social, and economic problems. While the Foundation endeavors to assure the accuracy and objectivity of each book it publishes, the conclusions and interpretations in Russell Sage Foundation publications are those of the authors and not of the Foundation, its Trustees, or its staff. Publication by Russell Sage, therefore, does not imply Foundation endorsement.

Library of Congress Cataloging-in-Publication Data

Deaux, Kay.
    To be an immigrant / Kay Deaux.
        p. cm.
    Includes bibliographical references (p. 222) and index.
    ISBN 10: 0-87154-086-X
    ISBN 13: 978-0-87154-086-7
    1. Immigrants—United States—Social conditions. 2. Immigrants—United States—Psychology. 3. Immigrants—United States—Public opinion. 4. Ethnicity—United States. 5. United States—Emigration and immigration—Public opinion. 6. Public opinion—United States. I. Title.

JV6475.D43 2006
304.8'73—dc22

2006042337

Text design by Genna Patacsil.

RUSSELL SAGE FOUNDATION
112 East 64th Street, New York, New York 10021
10   9   8   7   6   5   4   3   2   1

To Sam Glucksberg, my favorite immigrant

Contents

About the Author |

KAY DEAUX is Distinguished Professor of Psychology at the Graduate Center of the City University of New York.

Acknowledgments |

MY INTEREST IN immigration surely started long before I became a social scientist. As is true of so many of us who live in immigrant destinations, stories of the "old country" were part of early socialization. In my case, that old country was Finland, from which my paternal grandparents came to the United States through Ellis Island in the early years of the twentieth century. Although the stories were fewer in number and sparser in detail than I now wish they had been, the tangible evidence of photographs, fabrics, and foods were always part of the experience of visiting my grandmother. She spoke almost no English, and thus the Finnish language too was part of what I remember as a child. My father exemplified assimilation, making little reference to his origins and abandoning the language once his mother died. My uncle, in contrast, represented a different path, maintaining a social network with the Finnish community, even as he developed a successful mainstream architecture practice. It is from him that I have a two-century genealogy of the Finnish family line—though written entirely in Finnish, a language I never learned beyond the few phrases I used to speak to my grandmother as a child.

My professional interest in immigration is much more recent. Although the social psychological perspective and concepts that I bring to bear have been honed over several decades of practice, their application to the phenomena of immigration took shape only after I moved to New York City in 1987. New York is a city defined by its immigrant population, both internal and external migration, and the people and the places of the city speak volumes about immigrant experience, both present and past. The waves of immigration and the patterns of settlement have of course been documented extensively. Yet as I thought more about these patterns and trends, I began to see how the perspective of a social psychologist could add to our understanding and appreciation of the immigrant experience. And so the idea of this book was born.

Critical to the conceptualization and the tangible beginning of this project was the year that I spent as a Visiting Scholar at the Russell Sage Foundation. The history of the foundation's support of work in the field of immigration, under the leadership of Eric Wanner, is well known and the climate of the foundation is one that stimulates and expands one's understanding of the many forces at work to shape the lives of immigrants to the United States. I am grateful to all of the scholars and the staff members who were part of my experience that year.

Over the past few years, many people have advised and informed me as I have been writing this book. Three years ago I tried out some early versions of chapters in a course on immigration that I taught at the CUNY Graduate Center. I value the feedback that I received from the students in that class. Throughout my time at the Graduate Center I have benefited from the stories and experiences of my students, many of whom are both living and studying the immigrant experience themselves. Our ongoing research seminar on immigration continues to introduce new information and new perspectives, and I thank all who have been part of that ongoing conversation. Discussions and interactions with other immigration scholars at the CUNY Graduate Center, in particular Nancy Foner and Phil Kasinitz, have allowed me to cross disciplinary boundaries much more easily than I could otherwise have done. Many people have been willing to read portions of the book and offer helpful feedback. In particular, I want to acknowledge Nida Bikmen, Frances Cherry, Victoria Esses, Susan Fiske, Sam Glucksberg, Susan Meiklejohn, Suzanne Ouellette, Patricia Ruiz-Navarro, Taryn Tang, Teceta Thomas, Debora Upegui-Hernandez, and Shaun Wiley. Reviews of the entire manuscript from Tom Pettigrew and from an anonymous reviewer gave me very useful suggestions for final revisions. At Russell Sage, Suzanne Nichols was supportive at every step of the process. And, finally, my special thanks to Sam Glucksberg, who joins the pantheon of long-suffering and mostly good-spirited POAs—partners of authors who are engaged in what sometimes seems to be a writing process without end. He is surely my favorite immigrant.

Kay Deaux

Chapter One | Introduction

[Approximately] 34 million foreign-born people lived in the United States in 2002 . . . with the size of the U.S.-born second generation numbering around 32 million, so that immigrants and their children together totaled almost 66 million people, or about 23 percent of the U.S. population.

—Bean, Lee, Batalova, and Leach (2004)

Overall, respondents are more likely to be against immigration than in favor of it. When forced to choose between two positions, a majority of respondents said that we should "strictly limit" immigration (58.1 percent) rather than "keep our doors open" (41.9 percent).

—Mizrahi (2005)

I would like to speak as American people do. It's my dream. Sometimes I'm thinking, when am I going to think like American people?

—Shalamova (2004)

FROM EACH OF these voices of immigration—the dispassionate statistical accounts of aggregated movement of people from one country to another, the distilled summaries of attitude surveyors, and the often fervent statements from immigrants themselves—we learn something about the phenomenon of integration, but from none do we grasp a full picture. The story of immigration is one of tremendous scope, spanning centuries, continents, and diverse ethnic origins. In its magnitude, immigration raises questions that run the gamut from individual motives to international policies. Over the years many social scientists have devoted their energies to understanding parts of the picture, from the Chicago sociologists in the early twentieth century (perhaps most notably depicted in *The Polish Peasant in Europe and America*) to the rapidly developing coterie of immigration researchers at the beginning of the twenty-first century (Hirschman, Kasinitz, and DeWind 1999). Hundreds of books and thousands of articles have reported on some aspect of the immigration story.

Given this plenty, one might wonder what remains to be explored. From my perspective, despite the considerable work that has been done, unanswered—and indeed, in many cases, unasked—questions about the experience of immigration remain. At the risk of oversimplification, our current understandings of immigration can be said to be most thoroughly analyzed from two quite different perspectives. On the one side, demographers and other social scientists have extensively charted the large-scale movements of people from one country to another, and in some cases within a single country—in contemporary China, for example, where the massive movement of people from rural areas to major cities are being observed. Using the categorical tools of their trade, they have compared generational, ethnic, and (less frequently) gender groups on outcomes such as employment and education. From these accounts, we learn much about broad-gauge patterns and trends, about differences between groups from different countries and different areas of the world, and about generational differences in the achievements of immigrant populations. Yet, as Suzanne Model has said, "census analysis cannot uncover human motives" (2001, 79).

The perspective that emerges from autobiographies, journalistic accounts, and some ethnographies speaks more directly to these motivational issues. In this ever-increasing stock of stories, with their mixture of pain and humor and challenge, we gain a more vivid sense of the individual experience—of the choices, the obstacles, the opportunities, and the accomplishments. In these accounts we have a much greater sense of the immigration experience as a dynamic process rather than an easily tabulated change of location. So too do we begin to appreciate the importance of the context into which an immigrant comes and the ways in which the features of that context—the social networks, the opportunity structures, the confrontations with hostile or supportive members of resident host communities—play an important role in the overall experience. Yet here as well there are some limitations. Focusing exclusively on the individual case does not allow us to assess the generality of that experience or to explore the ways in which that experience could be altered by changed circumstances. My goal in this book is to take both of these broad perspectives into account and at the same time offer a new framework for understanding what it is to be an immigrant, a framework that is more individual than the demographer's and more general than the autobiographer's.

"Ask a different question and you may get the answer you want."
—Chinese fortune cookie

Different paradigms and different intellectual traditions bring to an area of investigation their unique lenses, which shape both the questions and the answers that emerge (Morawska 2003). To a demographer, for example, the categories of census reports become a key predictor (or independent variable, in the language of experimentation). Similarly, outcomes of interest are those that are represented in available quantitative records, such as rates of employment, levels of education, or indices of residential segregation. Anthropologists focus their attention on specific societies, locating patterns of behavior in a specific time and space and seeking to characterize the folkways of a particular society through observations gained by participating in the cultural milieu. More individualized accounts are adopted by those who speak to individual immigrants: both questions and answers are different, as narrative account takes precedence over quantitative indices. Family members, people in neighborhoods, churches, and workplaces, letters sent home—these are some of the building blocks of the storyteller. One of the earliest works in the immigration literature—*The Polish Peasant in Europe and America*—made rich use of the letters sent between immigrants to the United States and their families back in Poland.

I come to the topic of immigration as a social psychologist with a different set of paradigms and a different intellectual tradition, with the goal of exploring the domain that lies between the demographic category and the first-person account. Following the guidance offered me in a Chinese fortune cookie, I hope that in posing some different questions about the immigrant experience, I will reveal some new answers that will interest all who think about immigration today. As a psychologist, I pay attention to the perspective of the individual immigrant, as he or she views both the self and the surrounding society. As a social psychologist, I always consider the context in which people operate and negotiate their lives—contexts that include not only the immediate social and physical surroundings, but cultural belief systems and political and economic realities as well. Thus, the theoretical framework that I use throughout this book is one of persons in contexts. Such a framework gives priority neither to the individual as sole agent nor to the environment as sole determinant. Rather, the intersection of the two becomes the place of analytic exploration. Almost as a corollary of this assumption, I arrive at no single description of the immigration experience. Different individuals, as members of different groups, arrive in different cultural and historical contexts, and the ways in which their experience plays out depends on the mixture of elements.

A central concept in my analysis is the socially constructed identities of immigrants themselves. Although such identities are in some respects intensely personal, insofar as they are part of the way in which a person sees him- or herself, they are at the same time shaped by the social realities of the society in which the person lives. Thus factors as broad as cultural beliefs and as immediate as daily interactions with members of other ethnic groups shape the identity of the individual. To be an immigrant is to be part of this socially embedded experiential world.

I also assume that immigration is both a dynamic and a symbolic process rather than a discrete event. Immigration is an experience that begins before people move away from their country of origin and that continues long after they arrive in a new country. Immigration is not a "done deal" but instead a part of one's life that continues to have relevance in years and indeed generations to come. Here is where issues of meaning, of expectation and of memory, must be considered as well as the processes of active identity negotiation.

ELEMENTS OF THE ANALYSIS

In figure 1.1, I offer a general framework for the discussions that follow. This framework is adapted from a model of personality and social structure developed by Thomas Pettigrew (1997), whose approach is wholly consistent with the person in context approach I adopt. Three levels of analysis are considered, what Pettigrew terms the macro, meso, and micro levels. The macro level describes events and phenomena associated with the larger social structure—with the institutions, organizations, and cultural representations of a society. At the micro level is the individual—the person whose attitudes, values, motivations, and actions are the ultimate concern of most psychologists. Between these two levels of analysis is what Pettigrew terms a meso level, a point of focus that links the individual to the social system. Here is where social interaction takes place, as people engage one another and, in so doing, transmit their own positions and are impacted by the attitudes and behaviors of others. The meso level thus serves a critical mediational role, the vehicle by which the macro events in a society become represented in the individual psyches of its members and, from the other direction, by which the actions of individuals have an impact on the larger society. It is here that a social psychology of immigration makes its major contributions.

Let me describe more specifically how this general model can be applied to the analysis of immigration. At the macro level of social structure, I look to the political, demographic, and social factors that define the climate of immigration in a given society. Some aspects of this context, such as political policies and demographic patterns of immigration flow, are

Figure 1.1   Basic Elements of an Immigration Analysis

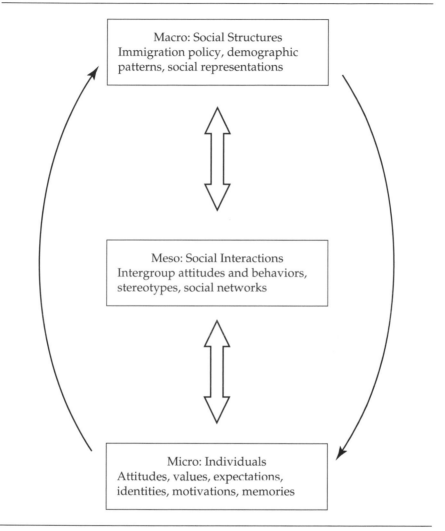

Macro: Social Structures
Immigration policy, demographic
patterns, social representations

Meso: Social Interactions
Intergroup attitudes and behaviors,
stereotypes, social networks

Micro: Individuals
Attitudes, values, expectations,
identities, motivations, memories

Source: Adapted from Pettigrew (1997).

primarily the domain of political scientists and demographers, respectively; yet insofar as they are part of the lived experience of immigrants, they must be considered in a psychological analysis as well. Policy and demographics are clearly interrelated: which people immigrate to a country and how many people immigrate depend directly on the specifics of political policy and legislation (for an analysis of Mexican immigration that emphasizes the interrelationships, see Massey, Durand, and Malone 2002). Further, it can be argued that the relationship between these two components is bidirectional. The influence of policy on immigration numbers is obvious, but it is also true that patterns of immigration can affect subsequent policy, mediated by the influence of the social and political attitudes of the citizenry.

Social representations are introduced as another aspect of the macro level of analysis. Here the emphasis is distinctly social psychological—a concern with the shared images that people have about immigration in their society. Is the dominant image one of a melting pot, as has been the tradition in the United States? Or does the prevailing image place more emphasis on maintaining cultural diversity, as is characteristic of Canada? As suggested by the Canadian case, in which diversity is official federal policy, social representations are intimately related to both demographics and doctrine. Policies are, at their roots, a reflection of the norms and values of a society. At the same time, a society's representations of immigrants are influenced by demographic realities—who is coming, how many are coming, and what political and economic challenges they present. Not surprisingly, then, social representations are considered to be a dynamic rather than static element—a process of representing as well as the representation itself (Moscovici 1988).

Both policies and social representations can have a direct impact on the individual immigrant—a visa granted, for example, or an image of the host country presented to the immigrant reader in a newspaper or television show. Many macro-level factors are filtered, however, through actions and interactions at what I am calling the meso level of analysis. Depicted at the meso level in figure 1.1 are some of the many forms of social interaction that operate between the individual and society. Social attitudes, for example, encompass a set of beliefs about both immigration policy and immigrants themselves that are more sharply articulated than general social representations of the phenomena. At a more specific level, the concept of group stereotypes is another element of the social context. People not only hold beliefs about the characteristics and contributions of immigrants in general, but also have attitudes about specific groups of immigrants. These attitudes and stereotypes are communicated to immigrants through the media as well as through direct social interactions, in abundance if not necessarily with consistency of message.

One part of understanding the meso-level processes requires a detailed analysis of the kinds of social interactions in which an immigrant is engaged, and what social networks constitute the lived space. Some of these interactions are with others who share a culture and immigration history; others are with members of the host country who may have few common experiences and limited understanding of the immigrant's life. These varied interactions and networks shape the social context in which the immigrant life is defined, creating both an ongoing climate as well as situational perturbations.

At the micro level of figure 1.1 are the immigrants themselves—those people who enter a context that is defined broadly by elements of policy and social representations and that is permeated by more targeted attitudes and stereotypes about their condition and their group. As conceptualized here, the immigrant is not simply a number or a static condition, but rather is the site for a variety of social psychological processes, which are captured by the general rubric of identity negotiation. It is at this site that the experience of being an immigrant becomes real, forming and changing within a societal context of people and places.

Identity here is conceived very broadly, including self-definition, language usage, social and cultural habits, friendship networks, and other significant aspects of social and psychological life. For the immigrant, identity negotiation is a continuing process of situating oneself—of defining the self in relation to other people and other groups, all taking place under the larger societal umbrella. Also included in the general model is a recognition that immigrants come from somewhere with some things—things in this case not in the sense of material possessions, though those are certainly not unimportant and worthy of study in their own right, but rather with a set of expectations about what the new country will provide and how one will establish a life for oneself, and in many cases one's family. This psychological suitcase also includes a set of memories and images of the people and places of one's origin, some of which will be discarded over time and others of which will continue to influence one's identity (though often in altered form). In this analysis, both expectation and memories are in part individual and in part collective. Although they have a reality in the life of individuals, they at the same time are often shared images that reflect a co-construction process during both pre- and post-immigration periods.

These three levels form the basis of my perspective on what it means to be an immigrant, together with the assumption that social context is a critical mediator between individual and social system. Much of the existing research in immigration considers the direct, unmediated paths between individual and social system, as when the occupational opportunity structure, for example, is analyzed for its impact on individual employment, or when individual motivations are considered the direct precursor of immigration flow. Like Pettigrew (1997), I believe that social psychology has an important role in the space between macro and micro. More interested in the individual than sociology as a whole, more aware of context and structure than most psychologists, the social psychologist has both the opportunity and responsibility to work within this middle kingdom. It is here that the knowledge of what happens in immigration can be supplemented with a deeper understanding of how and why.

Using the pivotal concept of immigrant identity, I have developed a framework that considers how social forces, both large and small, shape the contexts in which immigrants must locate and define themselves. Not all immigrants encounter the same contexts; not all immigrants make the same choices within the contexts that they experience. But as we become more fully aware of the contingencies of the immigrant experience, we will better understand how different pathways develop and different outcomes result. It is in pursuit of that understanding that this volume is developed.

A PREVIEW OF THINGS TO COME

In the chapters that follow, I present my case for a social psychological perspective on immigration. Consistent with the model shown in figure 1.1, this analysis incorporates phenomena and processes at the level of the system as well as the level of the individual. Immigrant identity is a key concept for my analysis, but it can only be understood within the broader frame of social structure and social settings.

Chapter 2 sets the stage as I consider the broad contextual factors—policies, demography, and social representations—that define the arena in which an immigrant's experience is played out. Policies such as the immigration laws of 1924 and 1965, which respectively narrowed and widened the windows of opportunity, are discussed as they affected the flow of immigrants to the United States. These concrete events are coupled with an analysis of the more abstract representations of immigration that have been prevalent. Further, as a way of appreciating the historical and cultural specifics of immigration, I make a comparison with the Canadian case, which both shares similarities and illustrates important differences. As will be shown, these cultural and political parameters serve to establish boundary conditions for an individual immigrant's possibilities and potentialities.

Chapter 3 reviews the considerable literature on attitudes toward immigrants and immigration policy and considers how those attitudes have both changed and not changed over decades. Through years of survey data collection, often containing the same questions repeated on a regular basis, we have learned much about the ways in which the citizenry as a whole views immigration policies. Should immigration quotas be reduced? Should policy be adjusted to allow more immigrants to enter the country? In addition to these questions about overarching policy are beliefs about the characteristics of immigrants in general: do they contribute to the economy and the social good or are they a drain on the resources of the country? Again, repeated surveys provide much information here. Beneath the simple numbers indicating approval or disapproval lies the stuff of social psychological analysis—the motives and attributions that support expressed beliefs. In this analysis I also consider the correspondence or divergence that exists between the attitudes of those in the host country and the attitudes of immigrants themselves, as they each define their goals for an optimal society.

In chapter 4 attitudes towards immigrants are particularized, considered at the level of stereotypes about specific ethnic groups. Stereotypes of ethnic and national groups have been documented for at least eighty years in the social science literature. In the course of these analyses, distinct profiles have emerged for most groups who have come to the United States in substantial numbers. These profiles often differ substantially, both in their overall evaluative tone and in the particular elements thought to characterize a group. Some immigrants are believed to be better than others— more desirable, better educated, more motivated, or more law-abiding. Others are thought to embody character deficits and moral depravity. Which group is perceived to be better or worse is not necessarily constant, however, if we look over a long span of history. As just one example, stereotypes of both Japanese and Chinese in the United States have changed dramatically over the past century, from being depicted as evil and immoral forces to what is now often labeled a model minority. Thus, like other elements of context, analysis of group stereotypes requires a consideration of change. Equally important, however, is an understanding of how stereotypes operate to influence the interactions between immigrant and host, often taking the form of discriminatory behavior directed at immigrant groups. These meso-level phenomena are critical to the experience of immigrants and to their definition of self.

At the heart of my analysis is the concept of ethnic and national identity, which will be the focus of chapter 5. As a social psychological concept, ethnic identity moves away from the static categorization of the census report to the subjectively claimed conception of self. Although identity is subjective, it is not wholly individual; rather, it can be understood as a marker of association with other people who share similar views and ways of identifying themselves at a particular place and time. Ethnic identity is a concept far more complex than was earlier recognized. It is multifaceted, it is dynamic in nature, and it combines with other aspects of social identification, such as religion, gender, and politics. Further, ethnic identities themselves can be multiple, as the growing body of literature on transnationalism suggests. Both specific examples and general structures of identity will be considered in this chapter.

Chapter 6 continues the analysis of identity with a detailed look at the processes of identity negotiation. In the literature of immigration, assimilation theory dominated the thinking about ethnic and national identification for much of the twentieth century. Initially these models posited a steady move from identification in terms of one's country of origin to identification with the new society (primarily the United States in these accounts). The comfortable predictability of this model began to falter, however, in the post-1965 immigration period as it became clear that not all groups took on the new American identity with equal ease. The recognition that different groups of immigrants might experience different trajectories of assimilation was a first step in a more complex analysis. I complicate that analysis further, shifting it to a more psychological plane on which persons negotiate their ethnic and national identities in varying contexts. By looking more closely at some of these contextual factors, I believe we gain a far deeper understanding of how immigrants are defining, negotiating, and combining identities to yield more differentiated patterns than early assimilation models allowed.

In chapter 7 I focus on one group of immigrants—those from the English-speaking countries of the Caribbean—and interpret their experience in terms of the overall framework that I have developed. Thus I begin with an analysis of immigration policies and demographic movements, as they pertain to West Indian immigrants, and then move on to consider specific attitudes toward these groups. Shifting to the perspective of the West Indian immigrant, I then look at the ways in which these primarily Afro-Caribbean immigrants define and negotiate their identities and how these identity positions influence other forms of behavior.

In the final chapter, I look in both directions—back in the sense of summarizing the overarching perspective that I have taken, and forward with the aim of considering what might come next. As a researcher, my comments will emphasize some directions that seem to me most likely to be empirically and theoretically productive. As a citizen concerned with the lives and experiences of immigrants, I will offer some thoughts on the possible policy implications that are suggested by the social psychological analysis I have undertaken here. What value is added by this approach, and how might policy makers become more effective if this new perspective was taken into account?

In his classic text *The Uprooted* (1951), Oscar Handlin claimed that he was reversing the direction of previous discussions of immigration by focusing on the effects of immigration on the immigrants themselves, rather than looking at their impact on society at large. To study these effects, Handlin looked at letters from immigrants to family and friends, at newspapers directed to the immigrant communities, and at immigrant fiction. The picture he painted was in many respects quite bleak. As he forecast in the book's preface, his story was one of "broken homes, interruptions of a familiar life, separation from known surroundings, the becoming a foreigner and ceasing to belong" (1951, 4). Alienation was a key theme for Handlin as he focused on the lives of first-generation immigrants.

Although I share Handlin's interest in focusing on the experiences of immigrants themselves, my view of those experiences is less dark than Handlin's. Without denying the feelings of loneliness, alienation, and helplessness that immigrants then and now experience, I also see evidence of a more positive dynamic of negotiation and change. Because of vast changes in communication availability and travel possibilities, initial information about the host country and the subsequent capability of connecting with others, both within this country and back to the place of origin, are very different than they were a half century ago. These changes do not mean that the immigrant experience today is inevitably better, but it is certainly different in many respects. As Nancy Foner (2000) reminds us, however, not everything about contemporary immigration is a new story; many similarities and continuities with past immigration can be found. Moreover, I deviate from Handlin in causal emphasis as well. In exploring the impact of transition and social forces on the immigrants, Handlin tended, perhaps inadvertently, to deprive the actors of agency. Their story, as he told it, was one of reacting to forces seemingly out of their control. My account is a more agentic one: while giving full consideration to the macro factors that influence the immigrant experience, I also look to the opposite direction of influence, as indicated in figure 1.1. The flow of causality runs in both directions, and the mediation by situational factors and social interaction contributes much to the form and the positivity of an immigrant's life. With acknowledged debts to Handlin and to all of the other scholars who have preceded me, I offer here my view of what it means to be an immigrant.

Chapter Two | Setting the Stage: Policies, Demography, and Social Representations

There she lies, the great Melting-Pot—listen! Can't you hear the roaring and the bubbling?

—Israel Zangwill (1909)

Immigration policy should be generous; it should be fair; it should be flexible. With such a policy we can turn to the world, and to our own past, with clean hands and a clear conscience.

—John F. Kennedy (1964)

THE CONTEXT FOR immigrants—the stage set, as I metaphorically refer to it— could be considered in terms of the immediate, interpersonal situations that immigrants encounter when they arrive in their new country. That is the level of analysis most familiar to social psychologists, who often focus intently on the micro-level aspects of interpersonal interaction, and it is a level of analysis that I will use in later chapters. Here, however, I begin with a wider lens, one that looks both at broader currents in the contemporary scene as well as historical events that have shaped immigration in the United States over the past century.

Three elements guide this analysis—policy, demography, and social representations—and their contributions are interlocked as figure 2.1 illustrates. Consider, for example, the policies of the United States with regard to immigration. Over the past one hundred years, key legislative actions have shifted the course of immigration, in terms of both source and numbers, in ways that are critical to the story. On the one hand, it is important

Figure 2.1   Cultural Elements of Immigration

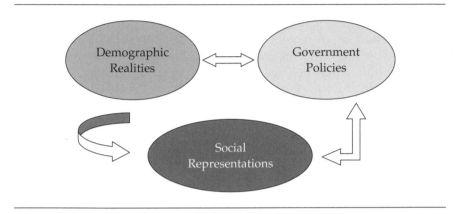

Source: Author's compilation.

to consider the impetus for these changes in policy, which can reflect particular political and social conditions within the country or that can, in the case of world wars and broad-ranging economic conditions, influence immigration in many countries simultaneously. On the other hand, it is important to consider how the enacted changes make the bar higher or lower for those who wish to enter the country, thereby affecting the immigrant flow and the demographic patterns.

Thus, in figure 2.1, the relationship between demographic patterns and social policy is depicted bidirectionally. Although the move from policy to population patterns is the most obvious direction, that is, evidence that raising or lowering the caps on entry will have a direct numerical impact, the rationale for the other direction is also strong. Once the population reaches a certain level—whether the level of the country as a whole, the immigrant share more particularly, or the number of specific types of immigrants—citizens and lawmakers often become energized in debates about the need for changes in current policies.

The third element of the triad is somewhat more elusive, or at least less concrete. Whereas one can look to the legal record for articulation of official policy, and to the census data files for a stipulation of numbers, social representations are less easily pinned down. Yet, this element of the attitudes and images that a community holds about immigration—in general, as well as about particular groups of immigrants—is a critical member of the triad. Policies are affected as much by subjective belief as by objective data, and the social process of interpretation and explanation of events drives the political actions.

The settings that I describe in this chapter—consisting of policy, demography, and social representation—are based primarily on the landscape of the United States, which "has admitted more immigrants than any other country" during the past two hundred years (Meyers 2004, 27). At times, however, it will be useful to consider alternative scenarios from other countries, where policies, demography, and representations can differ. In turning to these other models, the dynamics and interdependence of the three elements will be clearer, as will the possibilities for alternative scenarios.

A BRIEF HISTORY OF U.S. IMMIGRATION POLICY

The history of the United States is, as Oscar Handlin (1951) noted, a history of immigration.[1] Indeed, one could consider, as Christopher Jencks (2001) has, the movement of people from North Asia to the North and South American continents, some 13,000 years ago, as the first U.S. immigrant movement. I will leave the long history of immigration, from the discovery of America by Europeans and their early settlements through the forced immigration of Africans during the slave trade, to historians. Instead I focus on some of the key moments in U.S. immigration history that illustrate how the "theatrical set" of immigration can vary even within a single country in a time span of little more than a hundred years.

Prior to 1875, immigration to the United States was basically unrestricted. By executive order, the country's first president, George Washington, announced an open-door immigration policy which, despite some opposition, set the tone for nearly a century (DeLaet 2000). The first limits on immigration, enacted in 1875, were aimed primarily at categories of people deemed offensive to the society, such as those who were destitute, immoral, or physically handicapped (Edmonston and Passel 1994). Thus, although certain groups were stigmatized, the basis of categorization was not ethnically based, except for the provision that Asians could not be imported without their consent (DeLaet 2000). The Chinese Exclusion Acts of 1882 and 1884 were the first set of immigration laws to target people from a specific area of the world. The 1882 act barred all Chinese individuals from citizenship; the 1884 Act stopped a potential loophole by making the restriction apply to all Chinese persons, whether or not they had been citizens of China. The anti-Chinese provisions were strengthened further by denying Chinese even entry to the United States, unless they belonged to certain groups such as officials, merchants, or tourists. Not until 1943 were these bans lifted (DeLaet 2000; Xie and Goyette 2004).

The immigration of Chinese had been a concern for some time, particularly on the West Coast of the United States, where Chinese constituted more than 10 percent of the population in the mid-nineteenth century (Meyers 2004). In 1870, for example, Congressional debates on the specifics of the immigration policy focused on the criterion of "all free white persons." In the aftermath of the Civil War, people "of the African race or of African descent" were added to the category of eligible persons; however, anti-Asian sentiment prevented a totally nondiscriminatory passage that would have allowed all persons to be eligible for U.S. citizenship (Jacobson 1998). The focus on Asians developed in the context of substantial Asian immigration, especially on the West Coast. Objections to the entrance of Asians were in part based on concerns that the coolie trade was simply another form of slavery (DeLaet 2000). Other opposition was more economically based, as labor organizations viewed Chinese immigration as a threat to the jobs of U.S. workers. Mingled with these ethical and economic concerns were more specific stereotypes and prejudices against the Chinese, who were viewed as racially and culturally distinct from the dominant U.S. population. These early objections, focused specifically in this case on Asian immigration, became much more broadly framed as the twentieth century began.

The Immigration Acts of the 1920s

With the number and the ethnic diversity of immigrants rising sharply in the early part of the twentieth century, public sentiment against immigration rose as well. Public discourse and political debate culminated in two major pieces of legislation that sharply altered the course of immigration to the United States. Both the Quota Law of 1921 and the subsequent Immigration Act of 1924 established a new and far more restrictive stance for the country (DeLaet 2000; Meyers 2004). In the first of these, the Emergency Immigration Restriction Act, quotas on immigration were established for the first time. Using 1910 as the reference point, each country's immigration allowance was limited to 3 percent of the number of those peoples who lived in the United States in 1910. To take just one example, 104,000 people born in France lived in the United States in 1910 (Nugent 1992). Thus, according to the 1921 law, annual immigration of French citizens to the United States would henceforth be limited to 3,120 per year. This same calculation applied to all other countries of origin, with the exception of Asian nations, which continued to be excluded in total. The 1921 quota act was enacted initially for one year and then extended for two more years, at which point it was replaced by the Immigration Act of 1924.

National quotas were further reduced by the Immigration Act of 1924. The selection criterion was altered as well. The overall rate of immigration was reduced in two ways: first, by dropping the percentage from 3 to 2 percent, and second, by shifting the base year from 1910, a point ending the decade that represents the peak in immigration, to 1890, a point ending a decade in which immigration was approximately 20 percent less (Nugent 1992). The combined effect of these changes was to lower the overall cap on annual immigration "from approximately 356,000 to less than 165,000" (DeLaet 2000, 122). The shift to an earlier reference point had another, fully intended consequence: it altered the ethnic balance of potential immigrants, away from the more recent flow of southern and eastern Europeans and back toward the more traditional northern European sources.

Consider the difference that this choice made. In 1890, the immigrant population of the United States was dominated by people from three countries: Germany (2,785,000), Ireland (1,872,000), and England-Wales (1,009,000). Following this triad at some distance, each country the source of less than 500,000 immigrants, were Sweden, Norway, Scotland, and Austria. In contrast, the 1920 census showed five countries each supplying more than a million immigrants: Germany, Ireland, Italy, Russia, and Poland (Nugent 1992). Clearly the tilt of the immigrant population was in a southern and eastern direction; it also represented a shift from a primarily Protestant group to one that included substantial numbers of Catholics, Jews, and Greek Orthodox (Meyers 2004). The choice of 1890 as a marker was an attempt to alter the balance, returning the country to its northern European and Protestant base. In fact, it is notable that the single highest point for the immigrant count from England and Wales during the period from 1870 to 1920 was 1890 (Nugent 1992)—surely a data point that was not lost on the framers of the 1920 legislation.[2]

The Immigration Act of 1965

The door that was closed (or at least left only partly ajar) in 1924 was opened wide again with the Immigration Act of 1965. The act was originally proposed in July 1963 by President John F. Kennedy, whose arguments for liberalization can be found in his posthumously published treatise, *A Nation of Immigrants.* In that volume, he argued for an immigration policy that would be "generous," "fair," and "flexible" (1964, 83) and that would reaffirm the American stance of openness towards people from all countries—quoting George Washington, "not only the opulent and respectable stranger, but the oppressed and persecuted of all nations and religions" (Kennedy 1964, 83). These sentiments were consistent with more general concerns for civil rights and the elimination of racial oppression that had grown in the early 1960s, and in fact the immigration policies of Kennedy were originally set in the context of broadly based civil rights legislation (Isbister 1996).

The 1965 Immigration Act did away with national-origin quotas and all race-based criteria for immigrants. Some numerical limits were imposed, but these were broadly based. First was by hemisphere—170,000 for the Eastern Hemisphere and 120,000 for the Western. Second was within the Eastern Hemisphere—20,000 per country (compare DeLaet 2000; Meyers 2004). In addition, a category preference system was put in place such that certain occupations were favored, along with family members of citizens and resident aliens. For a few countries, the new cap was a decrease from what had existed. In the case of England, for example, the quota prior to the 1965 legislation was 65,361 per year (Congressional Digest 1965). England, however, was using less than half of its quota so the impact of the bill on immigration patterns was minimal. In contrast, many countries had quotas numbering only a few hundred, or even less than a hundred per year; for them, the cap of 20,000 represented a drastic shift in possibilities— a shift that became evident in subsequent decades.

These liberalizing moves did not mean that all doors were open. As President Lyndon Johnson commented in a speech made at Ellis Island at the time of the bill's passage, "the days of unlimited immigration are past" (quoted in DeLaet 2000, 40). Further, the cap on immigration from the Western Hemisphere was actually a more restrictive policy, in that no limits had been imposed on this hemisphere before. Nonetheless, the effect that the elimination of discriminatory quotas had on subsequent patterns of immigration—both qualitative and quantitative—was dramatic and attests to the significance of this legislation.

The principle underlying the more generous immigration policy was certainly not endorsed by all. An editorial in a California paper, for example, lamented the "strange kind of sentimentalism" that led President Kennedy to "long for a return to the melting pot of the decades between the Civil War and World War I" (quoted in Fernandez 2000). In debate preceding the bill's passage, Senator Sam Ervin raised issues that echoed the concerns of policymakers in 1924: "Immigrants are more readily assimilated by the United States," he stated, "if their national origins bear a reasonable ratio to Americans tracing their national origins to the same countries" (Congressional Digest 1965, 145). The Veterans of Foreign Wars worried about "the continuation of our way of life" (Congressional Digest 1965, 149). With an affecting show of concern for the fate of other nations, the American Coalition of Patriotic Societies worried about "those nations whose skilled elite would be decimated by their immigration to the United States" (Congressional Digest 1965, 151). Such concerns were less evident from the Daughters of the American Revolution, who voiced concern about "proliferating African nations" and the impact of their population growth on U.S. immigration (Congressional Digest 1965, 157).

Whereas conservative opponents of the bill worried about qualitative changes in immigration, that is, what kinds of people might enter the country, supporters of the bill were conservative in their estimates of the quantitative impact. Attorney General Nicholas Katzenbach stated that the measure would result in "an increase of only a small fraction in permissible immigration" (Congressional Digest 1965, 146). Senators Douglas and Kennedy gave estimates of approximately 60,000 additional immigrants per year. As subsequent data show, these estimates were not very accurate, though not all of the later increases can be attributed specifically to the 1965 legislation.

Recent U.S. Immigration Policy

The door that was opened to immigrants by the 1965 legislation remained a welcoming portal for a good number of years, supplemented by a positive stance toward political refugees from communist countries prior to the collapse of the Soviet Union and from Southeast Asia after the fall of Saigon (Meyers 2004). Gradually, however, the pendulum of public opinion shifted, and a discourse of deterrence began to drive policy decisions. By 1986, when the Immigration Reform and Control Act (IRCA) was finally passed after lengthy debate, open doors were replaced by guarded gates. IRCA was focused on ways to control illegal immigration and to punish those who contributed to an increasing flow of undocumented workers (DeLaet 2000; Massey, Durand, and Malone 2002). Among other provisions, the act substantially increased funds for enforcement and introduced sanctions on employers who knowingly hired undocumented immigrants (sanctions that have not, however, been consistently applied). At the same time, provisions were included to grant amnesty to some immigrants and to declare an antidiscriminatory policy.

The pendulum continued to swing away from immigrants, however, with subsequent legislation in 1990 and 1996. Although the 1990 Immigration Act emphasized family reunification, it also set a cap on legal immigration and, under a mantle of encouraging diversity, attempted to shift the ethnic balance of immigrants back toward more traditional northern European sources. With the 1996 Illegal Immigration Reform and Immigrant Responsibility Act, the dominance of illegality in the political discourse was clear. This act was unambiguously about deterrence and punishment. Key provisions included a restriction on welfare and public benefits for immigrants at federal, state, and local levels; limitations on the possibility of class action suits by noncitizens; greater penalties for illegal entry; and increased funding for the border patrol. Pervasive in this more recent legislative climate is the social representation of immigrant as illegal and the stigmatization of the category.

MACRO LEVEL INFLUENCES
ON IMMIGRATION

Immigration policy is multidetermined. Eytan Meyers (2004), in a broad-ranging analysis of international immigration policies, identified five key factors that shape a country's immigration policy: economic conditions, wars, foreign policy, demographic composition, and ideology. Although the last two are more directly related to a social psychology of immigration (and indeed, are considered first and third in importance by Meyers), the influence of the more macro-level factors is worth noting. Massey (1995), for one, has argued that these broader economic and political events are more critical to an understanding of shifts in immigration patterns than is the legislation of 1924 and 1965.[3]

In his historical analysis of U.S. immigration policy, Meyers (2004) points to economic expansion at the beginning of the twentieth century and immediately after World War II as forces contributing to a liberalization of immigration policy, just as the need for labor to build the railroads encouraged immigration in the century before (Massey, Durand, and Malone 2002; Meyers 2004). Similarly, one consequence of economic depression is often a slowdown in immigration. Immigration is, for many, the promise of a more productive life and economic security. When the economy is growing and jobs are plentiful, the call of the highly productive industrial society can be great. In contrast, when the economy is in a decline and unemployment is high, the benefits of immigration, for either those in the host country or those considering immigration, are far fewer. Such was the case in the United States in the 1930s and perhaps, relative to other countries, is an emergent factor today as well. Economic conditions in the country of origin can also be influential. The well-known case of the Irish potato famines, which created a flow of immigrants from Ireland to other countries in the mid-nineteenth century and again between 1880 and 1910 (Nugent 1992), is just one example of local economic conditions precipitating a mass movement of people from their own country to another.

Economic and foreign policy considerations do not always mesh. Douglas Massey, Jorge Durand, and Nolan Malone (2002) describe how patterns of immigration from Mexico to the United States have shifted over the past hundred years, the result of shifting and often contradictory policies enacted by the U.S. government. During World War II, when farm workers were needed in the United States for the war effort, a bracero program was developed that allowed the temporary importation of Mexican workers. As it developed, this program "allowed the United States to have its cake and eat it too" (Massey, Durand, and Malone 2002, 39), combining cheap labor with the belief that border traffic was controlled. At the end of the twentieth century, contradictions were still evident in policies affecting Mexican migration: on the one hand, the enactment of border control policies and specific restrictions and penalties on Mexican migrants and, on the other hand, the cross-border mobility fostered by the North American Free Trade Agreement.

War and foreign policy have their most obvious influence in the case of refugee groups. Immigration from Russia to the United States, for example, was very high in the first decade of the century but dropped sharply with the establishment of a communist state in Russia and a security apparatus that discouraged immigration (Massey 1995). Worries about what might happen if the radical ideas of the Russian Revolution were imported reduced receptivity in the United States as host country as well. More recently, Russian immigration to the United States increased again, primarily among the Jewish population seeking more religious freedom. Other recent examples of refugee movements also illustrate the mutual influence of push and pull factors. Thus, in the United States in the past fifty years, significant numbers of Cubans immigrated in reaction to the ascendancy of Castro and his Communist regime as well as the anti-Castro policies of the United States. In contrast, Haitians, though suffering at least as much in their home countries, have been less eagerly welcomed and supported in the United States.

More specific political events can have an impact on immigration policy as well. Although it is probably too early to assess the long-term effects of September 11, 2001, the rhetoric and anecdotal evidence of the day suggested that choices on both sides of the equation—the push and the pull of immigration—were altered. In the United States and in Canada as well, calls for regulation of immigration, especially immigration from Arab countries, were quick to surface (Esses, Dovidio, and Hodson 2002).[4] With the inception of the Department of Homeland Security in the United States, which came to incorporate the Immigration and Naturalization Service, processing requests for immigration slowed down considerably. Visa requests as well were subject to long delays, affecting not only those who intended to immigrate permanently but also those who wished to study in the United States or merely attend professional and scientific conferences.

From the immigrant side, it seems quite likely that the emergent suspicions and hostilities expressed in the United States will dampen the promise of immigration to the United States for people from countries suspected of harboring terrorists. Internal migration within the United States also appears to have decreased among this population (Kaushal, Kaestner, and Reimers 2004). Even if the barriers to their entrance were not actually raised, reports of attacks on Arabs and Muslims in the United States quickly circulated through the community and created a "chilly climate" for pursuing the

American dream. An immigrant from Ghana, for example, whose first name was Mohammed, described how the name that he had originally enjoyed when he came to the United States, because of its association with the famed American boxer, came to be "not cool anymore" following September 11 (Ali 2004). Certainly the examples could be multiplied, both for cases of migration to the United States as well as to other countries throughout the world.

The two factors cited by Meyers (2004) that are more social in their emphasis are the demographics of a population, and in particular the degree of dissimilarity between immigrant and host population, and the ideology, which Meyers defined as "fluctuations between racism and liberalism" (2004, 60). In the U.S. policy reviewed earlier in this chapter, we have already seen how ethnic distributions influence policy, exemplified by actions against the rising Chinese population beginning in the nineteenth century and the quotas established by the 1924 legislation. A more detailed analysis of demographic trends follows here. Meyers's ideology factor has also been in evidence in this brief historical review, but a more detailed analysis of ideology and belief will be presented later (see chapter 3).

DEMOGRAPHIC PATTERNS IN THE UNITED STATES

Influenced both by specific immigration policy within the United States and by broader political and economic conditions in the United States and in the world, the rate of immigration has shifted markedly over the past century. As figure 2.2 shows, rates were high at the beginning of the twentieth century, dipped in the middle, and accelerated steadily from the 1970s through the end. In the language of statistics, we see a bimodal distribution, with two peak times: early in the twentieth century and at the transition point between the twentieth and twenty-first centuries. In between these two peaks, immigration was, though never completely dormant, nevertheless a far less prominent contributor to the overall U.S. population.

As of 2002, 23 percent of the U.S. population is first- and second-generation immigrants (Bean et al. 2004). In urban centers in the United States, these figures are much higher. In New York City, for example, the 2000 census figures show that 40 percent of people living in the five boroughs of the city were born in other countries (that is, are first-generation immigrants), compared to just 28 percent in 1990 (Lambert 2000). In Los Angeles, the story is similar, with nearly 30 percent foreign-born population in 2000 (U.S. Census Bureau 2001). These two cities alone account for one-third of the foreign-born population in the United States, a figure that suggests the uneven distribution of immigrants in the country.

Figure 2.2   Immigration to United States

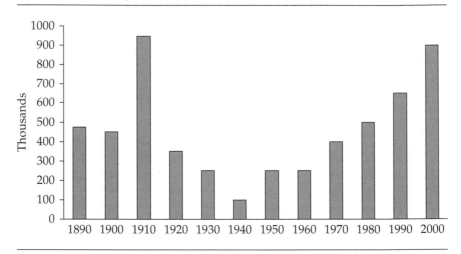

Source: Author's compilation from U.S. Bureau of the Census.

Numbers alone do not tell the whole story, however, particularly as we try to understand how the reality of numbers influences the social representations of the phenomenon. Over time, the countries of origin that account for the major immigrant movements have shifted dramatically. In the early years of the nation, immigration to the United States was primarily from England and its neighbors. As the nation grew, so did the diversity of immigrant populations, first expanding to include other countries in western and then in southern Europe. Between 1882 and 1896, 71 percent of immigrants to the United States were from the traditional base of northern Europe; between 1897 and 1914, 75 percent of immigrants came from countries in southern and eastern Europe (DeLaet 2000). Two centuries of slave trade, from the early 1600s to its prohibition in 1807, had already shifted the national demographics (though not, until much later, the citizenship rolls). Chinese immigration was also substantial at one point in the country's history, only to be restricted by the legislation of 1882.

Early in the history of the country, it was clear that the United States would not remain a British clone, either in its politics or its people. For some, this was a matter of concern. In 1751, for example, Benjamin Franklin worried that "the number of purely white people in the world is proportionably very small" (quoted in Jacobson 1998, 40). His palette was restricted—even Germans were viewed as "swarthy"—but his preferred balance was clear, wishing that the number of whites be increased. This

Figure 2.3   Changing Sources of Immigration to the United States

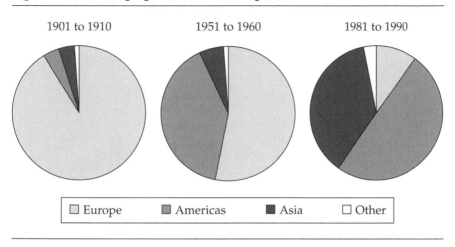

Source: Massey (1995).

concern for the whiteness of the country continued to be evident more than 150 years later when the Immigration Act of 1924 was formulated. As discussed earlier, that legislation not only reduced the numbers of immigrants to the United States but also created selective mechanisms for who those immigrants would be.

With the 1965 changes in immigration laws, the previous selective mechanisms were eliminated and the immigrant population could be drawn from a much broader population base. The consequences of this change have been dramatic, as figure 2.3 shows. In this figure we see the proportional representation of immigrants from Europe, the Americas, and Asia at three points in the twentieth century. As this graph clearly shows, European immigration, which was dominant in the first half of the century, now represents only a small fraction. In contrast, immigration from other countries in the Americas, very small at the beginning of the century, is now the dominant stream. Asian immigration—which includes people from a wide range of countries in East Asia (for example, China and Korea); Southeast Asia (for example, the Philippines and Vietnam); and South Asia (for example, Bangladesh and India)—is the other growth area in recent years. In 1980, Asian Americans represented 1.4 percent of the total U.S. population, and in 2000, 4 percent. Of these, 64 percent were born abroad, that is, were first-generation immigrants (Xie and Goyette 2004).

These patterns of change, both in number and nationality, are interesting in their own right because they tell the demographic history of the country.

They have added importance, however, as indices of social context into which new immigrants enter. Consider the situation at a few key points in time. At the beginning of the twentieth century, Italians and Russian Jews were the two dominant immigrant groups. In 1910 in New York City, a city that then had 4.8 million residents, there were 341,000 (7 percent) Italian immigrants and 484,000 (10 percent) Russian Jewish immigrants (Foner 2001a). By 1920, 43 percent of the citizens of New York were either first- or second-generation Italian-Americans and Jews. In contrast, fewer than 2 percent were African American and only a fraction were Hispanic. Thus the flavor of the city—its ethnic "hot spots"—was southern and eastern European. For the immigrants, this large numerical minority created communities in which culture and experience could be shared. For the resident host population, in contrast, the size of the group constituted an easy target for stereotypes and anxieties.

In the middle of the twentieth century, by contrast, immigration from all countries was relatively low, and immigrants constituted a considerably smaller proportion of the country's population. In New York City, for example, only 18 percent of the population was foreign-born in 1970 (Foner 2001a). The profile of the native-born American was much higher. In this context, the image of a melting pot seemed most apt. A process of assimilation, by which newcomers would blend in with the majority and give up aspects of their country of origin, seemed more feasible than it had when the numbers were larger and the differences between groups more noticeable.

The picture at the end of the twentieth century is a much different one. After thirty-five years of increasing immigration, communities of common ethnic origin have formed throughout the United States. In fact, residential ethnic segregation has increased in some major cities, such as New York. Both Asians and Latinos, for example, were more likely to live in highly ethnic neighborhoods there than in more integrated neighborhoods in 2000 than they were in 1990, as Janny Scott reported in the *New York Times* ("Races Still Tend to Live Apart in New York, Census Shows," March 23, 2001, p. B1). Within sections of the city and even within blocks, one can find specific ethnic groups developing communities that include groceries selling native foods, newsstands with papers covering both foreign and local ethnic events, churches that reflect the religious practices of a particular group, and parks that provide places for particular groups of people to meet. Further, because of the duration of increased immigration trends, first-generation immigrants are now arriving to communities in which second- and even third-generation immigrants from their country may still live. Being an immigrant today is less about finding one's way in a totally foreign country and more about relocating in a community that offers many familiar features of one's original home, though over time we can expect decreases in residential segregation, consistent with trends in other periods and other countries (see Massey 1985).

The importance of context to the immigrant experience has been described by Nancy Foner (1979, 1985, 2001b, 2005) with reference to Afro-Caribbean immigration, contrasting the British and U.S. context. West Indians who immigrated to Britain in the 1950s and 1960s were a distinct minority, joining with Indians and Pakistanis to inject color into what had been predominantly a white society. As such, they were both more visible and less segregated from the host country population than in the United States. As Henry Louis Gates observed, Brixton is not Harlem (1997, quoted in Foner 2001a): there is a noticeable black presence, but it coexists with a substantial white population. In contrast, West Indians who migrate to the United States encounter an established black community, from which their distinction is often not noted by the nonblack population. This difference has consequences both for how the immigrant group is regarded by others, and for how their identities are negotiated in the new context (both of which will be discussed in later chapters).

One other aspect of demographic patterns of immigration that needs to be recognized is the gender distribution. Often the image of immigration is that of a nuclear family—man and woman coming to the United States, perhaps with one or more children accompanying them. Alternatively, there is an image of the single male immigrant, coming with the hope of sending later for wife and family. In fact, sex ratios of immigration have varied considerably over time and between countries (Foner 2000; Nugent 1992). Before 1914, the majority of immigrants were male. For most of the twentieth century, however, women have been in the majority (Gordon 2005). This distribution is made dramatically clear in a display at the Ellis Island museum of orange and green wooden models, representing women and men and set out on a time line of twentieth century migration. Walter Nugent (1992) describes differences in the sex ratio between ethnic groups: from 55 to 60 percent male among East European Jews, Scandinavians, Germans, and British, to almost 90 percent for Greeks and Serbs. Foner (2000) presents data for New York City in the early 1990s, showing the number of men per hundred women varying from ninety-five for Polish immigrants to sixty-three for immigrants from the Philippines. There are numerous reasons for these differences, including both formal immigration policies that favor families or certain occupations, and the relative economic opportunities that women and men have in the United States but do not in have their home countries.

All these variations in demographic patterns have consequences for the immigration story, establishing specific contexts in which the immigrant establishes him or herself and posing particular challenges and opportunities for negotiation and adaptation.

SOCIAL REPRESENTATIONS OF IMMIGRATION

Social representations, the third element depicted in figure 2.1, are more abstract than demographic figures and policy enactments, but they are no less important to understanding the context of immigration. *Social representation* is a concept developed by the French social psychologist Serge Moscovici (1988), building on earlier work by Durkheim. Subsequently adopted by many social scientists who are attempting to extend the framework of explanation beyond the individual (Breakwell and Canter 1993; Deaux and Philogène 2001), social representations speak to the shared meanings in a culture. Beliefs about concepts or objects are jointly constructed by members of a society, and these consensually determined images in turn influence how relevant targets and events are viewed. Work on social representations has explored the meaning of psychoanalysis in French society (Moscovici 1976), definitions of madness (Jodelet 1991), and beliefs about human rights (Doise 2001). As these analyses show, shared understandings of abstract concepts influence individual day-to-day realities, and decisions that at first glance might seem to be totally personal can be viewed as expressions of a larger cultural frame.

Immigration as Melting Pot

Images of immigration exemplify the operation of a social representation—a concept that is widely shared within a culture or society, but that may differ sharply as one moves between societies. In the United States, throughout most of the twentieth century, the dominant social representation in discussions of immigration has been the melting pot. This cultural metaphor been called "a fundamental trait of American nationalism" (Kohn, cited in Gleason 1964), "stubbornly entrenched in our national subconscious" (Greely, quoted in Gleason 1964). The historian Arthur M. Schlesinger Sr. listed the melting pot—"the fusing of many different nationalities in a single society"—as one of America's top ten contributions to civilization (1959, 67). As Schlesinger noted, other nations may have people of mixed origin, but nowhere is the mix so extensive, so rapid, and so free of forcible incorporation—acknowledging the obvious exception of the slave trade and neglecting the history of American Indians.

Although a term like crucible that refers to a process of melting or blending was occasionally used when describing territories ranging from Europe to the American frontier (Gleason 1964), the clearly articulated image of the melting pot traces its origin to a play by Israel Zangwill first performed in Washington, D.C., in October 1908 and published in 1909. Zangwill dedicated *The Melting Pot* to Theodore Roosevelt, for what he saw as the president's "strenuous struggle against the forces that threaten to shipwreck the great republic" (1909/1994). In symbiotic spirit, President Roosevelt accompanied Zangwill to the Washington opening and enthusiastically declared it an "extraordinary able and powerful play" (Gleason 1964).

Zangwill's somewhat flowery dedication to Roosevelt reflects the text of the play itself, in which the spirit of music and lofty goals confront the scourge of discrimination and anti-Semitism. The play's hero, a young Russian immigrant who seeks to compose the great symphony, sees music as the transcendent force in a country where "all the races of Europe are melting and re-forming" (33). "America is God's Crucible," he states, as he envisions "the coming superman" that will represent a "fusion of all races" (33–34).

Zangwill himself was neither an American nor a first-generation immigrant. His parents had emigrated to Britain in the mid-nineteenth century—his father, from Russia, to avoid being conscripted into the tsar's army, and his mother from Poland with a cousin and aspirations for a better life. Zangwill was born and continued to live in London. Moreover, Zangwill's dreams of an ideal society appear less driven by the experience of being a second-generation immigrant than by the role that Judaism played in his life. Indeed, the fusion that he most clearly articulated was that between Judaic and Gentile, the evolution of a "new Hebraic man" (Udelson 1990). At the same time, he believed that similar possibilities existed for African Americans: "Even upon the negro the 'Melting Pot' of America will not fail to act in a measure as it has acted on the Red Indian" (Udelson 1990, 289, fn. 22). Whatever the particular mix of influence and inspiration, Zangwill viewed America, not Europe, as the site in which a multiethnic, multiracial civilization could emerge (Udelson 1990).

Although the image of the melting pot gained instant status as a social representation of the immigration process, it also elicited counter reactions from both the political right and left. From the right, perhaps the more vociferous of the two critiques, negative reactions to the image were based on the grounds of so-called racial integrity. From the left, objections were directed to the homogenization implied by an assimilationist image.

The sociologist Henry Pratt Fairchild (1926) was one of the most prominent voices arguing for racial separation. He described a pre-Zangwill era in which the appearance of "tolerant indifference" to immigration masked the fact that "it was not actually welcome" (9). Then, he caustically observed, "came the symbol, like a portent in the heavens" of America as a melting pot (10). The flaw in this symbol, from Fairchild's vantage point, was that it "did not take account of the true nature of group unity"— a unity that in his view is "primarily racial" (21). While a common nationality might be acquired through common group experience (if socialization is begun early enough), Fairchild argued that the hereditary basis of race precluded such a merger. "Racial dissimilarity always constitutes an element of weakness in group life" (79), he proclaimed. For the United States "to remain a stable nation, it must continue to be a white man's country for an indefinite period to come" (240). Thus, where Zangwill saw the melting pot as an ideal to be achieved, Fairchild regarded it as a "molten mass" that had little to commend it.

The increasingly influential genetics movement contributed to this critique as well, arguing that genetic defects—stereotypically associated with nonwhite, non–middle-class people—could proliferate and contaminate the good. As stated by Charles Davenport, the first director of the Cold Spring Harbor research station established for the experimental study of evolution, "The idea of a 'melting pot' belongs to a pre-Mendelian age" (Kevles 1985, 47). Madison Grant, then chairman of the New York Zoological Society, chimed in with similar arguments, pointing to Mexico as his evidence of the falsity of the melting pot (Grant 1921). By blending the blood of Spanish conquerors and native Indian populations, Mexicans evolved as a racial mixture that Grant saw as "now engaged in demonstrating its incapacity for self-government" (1921, 17).

These race-based arguments were pervasive during the years immediately following Zangwill's dramatic offering, and indeed foreshadowed the successful political movement in the United States to restrict immigration, keeping it smaller and more English-speaking than it had been. At the same time, other critics of the metaphorical melting pot focused more on the rights of the immigrant than on the tastes of the host citizenry. These critics, including Horace Kallen and Randall Bourne, were concerned with the assimilative connotations of the melting pot, insofar as they suggested that the immigrant was supposed to give up characteristics associated with the country of origin in favor of becoming 100 percent American (Gleason 1964). In the words of Kallen, "cultural pluralism," not a melting pot, should be the goal. Other liberals joined this chorus, including the well-known educator John Dewey, who epitomized an American as "Pole-German-English-French-Spanish-Italian-Greek-Irish-Scandinavian-Bohemian-Jew and so on" (cited in Gleason 1964, 40).

Despite these critiques, the representation of immigration as melting pot has endured for nearly a century. A 1993 Harris poll, for example, found that 63 percent of people surveyed believed that "the phrase 'melting pot' describes the United States today" (Harris 1993).[5] The longevity of the melting pot metaphor may be attributable in part to its ambiguity. Contained within the vivid imagery (perhaps not too different from the image of a pot of gold at the end of a rainbow) are a set of distinct and sometimes even discrepant assumptions. In various dictionaries that I consulted, the non-literal meaning of melting pot included "racial amalgamation," "social and cultural assimilation," a "remodeling of institutions," and "a place or situation where things are being mixed or reconstructed." Invoked in this set are ideas of location, of process, and of outcome. Gleason (1964) referred to this ambiguity in his analysis of the melting pot, aptly subtitled "symbol of fusion or confusion." "Its very ambiguity," he suggested, "allows its use by those who disagree about what it means" (45). The problematic aspect of this metaphor, he suggested, was the question of whether only the immigrant is changed or whether the melting pot implies a reformation of the host society as well. He also voiced other concerns: is the assumption one about biological blending, as in intermarriage, or more simply cultural assimilation? Is the theory of the melting pot meant to be prescriptive, as in the sense of a goal that the country wishes to attain? Or is it more aptly seen as descriptive, simply characterizing a state of affairs?

In the end, Gleason (1964) absolves the melting pot of the responsibility to answer these questions, according it importance as a symbol rather than requiring that it demonstrate the consistency and comprehensiveness of a theory. As symbol, it conveys an image of diversity and, though the process may be unclear, a sense of dynamics and change. The latter quality, for Gleason, is a key both to its longevity and to its continued applicability to the American immigration story.

Alternative Models and Metaphors

The social representation of the melting pot as a symbol for immigration in the popular discourse finds a parallel in social science's development of assimilation theory (Alba and Nee 2003; Gordon 1964; Portes and Rumbaut 1996). First introduced by Robert Park and the Chicago school of sociology, not long after Israel Zangwill put the phrase melting pot into popular discourse, "assimilation has historically been one of the foundational and far-reaching concepts in American social science" (Hirschman, Kasinitz, and DeWind 1999, 129). In chapter 6 I deal more directly with the theorized process of assimilation and what it implies (and what it misses) about immigrant adaptation and negotiation. At this point, I want only to note how pervasive the concept has been, serving as an explanatory framework within the social science community (tribal lore, as the late social psychologist Donald Campbell, might call it) just as the melting pot has dominated popular discourse. Like the image of a melting pot, assimilation theory has also used visual images to enrich and make more concrete the meanings implied. Thus, assimilation theory became known as a model of "straight line" transformation that suggested continuous upward movement by immigrant groups to the host norms (Gans 1973; Sandberg 1973). Then, in subsequent modifications of the theory, terms such as "bumpy line" and "segmented" were introduced to represent less steady and singular movement (Gans 1992; Portes and Zhou 1993; Zhou 1999). Social scientists, in their research and theorizing, attempt to remove the kinds of ambiguity that the metaphorical melting pot allows, and these later modifications of assimilation represent reactions to observed data. Nonetheless, the theory also provides a frame that allows some room for inference and speculation that may go beyond the data base, thus bringing social theory closer to social representation.

As I suggested earlier, an interdependence exists between social representations, demographic patterns, and social policy. Thus, it is not surprising to find that, in the face of reformulated immigration policies and shifting patterns of immigration, both the social representations in popular discourse and the theoretical models of social science show change. I've alluded to the changes in theories of assimilation and will deal more with these variations in chapter 6.

Shifts can be found in popular representations of immigration as well. In the 1960s and 1970s in the United States, notions of multiculturalism began to emerge (Rodriguez 2001). With this increased emphasis on the advantages of diversity as contrasted with homogeneity, a number of alternative metaphors came to the fore. Some of the new terms directly challenged the dominant metaphor, such as Richard Bourhis and David Marshall's (1999) reference to "undissolved lumps in the melting pot" (247). Others invoked culinary imagery, such as "salad bowl" and "banquet" (Fernandez 2000). Diversity of skin tone is suggested in terms such as colorful mosaic and rainbow coalition. Each of these images contests the notion of homogeneity implied in the melting pot and suggests an alternative model in which various groups maintain, whether by choice, by treatment, or by policy, distinctive characteristics of their culture.

Another social representation that, although not exclusively linked to immigration, nonetheless emerges frequently in the discourse is that of the American Dream (Hochschild 1995). Apparently this term was first introduced in a formal way by historian James Truslow Adams in 1931 to a country that was immersed in economic depression (McCharen 2004). At that time, immigrants were not coming to the United States in any substantial numbers. But in the post-1965 era, "millions of immigrants and internal migrants have moved to America . . . to fulfill their version of the American dream" (Hochschild 1995, 15). As defined by Hochschild, "the

American dream consists of tenets about achieving success" (1995, 15). Typically, this success is defined in economic terms—as establishing financial stability, perhaps starting one's own business, and owning a home. As defined within the U.S. context, the American dream is also infused with a heavy dose of individualism: individual success and entrepreneurial spirit are the incarnation of the American dream, extending perhaps to a nuclear family but rarely to the community beyond.

MAKING COMPARISONS: THE CASE OF CANADA

The history of immigration in the United States is a particular history, and the pattern that emerges from the interplay of its policy, demographics, and representations is a particular constellation. To appreciate the ways in which this pattern may share characteristics with others, yet have quite distinctive properties, it is useful to look at the development of immigration in other countries over a similar period. I choose Canada for a number of reasons. On the one hand, its proximity to the United States, the temporal parallels in its colonial settlement, and its current level of development might suggest that its immigration story would be much the same as that of the United States. Yet that assumption, in addition to the annoyance value it holds for most Canadians, is in fact a distortion. In policy, in demographics, and in the dominant social representations, Canada offers a unique case history.

Policy and Demography of Canadian Immigration

The early history of Canadian settlement represents an initial point of departure from the U.S. case. In Canada, both the British and the French established permanent settlements, the British in 1497 and the French in 1534. Despite the eventual governmental dominance of the British Empire, the French presence has continued to be a factor in Canadian politics over the years, as evidenced by the prolonged political debate over the province of Quebec. After capturing Quebec, the British attempted to impose a single culture with the Royal Proclamation of 1763, which defined a policy of "the absorption of the French nation by the English, which in matters of language, patriotism, law and religion is evidently what is most desirable" (cited in Day 2000, 106). The status of this proclamation was short-lived, however, and in the Quebec Act of 1774 greater privilege was accorded the Catholic church and the French population. Moving forward more than two hundred years in Canadian history, we see the 1992 referendum on a new constitution that would have given Quebec status as a "distinct society which includes a French-speaking majority, a unique culture and a civil law tradition" (cited in McLellan and Richmond 1994). Although this referendum failed, the recognition of two official languages by the Canadian government for all official transactions marks a clear departure from the U.S. case.

A second difference between the two countries concerns the position of indigenous peoples. Although neither country can claim bragging rights for their treatment of the original inhabitants, the territorial imperative in Canada was less complete. Some writers have contrasted, for example, a U.S. policy of elimination to a Canadian policy of assimilation with respect to the original inhabitants—although Richard Day (2000) warns against making that contrast too sharp, pointing to unfavorable treatment by Canadian settlers as well. Nonetheless, native populations have constituted a larger percentage of the total population of Canada than of the United States throughout most of the history of the two countries. Recent figures show, for example, that the aboriginal population in Canada in 1996 was 2.8 percent of the total (Statistics Canada 1999) compared to 1.5 percent in the United States identifying themselves in 2000 as American Indian and Alaska Native, either alone or in combination with one or more other races (U.S. Census Bureau 2000). If only those who identify solely as American Indian or Alaskan Native are considered, a number that may be more comparable to the Canadian data, the percentage drops to 0.9 percent.

During the nineteenth and early twentieth centuries, some trends that emerged in Canada showed certain similarities to the prevailing tone in the United States. Efforts to encourage immigration to Canada favored those of British origin, but people arrived from other countries as well—enough that the original system of categorizing immigrants as English, Scotch, Irish, and the term *foreigners* soon expanded to include Scandinavians, French, Germans, Mennonites, Icelanders, "Americans," and "other countries" (Day 2000). Without the specific target of a melting pot message to shape their views, some Canadian critics of immigration in the early twentieth century nonetheless expressed the same kinds of views that U.S. counterparts such as Henry Pratt Fairchild espoused. In *Strangers within Our Gates*, J. S. Woodsworth (1909/1972) offered a descriptive hierarchy of immigrant types. At the top of the pecking order, not surprisingly, were the British, who offered the promise of "more of our own blood" (46). Immigrants from the United States were next in line, followed by Scandinavians and Germans. The French, whom one might think would have some rights by virtue of settlement, ranked only fifth in Woodsworth's list. At the bottom of the list of immigrant groups were the "Orientals" (Chinese, Japanese, and Hindus), who apparently elicited the same kind of animus in Canada as they did in the United States and who, according to Woodsworth, "cannot be assimilated" (155).

The Chinese were the target of some of the earliest restrictive legislation in Canada, as they were in the United States. In 1885 the Canadian government enacted the Chinese Immigration Act, making this the first group to be singled out for exclusion. Legislative actions in Canada during the early decades of the 1900s also showed the exclusionary trend that was evident in the U.S. Immigration Act of 1924. The Canadian Immigration Act of 1906 established a policy of deportation, which appears to have been an effective curb on immigration rates (Day 2000). World War I had a negative impact on immigration attitudes in Canada and the United States alike, particularly with respect to people from Germany and Austria-Hungary. In 1919, amendments to the Immigration Act extended the number of specifically prohibited groups, at the same time expanding the language of exclusion. By this law, it was legal to exclude any immigrants who were "deemed undesirable owing to their peculiar customs, habits, modes of life and methods of holding property, and because of their probable inability to become readily assimilated" (cited in Day 2000, 141). Legislative restrictions continued to mount, such that by 1931, entrance to Canada was restricted to British and American citizens; wives, children, and fiancées of Canadian citizens; and agriculturalists, with all but direct relatives required to show proof of financial standing as well (Day 2000).

The Mosaic as a Canadian Social Representation

As legislation was becoming more restrictive, a social representation of immigration was developing in Canada that would prove to have the same durability that the melting pot has had in the United States. The first use of *mosaic* as a representation of the Canadian population is attributed to travel writer Victoria Hayward in her 1922 volume *Romantic Canada*. In describing the Canadian prairie country, Hayward speaks glowingly of the variety of visual and auditory experiences that different cultures present, and concludes that "it is indeed a mosaic of vast dimensions and great breadth" (quoted in Day 2000, 150).[6] In an introduction to that volume, E. J. O'Brien not only lauded the imagery that Hayward offered, but also specifically contrasted it with the dominant representation in the United States, where "the passion for conformity to a provincial process of standardization has crushed" unique traditions (quoted in Day 2000, 150).

The image of the cultural mosaic was reinforced with the publication of Kate Foster's *Our Canadian Mosaic* in 1926. Going beyond the pastoral images of Hayward, Foster specifically referred to the place of the cultural mosaic in the process of nation-building. Each person and group would represent a piece of the overall mosaic, yet each would maintain a distinctiveness—"no one tesserae encroaching in the very smallest degree upon another. All are required if the pattern is to be saved" (Foster 1926, 142). The glue for this mosaic was thought by Foster to be good will, respect, and positive bonds between the various peoples. Yet at the same time, she looked unfavorably at what she saw as an unregulated influx of "unemployable and undesirable immigrants" in the United States (1926, 11). Her solution for Canada? A mosaic that would consist primarily of British stock and "the more readily assimilable peoples of Europe" (11).

Like the metaphor of the melting pot, those of the mosaic can take varied forms, allowing different and not wholly consistent policies to emerge. Despite, and in part because of, this flexibility, the metaphor of a cultural mosaic has had longevity in the Canadian discourse, as policies of the latter half of the twentieth century illustrate.

Cultural Mosaic: From Social Representation to Public Policy

From the 1960s forward, multiculturalism has become increasingly central in official Canadian policy. One of the first markers of this trend was the activity of the Royal Commission on Bilingualism and Biculturalism in the mid 1960s. Exploring the circumstances of the "two founding races," the commission endorsed a principle of bilingualism including a guarantee of access to bilingual education (Day 2000). Although the document focused primarily on two groups, one volume of the commission report specifically reviewed other ethnic groups in Canada. In 1971, Premier Pierre Trudeau announced a White Paper on Multiculturalism, which would subsequently serve as the date of record as to when multiculturalism became official policy in Canada. Contained within this policy were declarations of support for "various cultures and ethnic groups that give structure and vitality to our society," encouragement of shared "cultural expression and values," and the expressed belief that a multicultural society would be stronger, richer, fairer, and more vital (Berry 1984). At the same time, the policy explicitly advocated the learning of both official languages, English and French, in order for groups to achieve full participation as citizens of Canada.

Three other more recent documents define the Canadian stance toward multiculturalism. First was *Multiculturalism: Building the Canadian Mosaic,* which was issued in 1987 to define a policy of "multiculturalism in a bicultural framework" and which was primarily addressed to legislators. Accompanying that document with an intended audience of the Canadian citizenry at large was "Multiculturalism: Being Canadian." A follow-up document

("Multiculturalism: What Is It Really About?") completed the package of reports, which firmly positioned the government with regard to a multicultural policy. The philosophy supporting these policies was conveyed in the official definition of multiculturalism, which outlined three principles: everyone has an ethnic origin; all cultures deserve respect; and cultural pluralism should be officially supported by the government (Day 2000). Ethnic was in turn defined as including cultural, national, and racial origins. Thus, the concept of a mosaic—and one with far more than two kinds of tiles—was firmly set into Canadian doctrine.

Representations, Policies, and Demographics

Canada's history of settlement, policy, and social representation illustrates the ways in which countries can develop distinctive profiles with regard to immigration. Jeffrey Reitz and Raymond Breton (1994) have argued that the differences between the United States and Canada are not terribly great. In partial support of their position, they report data showing greater support in the United States for the idea of cultural retention than in Canada. However, the place of this attitude in a broader belief system seems quite different between the two cultures. In the United States, support for diversity appears linked to an ideal of individualism, whereas in Canada the support is more closely linked to officially established policies (though endorsement of multiculturalism preceded the policies of the 1970s and 1980s, as the prevalence of the mosaic metaphor would suggest).

Other differences between the two countries can be seen in their demographics at the beginning of the twenty-first century. As noted earlier, the percentage of native Americans is somewhat higher in Canada than in the United States. At the same time, what some have termed the *visible minority* (or the more-often used phrase *people of color*) is much higher in the United States than in Canada: 25 percent in the United States versus only 9 percent in Canada (Bourhis and Marshall 1999).[7] Thus, even to the casual eye, particularly in urban centers, the countries look different.

Another difference between the two in terms of immigration patterns can be traced to the specifics of immigration policy. In Canada, following the 1966 White Paper on Immigration, a point system was instituted that gave preference to those who were termed *independent immigrants*—those who had both the language skills and the economic means to integrate rapidly into the country and to contribute to its economy (Reitz 2001). As a consequence of this policy, immigration statistics for the year 2000 in Canada show that 68 percent of immigrants were admitted in satisfaction of employment and business criteria, while only 31 percent entered on the principle of family reunification (Dovidio and Esses 2001). In contrast, the U.S. emphasis on family values resulted in proportions of 71 percent for family reunification and only 21 percent for skill and employment criteria.

Entrance differences such as these interact with the economic and social conditions existing in the country. Conditions of the economy, labor market conditions that favor skilled versus unskilled work, educational opportunities—these macro-level factors are unquestionably important in determining outcomes for immigrants. When combined with the factors that I have emphasized in this chapter—the official policies, the demographics of the immigrating people, and the social representations that shape the views of the immigration process—these conditions serve to describe the larger context.

I have focused on Canada as a point of comparison, to illustrate how different policies, representations, and demographics create a particular immigration landscape. For every country that is a destination for immigrants, a different picture can be painted. In Europe, for example, contemporary concerns with immigration emerge from a context quite different than that of Canada and the United States, which were both founded on a bedrock of immigration. Consider Germany, which was primarily a site of emigration rather than immigration until the mid-nineteenth century and which took an anti-immigration stance for most of the twentieth century (Meyers 2004). Within this generally nativist position, however, were two notable exceptions, one determined by ideology and the other by economics. The former is exemplified by the German policy on giving asylum to refugees, which for the last half of the twentieth century was the most liberal in Europe—a policy that evolved, it is thought, as a way of atoning for the horrors of the Nazi period (Meyers 2004). Economic conditions influenced practices developed to recruit temporary workers who ebbed and flowed with the state of the German economy. In principle, these guest workers (the greatest number of which are from Turkey) were contracted for specific jobs and were expected to return to their country of origin when the work was done. In practice, however, second- and third-generation immigrants who had never lived anywhere else but Germany were still considered guest workers.

The key to this apparent anomaly was, until very recently, the long-standing German definition of citizenship as based on blood line rather than territorial criteria. Thus, a person of German descent born in another country could be considered a citizen, whereas a person born in the country of foreign parents (an Auslaender) could not (Joppke 1998). As a result of this policy, substantial numbers of German residents (estimated at 7 to 8.4 percent by Meyers 2004, 154) had no political rights in the country in which they lived and worked. The German policy during much of the twentieth century thus displayed considerable ambivalence, supporting a growing foreign population while enacting legislation such as the 1983 "Law to Promote the Willingness of Foreigners to Return Home" (Meyers 2004).

The beginning of the twenty-first century marked a significant shift in official German government policy. In 1998 the newly elected liberal government declared that "Germany is a country of immigration" (cited in Meyers 2004, 155) and, in 2000, the definition of citizenship was changed to allow children born in Germany to foreign parents to qualify for German citizenship (Dovidio and Esses 2001; Meyers 2004). A few years later, in June 2002, Germany established its first formally regulated immigration system that both set limits on immigration while encouraging the integration of newcomers into the German culture.

Although the official policy in Germany has changed, attitudes toward immigrants remain mixed at best. Former German chancellor Helmut Schmidt recently remarked that Turkish guest workers should never have been invited in the first place, contending that multiculturalism can only work if a society is more authoritarian in structure (Bernstein 2004). Another leading politician was quoted as saying that "multiculturalism has failed, big time" (Bernstein 2004). Research finds that two contradictory beliefs about immigrants—assimilation and segregation—currently coexist in Germany (Zick et al. 2001). On the one hand, immigrants are expected to adapt to the prevailing norms of the native German population and give up their own culture; on the other hand, there are expectations that guest workers should remain segregated, better positioned to return eventually to their country of origin. The position of integration, which would endorse some form of multiculturalism, is not widely accepted, and instead is seen as a threat to the dominant culture or common base.

Contrast the German stance with that of France. France traditionally welcomed immigrants, and the percentage of immigrants in France has been the highest in Europe (Horowitz 1998). In a system of record-keeping in which the population is divided into two categories, French and foreigners, immigrants are readily moved from one column to the other. The prevailing representation in France, however, is not of a nation of immigrants but of a dominion of French. Census records are not even maintained on the number of minorities. France has, one writer claimed, a "collective amnesia" about immigrants (Horowitz 1998, 322) and the goal is not to glorify one's origins but to forget them. As a government adviser once stated: "When somebody emigrates, he changes not only his country, but also his history. Foreigners arriving in France must understand that henceforth their ancestors are the Gauls" (Fenby 1998, 202). Hyphenation of ethnicity (for example, Asian-American), so common in the United States despite its melting pot tradition, is virtually unheard of in France because uniformity to French traditions and definitions is more valued.

Although the historical policies of France and Germany have differed with regard to immigration and citizenship (Brubaker 1992), the two countries are quite similar now in their prevailing arguments for uniformity of culture. The perceived threat to the culture that immigrants pose is focused particularly on Muslim immigrants in both Germany and France, as well as in some other countries of Europe. Controversies over dress and the practice of religion have become more common. In France, for example, where the Muslim population now is estimated to be approximately 8 percent (including second- and third-generation immigrants), the question of whether young Muslim women can wear a headscarf to public schools has been a major controversy, provoking both school expulsions and revised state policies (Fleming and Carreyrou 2003). Once again, we can see the interaction of particular demographics, policies, and social representations and the ways in which the dynamics of this interaction change over time and place.

CONCLUDING COMMENTS

Without presuming to offer a full account of the history of U.S. immigration, much less a comprehensive international perspective, I have tried to illustrate the intricate relationships among public policy, demographic trends, and social representations of immigration. These components are, in the United States as elsewhere, inextricably linked and interdependent, such that a change in one alters the balance of the others. Policy affects patterns of immigration, and current demographics influence policy. Social representations operate within this space, sensitive to demographics as well as to history, and are influential in the instigation of new policies and support of old. Examples from Canada, Germany, and France show just how "un-fixed" these patterns are. Rather than inevitable sequences of events, movements and shifts emerge from particular combinations of forces and circumstances.

Acknowledging such flexibility is not to claim that the patterns are without regularity or that the processes are random. On the contrary, some predictability can be found within the diversity—but a predictability that comes only with detailed analysis of particular context. Thus, in the United States, the difference in demographics, for instance, from 1930 to 1960 as compared to 1970 to 2000 is considerable. These differences are apparent not only in how many people are entering the country and where they are coming from, but also in the types of communities they enter—ones in which they are original settlers versus ones in which one or more generations of people from their homeland have preceded them and established communities. Demographics and policy can also be clearly linked to the emergence and viability of particular representations of immigration, including the meaning of categories such as citizenship, guest worker, or illegal.

This is the stage for the immigrant's entrance—he or she a single number in the demographic summary, entering as a result of or in spite of national policy and subject to the laws and practices that are current in the country of destination. Cultural climate is also part of the stage setting, exemplified by the broad social representations discussed in this chapter. More focused beliefs directed at the immigrant, such as immigration attitudes and group stereotypes, contribute to the climate as well. However, whereas social representations generally speak to a common framework, the more specific attitudes and stereotypes can create quite different settings for groups who vary in ethnicity, religion, or language.

| Chapter Three | Rendering the Social Context: Attitudes Toward Immigration and Immigrants |

"There is clearly a need, at this juncture, for the use of a social lens to consider international migration and the situation of international migrants."

—United Nations Secretariat (2004)

SOCIAL REPRESENTATIONS SERVE as a broad framework for defining a country's views of immigration and of itself, setting up an iconic structure in which events can be played out. Yet the melting pot (or more recent derivatives, such as salad bowl) provides only vague outlines for the more specified attitudes that prevail in a society. Social representations, often evocative in their imagery and readily communicated as succinct phrases, can be inconsistently applied in their particulars; they can subsume a range of different, and sometimes conflicting, views on the phenomena of immigration. More specified beliefs about immigration policies and immigrant groups are "closer to the ground" and more readily understood in terms of varying degrees of positivity or negativity. These beliefs can also assume metaphorical form. An analysis of popular discourse surrounding immigration in the early 1900s in the United States, a period when new restrictions were being debated and eventually enacted, reveals images of diseased organisms, floods, and subhuman animals (O'Brien 2003). More often the lens of social science is the survey or questionnaire, less vivid in their depictions but equally informative about the public's views.

Here I consider general attitudes toward immigration as they have manifested themselves over the past several decades. These include both general measures of favorability—is it a good or bad thing for immigrants to come to this country?—as well as attitudes about what immigrants should do once they have arrived—what form of acculturation is most desirable? The second of these can be further complicated by consideration of not just the views of those in the host society, but also the opinions of the immigrants themselves, and by looking at the potential match or mismatch in these two views. Further consideration of the attitudinal climate encourages us to look for the beliefs and values that underlie expressed attitudes. These psychological processes and value orientations move us from a description of what to an understanding of why—a position that is useful and perhaps essential to the development of any intervention strategy or policy development.

PATTERNS OF IMMIGRATION ATTITUDES

Preparing for a conference on immigration in early 2004, the United Nations Office of the Secretariat observed that "probably in most regions and countries, and certainly according to the media that are creating an emerging world opinion, the current movements of people across borders represent a problem" (4). This diplomatically phrased understatement was followed by the observation that "these public perceptions reflect real issues and real problems, but they also reflect ignorance, prejudices and fear" (4).

International headlines emanating from several European countries in recent years, including Austria, France, and the Netherlands, support these UN observations. In the primary elections in France in the spring of 2002, for example, Jean-Marie Le Pen surprised many by finishing second, running on a platform that included proposing an end to all legal immigration and the deportation of all illegal immigrants.[1] Although the election results may have been a surprise, survey data collected throughout Europe in the late 1980s and early to mid-1990s showed increasing agreement with statements such as [there are] "too many non-European Union nationals in the country" and "the rights of non-EU nationals should be restricted" (Pettigrew 1998). More specifically stated attitudes suggesting prejudice and discrimination against particular immigrant groups are in evidence throughout Europe as well (Jackson, Brown, and Kirby 1998). Similar debates have emerged in Australia, which has seen a flow of immigrants, primarily from Asia, since it ended its White Australia policy in the early 1970s. Former Australian Prime Minister Robert Menzies helped to shape the tone of these debates with his frequent calls for the country to stand up to the so-called Yellow Peril from the north (Perlez 2002), recalling the racist discourse of an earlier era in the United States.

Attitudes toward U.S. Immigration Policy

In the United States, attitudes toward immigration and immigrant groups have been characterized by considerable ambivalence over the years. The policies described in chapter 2 provide discrete indices of public opinion, from the anti-immigrant feelings that prompted the restrictive legislation of 1924 to the far more open policy advocated by John F. Kennedy and enacted in 1965, followed in turn by the increasingly restrictive and punitive policies of the 1990s. Surrounding and underlying these distinct policy markers, however, is a far murkier picture of attitudes toward immigrant groups. Writing in the 1920s when anti-immigration feeling was strong, sociologists Robert Park and Herbert Miller claimed that the general American community "shows . . . a contempt for all the characteristics of the newcomer" (1921, 61). In 2000, Foner expressed her more charitable belief that "most white Americans would like to convey an image of themselves as unprejudiced and compassionate" (151). Yet in the 1920s there were staunch supporters of immigration just as there are strong opponents today. Both general patterns and individual variations are worth consideration.

Over the years, surveys of the attitudes of U.S. citizens toward immigration have recorded various ebbs and flows. In the 1930s and early 1940s, attitudes tended to be quite negative, emanating in part from the lengthy economic depression and isolationist sentiments at the beginning of World War II (Simon 1985). A 1939 poll, for example, found that 83 percent of the public opposed legislation that would increase allowances for the entrance of European refugees (Harwood 1986; Simon 1985). Survey questions are often phrased in terms of three options: should immigration be increased, decreased, or kept at its present level. Typically the percentage of people endorsing an increase in immigration is less than 10 percent—a figure that has remained relatively constant from the period between 1930 and 1960, when immigration was low, through the latter decades of the twentieth century, when immigration has been considerably higher. Differences in public opinion emerge, however, when we look at the percentage of those who endorse current rates of immigration versus those who favor reductions. By the mid-1960s, perhaps consistent with the passage of less restrictive legislation, attitudes toward immigration had become more favorable. Gallup poll data in 1964 showed 46 percent of the U.S. sample endorsing current levels of immigration and 38 percent preferring a decrease (with a typical low figure of 6 percent favoring an increase). This pattern shifted steadily over the next thirty years: in a 1995 Gallup poll only 28 percent of those surveyed favored then-current levels and 62 percent wanted fewer immigrants (Lapinski et al. 1997). A survey conducted in 2004 (Mizrahi 2005) showed slightly more favorable patterns, though a plurality still believed that immigration levels should be decreased (48 percent favored a decrease, 41 percent supported current levels, and only 10 percent favored an increase). In this same survey, 58 percent of the respondents agreed with the statement: "We should strictly limit the number of people who immigrate." Thus, despite some fluctuation, the trend over the past forty years in the United States has been toward diminished support for immigration.

A more vivid depiction of the negative trend is portrayed in an analysis of cover images from popular magazines during the past thirty years (Chavez 2001). Leo Chavez defined his sample as every magazine cover that dealt with immigration published between 1965 and 1999 in any of ten nationally distributed magazines, including *Time, Newsweek, Business Week,* and *The Nation.* He then classified each cover as representing a viewpoint that could be characterized as affirmative, alarmist, or neutral. Cover images considered affirmative showed some positive message, such as a celebration of immigrant contributions to the melting pot or a compassionate attitude toward immigrants. Alarmist messages, in contrast, pointed to presumed dangers of immigration, ranging from undesirable population growth to the "death of the nation" (2001, 21). As figure 3.1 shows, the trends are clear. In the decade of the 1970s, affirmative covers slightly outnumbered alarmist ones. From the 1970s to the 1990s, the number of affirmative images stepped steadily downward as alarmist images became more prominent. In both the 1980s and the 1990s, alarmist images accounted for approximately 75 percent of all covers published on the topic. My own statistical analyses on the Chavez data, comparing affirmative to alarmist messages over the three decades, shows a significant difference between time periods (X square = 9.84, df = 2, p < .01).

It is notable that Chavez (2001) found relative consistency in the use of more alarmist imagery across magazines that differed substantially in their position on the political spectrum. Beyond the vivid and often simplistic cover images, however, more varied and sometimes more nuanced tellings of the immigration story appeared in the accompanying articles. Here variations in political stance did emerge, much as Rita Simon (1985) found in an earlier analysis of media content between 1880 and 1980. In her study, as one example, the *Saturday Evening Post* took the most consistently anti-immigration positions. At the other end of the spectrum, *The Nation* was persistent in its stand against restrictions and its praise for the contributions that immigrants make to the society. Although varying somewhat in their position toward immigration policy, the magazine articles were often framed in similar terms, focusing on the change in immigrant origins, from Anglo-European to Asian and Latino, as a major cause for concern.

Just as popular magazines differ in their opposition to or endorsement of immigration, so are there variations within segments of the population.

Figure 3.1   Media Images of Immigration

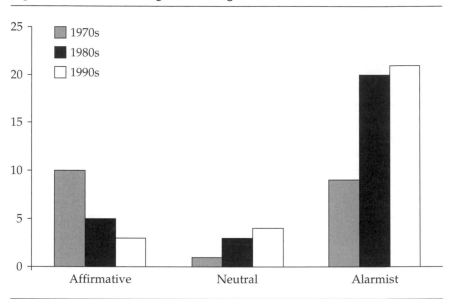

Source: Adapted from Chavez (2001).

Immigration is generally regarded more favorably by those higher in socio-economic status (Espenshade and Hempstead 1996; Simon 1985, 1987). In a 1980 Gallup poll, for example, 81 percent of those with only a grade school education favored halting immigration, compared to only 44 percent of those with a college education (Simon 1985). Similarly, Kim Mizrahi (2005) found that more education (but not greater income) was significantly associated with positive attitudes toward immigration. Studies in European Union countries are consistent, showing more positive attitudes among those with more education (Jackson et al. 2001; Pettigrew 1998). In these European studies, age served as a marker variable as well, with older people more likely than younger people to favor sending all immigrants back to their country of origin (Jackson et al. 2001) or to show both blatant and subtle prejudice against immigrant groups (Pettigrew 1998).

Ethnic differences in attitudes are often found in U.S. surveys, as are regional differences, though there is some inconsistency in the patterns across time and place. In a 1980 comparison of black and white respondents, Simon (1985) reported that blacks were more likely to favor stopping the flow of immigration than whites were, by a margin of 79 to 64 percent. Data from the mid-1990s reported by David Sears and his colleagues (Sears et al. 1999) found a smaller difference between these two groups with blacks either equal or only slightly more in favor of decreasing immigration than whites; both groups, however, were much less favorable to immigration than were the Hispanics and Asians who were part of this later sample. In contrast, Thomas Espenshade and Katherine Hempstead (1996) reported more favorable attitudes among Asians and African Americans and less favorable attitudes among Hispanic and non-Hispanic whites. In her 2004 national survey, Mizrahi found Hispanics to be the group most favorable toward immigration, whites the least favorable, and blacks midway between the two groups. These varying patterns surely suggest that more than one set of values or ideologies is driving the attitudes, creating both ambivalence within individuals and inconsistencies across studies. African Americans, for example, may view immigrants as an economic threat, while at the same time feeling solidarity with a group that also is subjected to discrimination, resulting in a mixed attitudinal picture (Diamond 1998; Thornton and Mizuno 1999).

Mizrahi also found that differences in attitudes toward immigration vary depending upon the region of the country in which respondents live. Dividing her sample into four U.S. Census Bureau regional categories, she found that people living in the eastern and the western states are generally more favorable toward immigration than those in the Midwest and the South. In a more timely analysis, based on the red state versus blue state distinction made popular in recent U.S. presidential elections, Mizrahi found that red state respondents (those living in states with a Republican majority) were significantly less favorable toward immigration than were blue state respondents (those living in states with a Democratic majority). In contemplating the political implications of this pattern, it is interesting to note that the traditional gateway cities for immigrants, such as New York City and Los Angeles, are in blue states. Thus, the presence of large numbers of immigrants in one's immediate environment does not, as some have assumed, necessarily create animosity.

Beliefs About Immigrants

Although a feeling that immigration should be decreased may be the modal position, respondents are often quite positive in their views of individual immigrants. Survey data show that a majority of respondents believe that those who emigrate from other countries "are basically good, honest people," hardworking, and likely to be "productive citizens once they get their feet on the ground" (Lapinski et al. 1997). The conditions under which immigrants enter the United States make a big difference in these and other views, however. Data reported by David Sears and his colleagues (1999) showed that although blacks and Hispanics make relatively little distinction between legal and illegal immigrants, both whites and Asians believe that legal immigrants are substantially more likely than illegal immigrants to be hardworking. Other data also reveal less favorable attitudes toward illegal immigrants (Harwood 1983; Simon 1987). Surveys, for example, often show a majority of people believing that the government should not provide health and education benefits to either adults or children who have entered the country illegally. This needs to be coupled with the recognition that people increasingly believe that the majority of people coming to the United States in recent years are illegal immigrants. A 1993 survey, for example, found that 68 percent of people believed that most immigrants are illegal (Lapinski et al. 1997). *Illegal immigrant* has in fact become a highly stigmatized category, adding an additional layer of negativity to the prevailing image of immigrants. Refugees also do not fare well in attitude surveys, despite what one might think would be some element of compassion for their plight (Simon 1987).

Attitudes also vary sharply as a function of country of immigrant origin. U.S. citizens are more likely to think the number of immigrants from European countries "about right," and the number from Asian and Latin American countries too high (Lapinski et al. 1997).[2] Even before 9/11, immigrants from Arab countries and the Middle East were rated among the least favorable groups, along with people from Latin America and the Caribbean (Yankelovich Partners 1993). A 1993 Gallup poll asked respondents whether particular groups of immigrants created "more benefits" or "more problems" for the country. A majority of respondents believed that the Irish, Poles, Chinese, and Koreans (in that order) have benefited the country; immigrants seen as most likely to create problems were Iranians, Haitians, Cubans, and Mexicans, with Mexicans and Haitians showing the sharpest rise in negative ratings compared to an earlier 1985 survey (Lapinski et al. 1997).

In her recent survey of U.S. attitudes toward immigrants, Mizrahi (2005) specifically targeted China, Jamaica, Mexico, and Poland, countries selected because they represented some of the most numerous immigrant groups from major source regions. Mexican immigrants were generally viewed the most negatively among the four groups, more likely to be seen as not bringing needed skills into the country and as draining the economy. Polish and Chinese immigrants, by contrast, were most likely to be seen as bringing such skills, as hardworking, and as contributing positively to the economy. Immigrants from Jamaica were generally downgraded, though not as severely as the Mexicans.

These general attitudes toward the desirability of different immigrant groups can be linked to specific ethnic group stereotypes, which are pervasive if not wholly consistent. In the next chapter I will look at those stereotypes more carefully. First, however, I think it is helpful to consider two other aspects of attitudes toward immigration. First are the reasons that people give or that seem to underlie their positive and negative attitudes. Second are the endorsement of general assimilation goals and the match of those goals between citizens of the host country and immigrants.

REASONS AND RATIONALE FOR IMMIGRATION ATTITUDES

Despite the risk of oversimplifying, I divide the reasons for being unfavorable toward immigration into three general categories. First is a set of economic arguments, framed either as the potential economic drain on the economy that immigrants might represent or as a threat to one's livelihood that potentially competitive workers pose. A second set of reactions deals with general quality of life concerns. In this case, the perceived threats are more symbolic than material, framed in terms of core values that the society is seen to represent. Sometimes related, either explicitly or implicitly, to these symbolic values is a third category of beliefs that focuses on the place and operation of status hierarchies within the society. All three types of reactions have long histories, as much in evidence at the beginning of the twentieth century as at the beginning of the twenty-first, though the particular exemplars and targets have sometimes changed in response to shifting demographic patterns.

Perceived Economic Threats

Consider some of the survey data that speak to people's economic concerns. In general, people who believe that economic conditions are unfavorable are prone to have negative attitudes toward immigration (Espenshade and Hempstead 1996). More direct in suggesting the causal beliefs that are at work are 1994 data showing that a majority of people believed that "new immigrants joining the labor force drive down wages" and that "new immigrants take jobs away from American workers"—66 percent and 64 percent respectively (Lapinski et al. 1997). At the same time, 78 percent of respondents in a 1993 poll believed that "many immigrants work hard, often taking jobs that Americans don't want" (Lapinski et al. 1997). Similar patterns of push and pull are reported by Mizrahi (2005): slightly fewer agreed with the first two questions (54 percent and 48 percent) and 89 percent agreed with the statement that hardworking immigrants take unwanted jobs. Not surprisingly, expression of these concerns depends on one's perspective. In a Los Angeles survey, 57 percent of white respondents and 47 percent of black respondents thought they would have "less" or "a lot less" economic opportunity than they currently had if immigration continued at its present rate. In contrast, groups more likely to contain first- and second-generation immigrants themselves were less worried about potential economic costs: 33 percent of Hispanics, 15 percent of Chinese, 13 percent of Japanese, and 6 percent of Koreans saw a negative impact from continuing immigration (Johnson, Farrell, and Guinn 1997).

These attitudes about immigrant employment potential and its consequent personal economic threat coexist with beliefs about the employability of immigrants. A majority believe, for example, that "many immigrants wind up on welfare and raise taxes for Americans" (59 percent in a 1993 survey) and that "immigrants use more than their fair share of government services, such as welfare, medical care, and food stamps" (from 60 to 74 percent in polls conducted over the last ten years) (Lapinski et al. 1997; Mizrahi 2005). As Victoria Esses et al. (2001) point out, attitudes such as these often suggest a kind of no-win position for the immigrant. On the one hand, they are expected to fail and are judged negatively for their perceived burden on taxpayers in the form of welfare and unemployment insurance. On the other, their potential success on the job market is seen as a threat, creating a more precarious position for the native-born worker.

Esses and her colleagues argue that a basic competition for resources underlies negative attitudes toward immigrants, framing the argument in what they term an "instrumental model of group conflict" (Esses, Jackson, and Armstrong 1998). The key elements of this model are illustrated in figure 3.2. First, there must be some perception that resources are limited, most often defined in terms of economic resources but applicable to the perception of power differentials as well. These perceptions precipitate group competition, based on a belief that resources are a zero-sum game, that is, that greater access to resources by another group means less access for me and my group. Affectively, these zero sum beliefs are represented as feelings of anxiety or fear, conditions that generate efforts to remove the competition and to improve one's actual or potential position. How that competition plays out depends on whom the relevant outgroup is seen to be. Some outgroups are clearly viewed as more threatening than others: those who share similar skills or potential access to resources, for example, are regarded as more dangerous than those who are more distinct. The specificity of some of these comparisons is suggested in data that James Johnson, Walter Farrell, and Chandra Guinn (1997) report in Los Angeles. When asked whether more good jobs for members of other ethnic groups would mean fewer jobs for one's own group, whites saw relatively little cause for concern, whether the targeted group was Asian, black, or Hispanic.

Figure 3.2   An Instrumental Model of Group Conflict

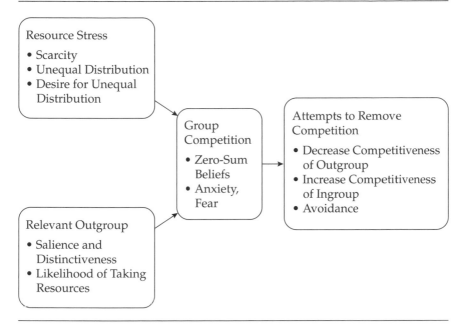

Resource Stress
• Scarcity
• Unequal Distribution
• Desire for Unequal
  Distribution

Group
Competition
• Zero-Sum
  Beliefs
• Anxiety,
  Fear

Attempts to Remove
Competition
• Decrease Competitiveness
  of Outgroup
• Increase Competitiveness
  of Ingroup
• Avoidance

Relevant Outgroup
• Salience and
  Distinctiveness
• Likelihood of Taking
  Resources

Source: Adapted from Esses, Jackson, and Armstrong (1998, 703).

A majority of black respondents, however, saw both Asians and Hispanics as direct competition for them. Hispanic respondents saw Asians as their primary threat, with blacks of somewhat less concern.

Specifically directing a person's attention to a potential comparison group can intensify negative reactions. As an example, participants in an experimental study conducted in the border city of El Paso, Texas, were asked to evaluate Mexican immigrants on a set of work-related traits (for example, hardworking, competitive, punctual). These student participants were more negative in their evaluations when asked how members of this group were similar to themselves than when the question was framed in terms of difference (Zárate et al. 2004). The potential if hypothetical threat to economic well-being, when heightened by a question about similarities, led respondents to see more possibility for realistic group conflict and, as a psychological consequence, to establish more distance between themselves and the rival group by downgrading their characters.

More generally, the relevance of the comparison group may help to explain the survey data that often show more negative attitudes toward immigration among groups with less education and lower socioeconomic status. For them, the potential loss of jobs to relatively unskilled immigrants appears to pose a far greater threat than it does to middle-class white-collar workers. On the other hand, one can imagine that if the immigrant flow showed a preponderance of higher skilled workers—perhaps a segment of the financial community from Hong Kong when the transition to Chinese rule was under way—then those with higher socioeconomic status would become more negative in their views.

In their work, Victoria Esses and her colleagues (Esses, Jackson, and Armstrong 1998; Esses et al. 1999) have shown that perceived economic threat is not simply a correlate of attitudes toward immigrants, but rather is a direct cause of negative attitudes. Participants in an experimental study who read an article about immigration in which immigrants were described as competing with Canadians for jobs were not only more negative in their evaluations of a fictitious immigrant group than participants who read a more neutral article, but also more negative about immigration in general. In related work, investigators in Switzerland (Falomir-Pichastor et al. 2004) manipulated perceived economic threat by telling experimental participants that studies have shown a relationship between rate of immigration and the unemployment rate of native Swiss. Participants who perceived a high degree of threat were more likely to discriminate against foreign-born residents than those who believed the threat was low. If antidiscrimination norms were made salient in this context, by informing participants of a national survey showing high levels of tolerance for foreigners, discrimination was somewhat reduced. The reduction was primarily evident among people in a low threat condition, however, and seemed to have relatively little impact on those who perceived high levels of economic threat.

We need to ask whether the fears of economic loss are realistically based. Do immigrants actually take jobs away from native-born workers? This question is one that has engaged the interest and ingenuity of a cadre of economists over the years. It is a difficult question to answer at any time, given the number of factors that must be considered. Further challenging the efforts to answer the question for a specific period in history are shifts in economic conditions and opportunities for employment. In the United States, in the latter part of the twentieth century, for example, the move to a more highly skilled workforce has changed the opportunity structure for less educated, less skilled immigrants. These conditions may have made it more difficult for unskilled immigrants to experience the kind of wage mobility that earlier generations of immigrants enjoyed. Yet if these workers are primarily competing with one another, rather than with native-born Americans (see Raijman and Tienda 1999), then the basis for job fears is misplaced.

Not being an economist, I offer no definitive analyses of this issue. However, statements from those who have studied the problem seem to indicate that, on balance, immigrants do not have an appreciable impact on wages or employment of native-born Americans (Friedberg and Hunt 1999; Raijman and Tienda 1999). At least two trends are suggested in comparing immigrant to native-born workers over the past twenty or thirty years. First, the previously higher employment rate of immigrants compared to native-born workers is decreasing; and second, the wage gap between the two groups has increased in favor of native-born workers (Raijman and Tienda 1999). Reitz (2001) reports similar trends in Canada between 1970 and 1995: lower rates of labor force participation and lower earnings for immigrants relative to native-born Canadians. Thus, it is difficult to sustain the argument that immigrants are a direct threat to the employment of native-born citizens.

Nor does there seem to be any good evidence that immigrants are a disproportionate drain on civic services. Gregory DeFreitas (1992) concluded that immigrant families are significantly less likely to receive public assistance than are native-borns, and when they do get public assistance, they receive less money. In contrast, some have concluded that the impact of immigrants is greater on the upside, in terms of increasing demand and overall productivity (DeFreitas 1992), though the magnitude of this gain may be limited as well (Friedberg and Hunt 1999). Such an effect, if true, clearly challenges the zero-sum beliefs that often underlie negative attitudes toward immigration, where it is assumed that any gain for another means a loss to the self.

Nonetheless, negative attitudes persist. As Rebeca Raijman and Marta Tienda conclude, "the belief [by researchers] that immigrants are a net, albeit modest, economic benefit for the U.S. economy is less important than the popular perception that the foreign-born (and their children) drain public coffers . . . and compete with U.S. workers" (1999, 254). Friedberg and Hunt concur: "The social dimensions of immigration may in fact play a more important role than economic factors in shaping public opinion on immigration" (1999, 358).

Accordingly, we turn to the second and third categories of reasons and rationale that I identified earlier: one concerned with quality of life and perceived threats to a society's core values, and the other related to beliefs about the legitimacy of status hierarchies within a society.

Quality of Life and Symbolic Values

People arriving from other countries are often believed, quite reasonably, to be different from oneself and one's own group in a variety of ways—

in religion, in cultural habits, in food preferences, in shared history. One stance taken toward these perceived differences is positive, seeing potential contributions to the fabric of the country in the diversity of its citizenry. An item included in a number of national surveys illustrates this perspective: "Immigrants help improve our country with their different cultures and talents." Between 60 and 70 percent of those questioned agreed with this statement in surveys administered on three separate occasions in the early 1990s (Lapinski et al. 1997). A statement from the United Nations Secretariat develops this position more fully, when it says that social integration implies "that what separates people is not negated but kept within the boundaries of commonly accepted rules and norms of behavior . . . groups . . . are asked to adhere freely to a social contract whereby they agree to live together in reasonable harmony" (2004, 9).

The endorsement of diversity is articulated most clearly in the policies of the Canadian government, as discussed in chapter 2. Guidelines for distinctiveness versus merger are laid out in some detail, calling for unification on civic responsibilities and allegiance to country while maintaining separation in culture and traditions. Such recognition of difference, it is believed, will strengthen the country and provide a vitality that strong homogenization policies would not.

In the United States, conceptions of diversity are less clearly articulated and more conflicted. On the one hand, celebrations of diverse cultures and cuisines are common and valued; on the other hand, commentators observe an underlying belief that "people are really all the same" (Markus, Steele, and Steele 2001). One ramification of these latter beliefs is the endorsement of a color-blind stance—the idea that we should not pay attention to group differences because they don't really matter. Yet the endorsement of a color-blind policy depends on who is being asked. In comparing majority and minority students in the United States, Hazel Markus, Claude Steele, and Dorothy Steele (2000) find that white students tend to support assimilation and see too much diversity as harmful. In contrast, minority students are more likely to endorse the presence of multiple perspectives and diversity on campus. Although the work of Markus and her colleagues is based on nonimmigrant groups within the United States, it seems quite applicable to the case of immigrants as well. For members of the white majority, it is far easier to support a position of assimilation to the norm, namely the dominant white group, while paying some lip service to diversity. For the immigrant (and minority) group, in contrast, diversity is a reality and one that cannot be so readily disclaimed.

To state that one is generally in favor of diversity is to say that one is ready to accept difference in the particular. That is, one must at some level be willing to accept that a group displaying differences in some domain is all right in doing so, and does not threaten one's position or beliefs. Unfortunately, that is not so easily accomplished. Considerable evidence points to the conclusion that people often view difference as a threat to the integrity of their positions. In the Juan Falomir-Pichastor et al. (2004) study, identity threat was found to be a major element in the negative attitudes that Swiss citizens held toward foreigners. Statements such as "a high rate of foreigners is a threat to the Swiss national identity" and "it is important to safeguard national identity" represented these views. In another example, from the Michael Zárate et al. (2004) study, participants in one condition of the experiment were asked to rate Mexican immigrants on interpersonal traits, such as friendly, generous, and traditional. In this condition, the Texas students were more negative in their judgments when they were asked to focus on differences between themselves and the Mexican immigrants, than when asked to focus on similarity. Recall that this is the opposite effect from that found when students were asked to make judgments on work-related traits. Thus, the attention to possible differences in personality and character—rather than making the observer feel less threatened, which a disparity in job skills did—was instead a reason to dislike the targeted group and what they represented. Still other research has shown that people, specifically, members of a host country such as Spain or Israel, feel anxiety about interacting with members of immigrant groups, in this case Moroccans, Russians, and Ethiopians (Stephan et al. 1998). Feelings of anxiety, such as uncertainty, worry, and apprehension, though not reported at high levels in absolute terms, nonetheless predict negative attitudes toward immigrant groups (Stephan et al. 1998).

Stephan and his colleagues suggest that negative attitudes toward other groups emerge from a matrix of four elements: realistic threats, such as the zero sum resources that Esses and her colleagues have studied; symbolic threats, based on perceived differences in values; intergroup anxiety; and negative stereotypes about the group (1998). In their research in Spain and in Israel, intergroup anxiety and negative stereotypes carried the greatest weight, though all factors were related to each other to a reasonably high degree.

Research on European attitudes toward immigration also reveals the important influence that value threat can have (Jackson et al. 2001). Citizens who appreciate the contributions that immigrants can make—by endorsing, for example, statements such as "people from these minority groups are enriching the cultural life of [my country]"—are also likely to be opposed to policies that advocate restriction or cessation of immigration. In contrast, restrictive policies are favored by those who see immigrants encroaching on their way of life, as indicated by statements such as "the religious practices of people from these minority groups threaten our way of life" or "in schools where there are too many children from these minority groups, the quality of education suffers." In each of the fifteen European countries that Jackson and his colleagues surveyed, these beliefs in cultural encroachment were significantly associated with restrictive immigration attitudes.

Whether in the United States, in Europe, or in Israel, there is ample evidence of the importance of social psychological factors at work, creating a web of attitudes that serves to distance one group from another, and in particular to separate the dominant host group from the incoming immigrant group. Difference is a difficult concept in many respects. On the one hand, it can be considered value-neutral, simply referring to two points that occupy different positions in some undefined space. On the other hand, it can imply, in varying degrees of certainty, different positions in a clear hierarchy of value. In a period of intense globalization, it is difficult to avoid the recognition of difference. As Clifford Geertz has observed, "Differences of belief, sometimes quite radical ones, are more and more often directly visible, directly encountered: ready-to-hand for suspicion, worry, repugnance, and dispute. Or, I suppose, for tolerance and reconciliation, even for attraction and conversion. Though that, right now, is not exactly common" (quoted in Shweder, Minow, and Markus 2000, 146). As Geertz suggests, awareness of difference seems less likely to result in attraction than in suspicion. One reason for the tilt in this direction is, I believe, that difference is not seen as neutral but far more often implies a hierarchical ordering. Further, it is most often the case that members of the host society see themselves at the top of that hierarchy and have some vested interests in remaining in that position.

Beliefs in a Status Hierarchy

George Frederickson claims that ethnic hierarchy is the "most influential and durable conception" (1999, 24) of intergroup relations in the United States, whereby "a dominant group . . . has claimed rights and privileges not to be fully shared with outsiders" (1999, 24). Similarly, Jim Sidanius and Felicia Pratto refer to "systems of group-based social hierarchies" (1999, 31). Characteristics such as race, ethnicity, and nation represent what Sidanius and Pratto call an arbitrary-set system, in which the distinctions between groups are socially constructed, leading to the development of a hierarchy in which one group is dominant over another. Within a society, social practices consistent with the hierarchy are sustained by a system of legitimizing myths—a set of attitudes and values that justify the particular arrangement. As an aside, I should note that these myths may be sufficiently pervasive that they can be endorsed by those low on the hierarchy as well as those who are high (see Jost and Banaji 1994; Jost, Burgess, and Mosso 2001).

Frederickson tracked the history of ethnic hierarchy back to the treatment of American Indians by the original British settlers and to the black slavery of the colonial period. Attitudes and policies toward Asian immigration, described in the previous chapter, represent another chapter in the hierarchy story. Throughout the history of immigration in the United States, one can readily find evidence of orders of preference and a favoring of the original northern European stock over immigrants from other regions.

Often the analysis of hierarchy reveals a philosophy of pigmentation rights. Consider the statement "Public opinion polls and other data indicate that there is a steadily increasing fear of the so-called 'browning of America,' a growing intolerance among native Americans . . . of immigrants" (Johnson, Farrell, and Guinn 1997). The use of browning to characterize the attitudes toward immigrants reflects a color line that has always been evident in the views of U.S. citizens toward immigrants (Deaux 2004).

Most often, the poles of the dimension have been black and white, with other groups assessed by their presumed similarity to one or the other pole. Attitudes toward Irish immigrants are a case in point. During the nineteenth century, Irish immigration was substantial: approximately 1 million in the first four or five decades and 1.8 million between 1845 and 1855 (Ignatiev 1995). In his informative volume *How the Irish Became White,* Ignatiev describes how Irish immigrants and black Americans were often restricted to the same poor neighborhoods and competed for the same low-paying jobs. Although the Irish often fared better in these competitions, stereotypical images of the two groups frequently merged. The Irish were called "niggers turned inside out" (Ignatiev 1995, 41); Celtic characteristics were said to include "the black tint of the skin" (Jacobson 1998, 48). Frederick Douglass saw the Irish as doing the "black man's work." "If they cannot rise to the dignity of white men, they show that they cannot fall to the degration of black men" (quoted in Ignatiev 1995, 111).

Although the Irish were sometimes viewed as more similar to black than white in the early years of their U.S. residence, they became, over time, what Nancy Foner has referred to as "probationary whites" (2000). This shift was part of a change in the language of ethnic distinction, wherein references to separate European nationalities became replaced with what Jacobson has called "the ascent of monolithic whiteness" (1998, 93). Previously ethnic groups had been measured against a northern European standard, whereby Italians, Slovaks, and other groups were found wanting; now Caucasian became the white standard and European immigrants were merged in contradistinction to groups whose heritage was Asian or African. From the frame of what has been termed racial consolidation theory, the cause of these shifts lay in the increasing numbers of nonwhite immigrants and the symbolic threat that they posed. Accordingly, unification of previously distinct white groups increased their size and presumed power (Shanahan and Olzak 2002).

The language of social sciences reified distinctions between what were termed the Negroid, Caucasoid, and Mongoloid races—groupings the late anthropologist Melville Herskovits said were derived "from commonsense observation as well as from the scientist's classification" (1935, 207). In large measure, the dominant paradigm shifted from an emphasis on ethnicity, as exemplified in the work of the Chicago school, perhaps best known through *The Polish Peasant in Europe and America*, to categorizing by race. In the race-based scheme, a white-at-the-top hierarchy was evident. Its simplicity is clear in comments recorded by James Loewen (1971) in his history of Chinese-Americans in Mississippi. A Baptist minister tells his interviewer: "You're either a white man or a nigger, here. Now, that's the whole story. When I first came to the Delta, the Chinese were classed as nigras." The interviewer inquires: "And now they are called whites?" "That's right!" is the reply.

As Jim Sidanius and Felicia Pratto (1999) have shown, this hierarchy of color continues today, though the perceived distance between top and bottom is not as great as it once was. Whites are accorded the highest status, black and Latinos are ranked at the bottom, and Asians typically fall in between.[3] Thus, for the contemporary immigrant to the United States, a majority of whom are either from Asia or from Latin America, entry can mean an almost automatic positioning on the color hierarchy, some distance below the dominant white.[4] This hierarchy is reflected in the perceptions of group competition reported earlier in describing the James Johnson, Walter Farrell, and Chandra Guinn (1997) data. Blacks saw Asians and Hispanics, both of whom typically rank higher, as their competitors. Hispanics saw Asians as their primary threat, but not blacks, who are typically lower. Whites saw little basis for competitive threat from any of the other groups.

Beliefs in a dominance hierarchy can be assessed at the level of individual predisposition as well as the outcome of group ranking. As defined by Sidanius and Pratto, social dominance orientation (SDO) "is defined as a very general individual differences orientation expressing the value that people place on nonegalitarian and hierarchically structured relationships among social groups" (1999, 61). Using the scale they developed to assess this tendency, one can identify those who are more or less likely to endorse and support social hierarchies. Those whose scores indicate high social dominance are more likely to endorse items such as "inferior groups should stay in their place" and less likely to support propositions such as "all groups should be given an equal chance in life." It should be noted that in the United States, where beliefs in hierarchy would seem to fly in the face of democratic ideals, the average score on the SDO tends to be quite low (varying between 2 and 3 on a 7-point scale). Nonetheless, the relative positioning on the scale is predictive of a variety of behaviors, including some related directly to attitudes toward immigrants.

In research conducted both in Canada and the United States, Esses and her colleagues (2001) found strong negative correlations between SDO and attitudes toward immigration. People higher in SDO were more likely to believe that immigration has a negative effect on jobs for the native-born and were less likely to be favorable toward immigrants or liberal immigration policies. The major reason for this relationship, as statistical mediation analyses showed, was the belief of high SDO individuals in the principle of zero-sum outcomes. Negative attitudes toward immigrant groups thus appear not to be an expression of ethnic prejudice per se, but rather a more economically driven belief in group competition for limited resources, which, as noted earlier, could refer to political capital as well.

Whereas strong endorsement of dominance hierarchies mitigates against a favorable attitudes toward immigrants, other social attitudes can serve as facilitators. Beliefs about equality of opportunity and the importance of social justice, on the face of it, provide countervailing pressures to the hierarchical beliefs just discussed. At the same time, these beliefs are complex and often, when in conjunction with the reflexive American endorsement of individualism, create ambivalence rather than unrestricted favorability. Further, as we saw earlier (Falomir-Pichastor et al. 2004), even deliberately making norms of antidiscrimination salient has a limited effect when perceived threats are great.

Beliefs in the value of equality reflect the climate of a host country and the principles of democracy that are at work. The focus in this case is less on the particular immigrant group and what it might bring to the table, but rather on the table that the host will provide. As we have seen, conceptions of the melting pot as dominant metaphor for immigration, though often ambiguous, frequently implied that the host country offered a clear opportunity for the immigrant to blend into the prevailing context to the extent that he or she was motivated to do so. In essence, beliefs in equality tend to weigh in on the side of equal opportunity: give everyone an equal chance and with hard work, all can succeed.

Beliefs in equality carry some ambivalence, however, as debates over affirmative action have often revealed (Crosby 2004; Crosby et al. 2003). A key point of distinction and dispute is whether equality refers to opportunity or to outcome. Relatively few citizens in the United States would dispute that everyone should have equal opportunity to jobs, education, and other fundamental activities of the society. The divergence begins when one moves beyond general statements of opportunity to beliefs about outcome, and the capability of members of all groups to attain those outcomes. Consider the following two statements, alternative ways of framing a general policy about a hypothetical intensive learning program to be required of immigrants: "this policy will help immigrants to become equal participants in our society" and "this policy will ensure that only those who can really succeed here can join our society" (Pratto and Lemieux 2001). In the first case, a belief that the policy would ensure equality of outcomes is at stake. In the second case, the statement reflects a belief that equality of experience will act as a monitor, allowing some to succeed and others to fail. Not surprisingly, Felicia Pratto and Anthony Lemieux (2001) find that those low in social dominance are more drawn to the first argument and less persuaded by the second compared to those high in social dominance.

Evidence suggests that U.S. citizens strongly endorse the belief that one's outcomes are the consequence of one's own efforts—the cult of rugged individualism that has so often been applied to the country's value system. In what James Kleugel and Eliot Smith termed the "dominant ideology" in the United States, "people tend to believe that the opportunity for economic advancement based on hard work is plentiful" (1986, 5). Endorsement of this belief moves the discussion away from the structural perspective of dominance hierarchy to the "up by your own bootstraps" perspective, thus seeming to reject the possibility of systematic group discrimination and endorsing individual accomplishment as a standard and a panacea.

COMPARATIVE BELIEFS IN IMMIGRATION STRATEGIES

The process of immigration has at least two sides: the views of those in the host country and those of the immigrants. What do they think about their new country? How do they choose to negotiate and adapt to the new social terrain? Is their ideal a melting pot or a salad bowl? Further, it is useful to consider whether these two perspectives mesh. Are host and immigrant of a similar mind when it comes to a preferred immigration strategy?

When asked whether their society should encourage a blended melting pot rather than maintain distinct ethnic cultures, the majority of U.S. citizens favor the melting pot (Sears et al. 1999). The relative preference for a blended culture was strongest among Hispanic respondents and weakest for the white respondents. Although seemingly inconsistent with some of the beliefs just discussed, this endorsement confirms the continuing influence of the melting pot metaphor, as applied at a general level.

Figure 3.3   Four Varieties of Acculturation

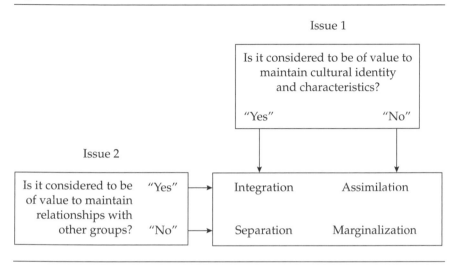

Source: Adapted from Berry et al. (1987). Permission granted by Blackwell Publishing.

In the survey data just described, respondents were forced to choose between two presumably polar opposites: blending in or remaining distinct. A somewhat more complex analysis of views on assimilation versus multi-culturalism draws on a two-dimensional model offered by John Berry (1990, 1997).[5] In this construction, attitudes about immigration are assessed by simultaneously considering positions on two questions. The first focuses on people's attitudes toward cultural maintenance, or the degree to which they want (or are believed by others to want) to maintain aspects of the country of origin, such as religion, language, and way of life. The second question concerns contact of immigrants with their new country. To what extent does the immigrant want to have day-to-day contact with members of the host society? If these questions are asked on a simple Likert scale of favorability, which ranges from strong agreement to strong disagreement, it is then possible to create a 2 × 2 taxonomy by using the mid-point of each scale as a dividing point. The result of such a strategy is shown in figure 3.3. Integration is the term applied to those who endorse both positions: maintaining cultural identity and relationships with other groups. Those who endorse neither are considered marginalized, unable to connect with either culture. Assimilation most closely represents the melting pot, as it is typically conceived, in which a person takes on the values of the host country and gives up allegiance to the culture of origin. Separation refers to those who maintain their original culture and choose not to relate to the new groups they encounter.

Several studies in recent years have considered how both immigrants and members of the host country match up when this particular categorization system is used. Most of these studies have been done in Europe, giving us a broader perspective and showing variety within Europe when it comes to issues of immigration. When asked their position, residents of countries such as the Netherlands, Finland, Israel, and Germany are fairly consistent in their beliefs that immigrants should establish some contact with the host country (Horencyzk 1996; Liebkind et al. 2002; van Oudenhoven, Prins, and Buunk 1998; Zagefka and Brown 2002). Native-born Germans, for example, typically endorse statements such as "I think it is important that immigrants have German friends" (Zagefka and Brown 2002). There is some variation, however, as to whether this contact should be accompanied by a maintenance of the culture of origin or should represent full assimilation to the new country. Hanna Zagefka and Rupert Brown (2002) found that German citizens preferred immigrants to adopt integration over assimilation by a 61 percent to 18 percent margin, though 19 percent of their sample also favored a strategy of marginalization, in which neither home country nor host country would be chosen. In another German sample, Ursula Piontkowski and her colleagues (2000) found similar rates of support for integration, less endorsement of marginalization, and somewhat more support for assimilation. These investigators also surveyed Swiss citizens with reference to Yugoslavian immigrants and Slovaks with reference to Hungarian immigrants. Approximately half of the Swiss favored integration, followed more closely by assimilation than in the German sample. The Swiss also gave more support to separation and marginalization than did the Germans. In contrast, the Slovaks showed relatively equal preferences for integration, assimilation, and marginalization strategies. Surveying Dutch citizens, Jan Pieter van Oudenhoven, Karen Prins, and Bram Buunk (1998) found that though both assimilation and immigration strategies were regarded favorably, native-born citizens endorsed assimilation most strongly when they were asked what they preferred immigrants to do. Interestingly, the same respondents believed that the immigrants, primarily Turks and Moroccans, favored separatism.

In sum, a reasonable consensus position emerges in most countries that immigrants should learn the ways of the new country. The differences appear to lie in how strongly host country citizens are willing to endorse simultaneously maintaining country of origin customs.

What about the immigrants? How do the people who have actually made the choice to move to another country weigh the four options of immigration, assimilation, marginalization, and separatism? Available research, again based mostly but not exclusively in western Europe, suggests that integration is the favored position. Such findings have been reported for Yugoslav immigrants to Germany and Switzerland (Piontkowski et al. 2000), Hungarian immigrants to Slovakia (Piontkowski et al. 2000), Moroccan and Turkish immigrants to the Netherlands (van Oudenhoven, Prins, and Bruut 1998), Turkish and Aussiedler immigrants in Germany (Zagefka and Brown 2002), Soviet immigrants to Israel (Roccas, Horenczyk, and Schwartz 2000), Vietnamese in Finland (Liebkind 1996a, 1996b), and Vietnamese and Hong Kong immigrants to Australia (Nesdale and Mak 2000). In addition, extensive research by John Berry and his colleagues in Canada finds that integration is the preferred strategy, with either assimilation or separation vying for second place (1989).

I know of two exceptions to this tendency: a study finding that Turkish immigrants in Germany preferred separation to integration by almost a two to one margin (Piontkowski et al. 2000) and a report that New Zealand immigrants prefer assimilation to integration (Nesdale and Mak 2000). The Piontkowski findings seem to contradict those of Zagefka and Brown, who also surveyed Turkish immigrants in Germany and found a strong preference for integration. The difference, I suspect, may lie in how the statements of acculturation beliefs were worded. In Piontkowski et al., a positive relationship with the new country is shown by the endorsement of "we Turks should try to participate completely in the German life" (2000, 8). In Zagefka and Brown, less involvement was enough to indicate acculturation, as indexed by statements such as "I think it is important that members of my cultural group have German friends" (2002, 176). Thus, the level of involvement or relationship may be critical to definition of acculturation attitudes, a point to which I shall return.

The case of New Zealanders in Australia, who preferred assimilation, is a second exception. It raises a different point in our attempt to understand just what acculturation attitudes imply. New Zealanders and Australians are, in many respects, quite similar in appearance, language, and culture—certainly more similar than Vietnamese or Hong Kong immigrants would be to either one. The possibility of assimilation—blending in completely with the country of immigration—may thus be an option that is much more viable for this group in these circumstances than for other immigrant groups. Cross-border immigration between Canada and the United States, in either direction, is likely to show a similar endorsement of assimilation.

Although the preference of immigrants for an integrative strategy is reasonably consistent, their preferences are not always recognized by members of the host country. In the van Oudenhoven, Prins, and Bruut (1998) survey of Dutch citizens, for example, a plurality believed that Turkish and Moroccan immigrants favored separatism, though they reacted most negatively to immigrants who did so, as compared to those who adopted other strategies. Zagefka and Brown (2002) reported less striking discrepancies. Although their German respondents thought that integration was the strategy favored by most Turk and Aussiedler immigrants, a substantial minority (28 percent) believed that separatism was the preferred acculturation mode of immigrants, a strategy that only 2 percent regarded as being the most desirable choice. Considered from the reverse perspective, immigrants believed the host less supportive of integration and more supportive of assimilation or marginalization than they were themselves. Similarly, Sonia Roccas, Gabriel Horenczyk, and Shalom Schwartz (2000) report that Soviet immigrants to Israel think that Israelis are less favorable to integration and far more favorable to assimilation than they themselves are.

The discrepancies that are apparent when we look at attitudes of host country citizens versus those of immigrants, in terms of what mode of acculturation should be adopted, suggest that the course of immigration may be marked by considerable misunderstanding and incompatibility of goals. Richard Bourhis and his colleagues have addressed this question of fit in their interactive acculturation model, developed first in the Canadian context but now tested in several European countries as well (Bourhis et al. 1997; Bourhis, Montreuil, and Barrette 1999). Using the 2×2 categorization offered by Berry, with some modifications,[6] and considering both host and immigrant attitudes simultaneously, Bourhis et al. (1997) propose a model in which relations, what they term relational outcomes, between host and immigrant communities can be characterized as consensual, problematic, or conflictual. Consensual relations are considered most likely when both host and immigrant favor either integration or assimilation strategies. Mismatches involving preferences for integration by one group and assimilation by another are likely to result in problematic relationships, according to Bourhis and his colleagues. When separation or segregation is endorsed by either or both groups, Bourhis predicts that conflict is the most likely outcome.

The implications of this model, in terms of both how discrepancy is to be assessed and what outcomes are most relevant to a state of fit or nonfit between orientations, are just beginning to be explored (for example, Roccas, Horenczyk, and Schwartz 2000; Zagefka and Brown 2002). As a predictor of intergroup relations, this model will be considered again in chapter 6. In the present context, however, the major point to be made is that attitudes toward immigration strategies can differ markedly between host and immigrant group. Such discrepancies can exist in objective reality, in that the assessed views of host and immigrant differ; or they can exist in perceived reality, such that either group's belief about the other's preference is discordant with one's beliefs (Zagefka and Brown 2002). Charting these attitudinal patterns can provide a more articulated view of the context in which immigrants function.

Although the idea that there are different strategies of acculturation is a sensible one, the simple 2×2 categorization system is not without problems. At least three critical issues can be raised here: definitions of intergroup contact, the dimensionality of strategies, and the implicit assumption of independence of strategies by host and immigrant communities. The first of these issues has been alluded to previously. Definitions of what it means to connect to the host society have differed substantially across studies. Thus, whereas Berry's early statement and some translations of that position refer to maintaining relationships with the host country or having some unspecified number of friends in the new country (Zagefka and Brown 2002), other researchers have set a higher bar. Examples of the latter are statements that refer to complete participation (Piontkowski et al. 2000) or to adoption of the cultural identity (Bourhis et al. 1997). Some investigators have assessed the two domains of culture separately and inferred integration by looking at deviations from the mean on both scales. Others have explicitly defined the two domains in conjunction with one another, for example, "I would like to celebrate the Jewish holidays without abandoning the holidays we used to celebrate in the Soviet Union" (Roccas, Horencyzk, and Schwartz 2000).

These varying definitions of cultural integration imply very different levels of involvement for the immigrant. To have a number of friends in the new country may be quite easy, depending on how friendship is defined. Casual friendships at the workplace, for example, might seem enough to answer positively when asked whether one has developed a relationship with the host country. Such an avowal might be quite far from "complete participation" or "adoption of the cultural identity." First-person accounts from immigrants whose religion or values are notably different from the dominant group, for example, often refer to casual friendships but not to deep social ties, or to participation in a common work world, but to rejection of social activities that might involve alcohol, open sexuality, or other behaviors inconsistent with religious tenets. Understanding the degree to which an immigrant immerses himself or herself in a new culture undoubtedly requires more than a simple set of scaled questionnaire items. More qualitative work would be helpful for probing these issues.

A related question concerns the multiple domains or dimensions on which acculturation might operate. Is acculturation a single concept or does it operate on several planes, not all of which are in tandem at any point? Gabriel Horenczyk (1996) studied the acculturation attitudes of Russian immigrants to Israel, distinguishing between culture, language, religion, and friendship in each case. Although he found the typical pattern of preference for integration among both immigrant and host country respondents, some differences were evident as the focus shifted from one domain to another. Immigrants were more likely to endorse a separation strategy in the domain of language, for example, than they were in the domain of culture (though they viewed integration as the preferred strategy in both domains). Israelis also preferred integration as an overall strategy to be adopted by their immigrant population, but the preference was stronger regarding language than culture. In both cases, language is an important point of the acculturation process—but which language is to be dominant becomes a critical point of contention. These variations add complexity to the attitudinal picture; they may also create ambiguity for the immigrant who is trying to decipher the attitudinal stance of the native population.

The third issue I raise concerns the assumed independence of host and immigrant attitudes and their definition apart from a particular immigration context. In assessing attitudes of host country citizens and immigrants, some investigators assume that the measured attitudes assess general orientations toward immigration. In reality, I would argue, attitudes are formed within the current context, and do not reflect general beliefs about how immigrants should acculturate, but instead are framed in terms of specific individuals currently immigrating to the country. If only one major immigrant group is arriving in a relatively homogeneous country, then the general attitudes of both host and immigrant group are probably quite similar to any target-specific issues that might be raised. In more complex settings, however, a number of additional questions arise. From the perspective of the host, preferences for immigration strategy—for example, for assimilation versus separation—undoubtedly is influenced by what group the host has in mind. Immigrant groups who are very similar to the host—for example, New Zealand immigrants to Australia or Canadian immigrants to the United States, versus Vietnamese immigrants to the same countries—in all probability elicit quite different attitudes on the part of the host. The recent controversial work of Samuel Huntington (2004), reacting against what he sees as the Hispanicization of the United States, is a clear case in point. From the perspective of the immigrant, the possibilities for assimilation or integration may also appear quite different for the Muslim Turk to the Netherlands than they would for a British Protestant immigrant.

The interactive acculturation model of Bourhis takes a generic stance on the issue of fit, implying that the major source of concordance or discordance is attitudinal preferences. Thus if, for example, both host and immigrant communities believe in a general way that assimilation is the preferred strategy, according to the model, there should be no problems. Yet as was suggested by some of the data focusing on Turkish immigrants in Germany (Piontkowski et al. 2000) or by studies of Vietnamese in Finland (Liebkind 1996a, 1996b), the specificities of groups can create some conceptual noise for the model, requiring us to look at attitudes and preferences in a more targeted way.

In the next chapter, I do just that, looking at the group stereotypes about different national and ethnic groups, and considering how those beliefs further establish a context in which an immigrant negotiates an identity and finds a place in society. Just as the move from general social representations about immigration to more specific attitudes about immigration policies and immigrant groups is a form of conceptual ratcheting down, so does a shift from general attitudes about immigrants to beliefs about particular target groups entail another sharpening of focus. From this vantage point, we will see more clearly that not everyone's immigration is the same—that both host and immigrant groups define microclimates that need to be understood as both examples of general process and as unique sites of negotiation.

Chapter Four | Images and Actions: Contending with Stereotypes and Discrimination

Different races and nationalities differ widely in the details of their conception and practice of life.

—Robert E. Park and Herbert A. Miller (1921)

Stereotypes are substitutes for real knowledge—which is never of anything so simple or permanent as a particular generalized image of foreigners.

—Isaiah Berlin (2001)

Japanese by blood, hearts and minds American, with honor unbowed bore the sting of injustice for future generations.

—Inscription on memorial in Washington, D.C.
Akemi Matsumoto Ehrlich, *The Legacy*

THE CONCEPT OF immigrant, like immigrants themselves, comes with baggage. At the conceptual level, this additional weight consists of meanings associated with the targeted group. Some of these meanings are obvious and literal, as in thinking about an immigrant as someone who is new to the country, whose first language may be something other than English, who probably has relatives living in another country, and so forth. Other meanings, as we have seen, involve beliefs about the motivations and intentions of immigrants or the perceived impact it is thought they will have on

66

the country of destination. More sharply focused than these images of the generic immigrant are specific beliefs about certain groups of people, defined by their country of origin. From this perspective, not all immigrants are alike in the eyes of the host. Instead, group-specific stereotypes become a set of distinctive frames through which immigrants from differing parts of the world are viewed. Moreover, these frames have consequences: immigrants are not only thought to be different from one another, but are treated differently as well. Who they are thus becomes shaped by what people think they are, attesting to the interactive dynamic that defines the immigrant experience. It is these issues of stereotypes, prejudice, discrimination, and their consequences that I now consider.

IMAGES OF IMMIGRANTS

Our seemingly irresistible urge to characterize, often in highly personal and dispositional terms, those who are different from us has been evident in studies of immigration from the beginning. As early as 1911, an official commission on immigration produced the Dillingham report, *A Dictionary of Races and Peoples* (Jacobson 1998). Forty-five separate immigrant groups were recognized (thirty indigenous to Europe), and all were characterized in racial, physical, and dispositional terms. The Bohemian's brain, for example, was said to be the heaviest, and the Jewish nose more prominent than other immigrant noses. Shifting to psychological turf, the commission commented on the savage manners of Serbo-Croatians, the individualism of southern Italians, the high-strung nature of the Poles, and both the affability and the suspiciousness of Sicilians (Jacobson 1998).

Less physical determinism and more social context is found in Park and Miller's *Old World Traits Transplanted*, which was published ten years after the Dillingham report.[1] This book marks one of the first extensive discussions of immigrant characteristics, as perceived and reported by the social scientists involved in the early University of Chicago research projects. Park and Miller presented their work as objective observation, not as the creation or application of cultural stereotypes. In reading their work through a twenty-first century lens, however, the line between objective observation and subjective interpretation seems fuzzier than they acknowledged.

As noted, Park and Miller began with the assumption that "different races and nationalities differ widely in the details of their conception and practice of life" (1921, 2). At the same time, these authors suggested that differences might mean little to the American community, which "shows . . . a contempt for all the characteristics of the newcomers" (61). Persisting in their aim to document differences, Park and Miller offered a typology of six kinds of immigrants, each defined in terms of the motives or goals that presumably influenced their move to the United States and their attitudes toward assimilation. These designated types included the *settler*, whose move was typically precipitated by economic crisis and whose major goal was to "secure an existence"; the *all right Nick*, an opportunistic type who wanted to pass into the dominant group; and the *intellectual*, a type that Park and Miller saw as misadapted to the United States with no marketable skills. These general functional descriptions then yielded to more stereotyped images of specific nationalities. Consider the *colonist*, for example, a group the authors described as maintaining memories and values of their home country rather than assimilating with the new country (at the same time believing that they were contributing more to the United States than they were gaining from it). To illustrate this type, the authors used a lengthy quote from a German immigrant who was protesting the ideal of the melting pot: "We regard this uniformity as equivalent to the destruction of all that we regard as the holiest part of our people and its culture" and "the undertaking itself appears to the German spirit as repulsive" (95). The categories of colonist and German thus become fused, creating a specific ethnic stereotype. Park and Miller went on to describe what they saw as the outstanding characteristics of a variety of immigrant groups included in their early twentieth-century study, pointing to the "family pride" of Italians, the "thrift, cleanliness, quickness, sobriety, industry, adaptability, [and] eagerness to learn" of the Japanese, and the "surprising interest in education" on the part of the Mexicans.

Good intentions do not preclude stereotypic attributions. Some years before Park and Miller, the social activist Jacob Riis made ample use of stereotypes while advocating for improvements in tenement housing. He viewed the Italian as "gay, lighthearted . . . as honest as he is hot-headed," and saw the Jewish people as concerned with thriftiness, "at once its strength and its fatal weakness, its cardinal virtue and its foul disgrace" (quoted in Foner 2000, 146). In these and other comments we find substantial evidence of the pervasive tendency, among both scientists and reformers and the population at large, to use categories and to infer traits of those in the category.

Stereotypes can mix good traits with bad in characterizing a particular group, but it is often the bad traits that predominate when a group is new and unfamiliar. At the beginning of the twentieth century, for example, many people had little good to say about Italian and Jewish immigrants, often couching their critiques in racial terms that linked the new immigrant groups to the already devalued black groups. This tendency to draw parallels between one devalued group and another—a way of anchoring the new and unfamiliar to the old and familiar, in the language of social representation theory (Moscovici 1988)—took many forms. Consider Henry

Cabot Lodge's advice in 1891 on the suitability of Slovak immigrants: "not a good acquisition for us to make, since they appear to have so many items in common with the Chinese" (quoted in Jacobson 1998, 42).

Irving Lewis Allen (1983) compiled a lexicon of epithets applied to immigrants (as well as to American minority groups), collected from scholarly collections of slang and dialectic speech in American English between the colonial period and 1970.[2] As Abraham Roback (1944) implied when he coined the term ethnophaulisms, defined as ethnic slurs referring to some outgroup, many are negative in their connotations. Australians and New Zealanders, for example, have been called "cornstalks," "diggers," and "currency-lads"; the Dutch as "cabbage heads," "butter mouths," and "wooden shoes"; and Puerto Ricans as "greaseballs" and "hicks" (Allen 1983). The negativity of these terms is clear. Is there any pattern to their being invoked?

In analyzing the variation among groups, Allen (1983) posited that the size of the ethnic group is related to the frequency of names that are generated, and indeed, his data supported that hypothesis. His results were heavily influenced, however, by the exceedingly large number of names associated with African Americans. Even excluding this group, however, there is an association between group size and number of epithets. It is also apparent that numbers—which perhaps serve as an index of the frequency with which the majority of people encounter members of the particular group—do not alone account for all of the variance. Looking at Allen's data, one finds, for example, that the population of British Canadians in the United States was four times larger than that of Chinese, yet the Chinese garnered more than five times as many terms. Terms applied to nonwhite groups also differed in type, including a higher proportion of physical descriptors. Whereas 19 percent of all terms collected refer to physical characteristics, the proportion for African Americans is 45 percent and for Chinese is 47 percent. The difference is less pronounced with other Asian groups, such as Japanese or Vietnamese. Typically, physically based terms refer to color, such as black, brown, or dark in the case of African Americans, and yellow or mustard in the case of Chinese. Such color descriptors are not inherently negative. When embedded in a social system in which a hierarchy of color exists, however, they serve as powerful evaluative markers.

It might be easy to dismiss the views and comments of those who lived in the past, several decades ago in some of the data I have cited, by airily saying that times have changed. It would be a mistake, however, to believe that differentiated attitudes and stereotypes about immigrant groups no longer exist. Recent Gallup and Yankelovich surveys suggest numerous perceived differences between nationality and ethnicity. When asked, for example, whether a particular group has generally benefited the country or created problems, respondents in these surveys generally report that Polish, Irish, and Chinese immigrants have been beneficial for the country, and that Cubans, Haitians, Iranians, and Mexicans have caused problems (Lapinski et al. 1997).

Data we have collected shows continuing differences in the evaluations of various nationality groups. In a nationwide sample of adults taken in late 2004, Kim Mizrahi (2005) asked respondents about their positive and negative feelings toward four specific groups of immigrants—Polish, Chinese, Mexican, and Jamaican—chosen as countries that have substantial immigration to the United States and that represent different areas of the world. On an overall index of attitudes, based primarily on issues related to work and the economy, respondents were significantly more favorable toward immigrants from China and Poland than those from Mexico and Jamaica. A closer look at the data, however, reveals an interesting pattern of ambivalence. In separate measures of positive and negative attitudes that tapped into aspects of culture and character, both Mexican and Jamaican immigrants were rated more extremely on both dimensions, that is, more positively and more negatively, than immigrants from China and Poland were. Thus, on the one hand, respondents seem to acknowledge the contributions that Mexican and Jamaican immigrants make and the obstacles they face, yet fault them for failing to overcome their difficulties.

A few years ago, we asked New York City college students to evaluate the favorability (on a 100-point scale) of ten selected immigrant groups, representing countries in eastern and western Europe and in the Caribbean and Latin America. In general, immigrants from western European countries were rated more favorably than those from eastern Europe. In turn, immigrants from both European regions were rated more favorably than immigrants from the Caribbean, with Mexicans rated most negatively. Because the sample was drawn from the colleges of the City University of New York system, in which approximately 50 percent of the students are first-generation immigrants themselves, we were able to make a further comparison between judgments of those who were or were not born in the United States.

Figure 4.1 shows the results of this comparison. Two interesting observations emerge from these data. First, and perhaps not surprisingly, immigrants are more favorable in their views toward every immigrant group than native-born respondents are. At the same time, the differences are not enormous, typically representing 5 to 10 percent increases in favorability. More striking, in my view, is the fact that the rank order of groups is virtually identical between immigrants and nonimmigrants. Thus, whether born in this country or not, respondents consistently used a calculus by which, for example, Italians are better than Russians and Russians are better than

Figure 4.1   Favorability Ratings of National Groups

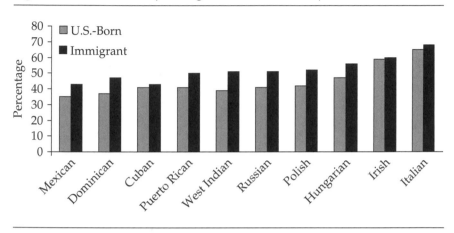

Source: Author's compilations.

Mexicans. Although more specific in their nationality reference, these findings are wholly consistent with more general analyses of the rank ordering
of major ethnic and racial groups (African, Asian, European, and Latino)
that have been reported in a variety of U.S. surveys (Bobo and Massagli
2001; Sidanius and Pratto 1999). Apparently these dominant representations in the United States are either learned very quickly or are more generally shared beyond U.S. borders, despite presumed differences in the
extent of previous experience with the various groups.

SOURCES AND INFLUENCES ON IMMIGRANT STEREOTYPES

If differences between immigrant groups are so widely believed to exist,
how are they explained? Perhaps the most ready explanation is to point to
the country of origin as determining the nature of immigrant stereotypes,
drawing from "old country" soil to account for "new country" manifestations. Thus, it would be said, Polish immigrants are like they are because
Poles are that way, or Mexican immigrants are simply a transported case
of what Mexicans in general are all about. Park and Miller (1921) suggested
this causal explanation in their classic analysis *Old World Traits Transplanted*,
invoking both heredity and environment to explain the predispositions
they noted. At one point they suggested that the character of an immigrant group "may be connected with their original, inborn, temperamental

dispositions"; at another they say that varying patterns are not due to any "inborn and ineradicable traits" but rather to "a long train of common experiences" (303–4).

National Stereotypes

Some of the earliest research in social psychology, undertaken by Daniel Katz and Kenneth Braly in the early 1930s, was an assessment of national stereotypes (1933). In this classic study, Princeton students were asked to indicate which traits, chosen from a set of eighty-four adjectives provided by the investigators and varying in favorability, were characteristic of the people from each of ten ethnic-national groups, seven of which could be considered potential immigrant groups—Chinese, English, Germans, Irish, Italians, Japanese, and Turks. This work showed how easily people were able to describe citizens of other countries, from images of Germans as industrious and scientifically minded to English as sportsmanlike and intelligent. Even Turks, whom we can assume that few of the Princeton students in the 1932 study had ever encountered, were readily characterized as cruel by nearly 50 percent of the sample, answers presumably influenced by knowledge of the 1915 Armenian massacres.

The procedures of Katz and Braly (1933) have been replicated by three subsequent generations of researchers (Gilbert 1951; Karlins, Coffman, and Walters 1969; Leslie et al. 2005).[3] Over the four periods, some interesting changes in content emerge, which I will consider in more detail later. Contemporary students show more variety in their characterizations of all the groups, as assessed by the number of adjectives that would be required to capture 50 percent of the total responses given by participants, a shift from 8.5 in 1933 to 10.9 in 1969 and 2000 (Leslie et al. 2005).[4] Evidence of consistency across time is also evident, however, when one compares the relative use of specific traits, defined by Leslie et al. (2005) as the top ten traits used to characterize each group. With this measure, one sees significant consensus across the time periods for most of the groups, with the exception of the Turks and Japanese. For the Japanese, the shift represents a significant move from negative to more positive; for the Turks, negative traits are endorsed less frequently but are not replaced with other characterizations, indicating both a lack of familiarity with the group and the likelihood of faded memories of the Armenian tragedy.

In their more general work on the stereotyping process, Fiske and her colleagues have proposed a two-dimensional stereotype content model for locating images in semantic space (Fiske et al. 2002; Cuddy, Fiske, and Glick 2004). Warmth, assessed by ratings on traits such as friendly and

Figure 4.2   Spatial Mapping of Ethnic Group Stereotypes

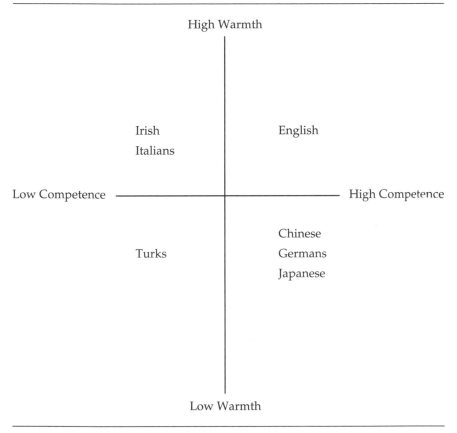

High Warmth

Irish   English

Italians

Low Competence ——————————————— High Competence

                         Chinese

Turks   Germans

                         Japanese

Low Warmth

Source: Adapted from Cuddy, Fiske, and Glick (2004); Leslie et al. (2005).

warm, and competence, assessed by ratings on traits such as confident and competent, constitute the two dimensions of this model, which when juxtaposed yield four distinct quadrants, as shown in figure 4.2. As Fiske and her colleagues have shown in their research, these four quadrants are associated with different kinds of affective judgments. Admiration is felt for those groups in the upper right quadrant, and contempt for those in the lower left quadrant (low in both competence and warmth). Pity and envy characterize the upper-left and lower-right quadrants, respectively, both indicating some ambivalence in affective tone. Lisa Leslie and her colleagues (2005) used this framework to obtain judgments of the seven ethnic groups from the original Katz and Braly set, and their results are shown in figure 4.2. As can be seen, only the English occupy the most favorable (upper right) quadrant where admiration is predominant—a location that, not incidentally, is shared by Americans when they are included in the ratings. Italians and the Irish are generally considered to have warmth but less competence, a position associated with feelings of sympathy. The lower right quadrant of this model is represented by the Chinese, Germans, and Japanese. Here the main emotion is said to be envy. One also thinks in this quadrant of the so-called model minority, considered capable but somewhat distant. Only the Turks, among the countries included in the Katz and Braly set, are relegated to the lower left quadrant, representing lesser degrees of both competence and warmth and resultant feelings of contempt. Clearly these data indicate that not all potential immigrant sources are viewed in identical terms.

Typically, these assessments of national stereotypes are defined in ungendered terms, asking people simply to consider the French or the Dominican, to take two examples. Gender is not irrelevant, however, as work by Alice Eagly and Mary Kite (1987) has shown. These investigators found that stereotypes of men from a particular country are generally quite similar to the national stereotypes as described in gender-neutral terms. For example, there is a close correspondence between answers to "what are Germans like?" and "what are German men like?" In contrast, stereotypes of women from the same country often differ markedly, both from the national stereotype and from the men of that country. As an example, Iranian men were rated lower on traits of warmth and communion than any of the other twenty-seven nationalities included in the Alice Eagly and Mary Kite (1987) study, and moderately high on characteristics of agency and assertion. In contrast, Iranian women were rated lower than any other group on the agentic dimension, but were seen as more moderate in terms of communion. Traits most often used to describe Iranian men included egoistical, hostile, and aggressive, whereas the most common descriptors of Iranian women were traditional, religious, and family-oriented. Comparison of each group with the stereotypes of gender-unspecified Iranians showed a correlation of +.95 for the male stereotype and only +.12 for the female stereotype. Interestingly, differences in the male and female stereotypes, considered in reference to the general national stereotype, were greater when a rater's overall evaluation of the country was more negative. Negativity, in these cases, was defined by traits such as aggressiveness and competitiveness that are typically more associated with the male stereotype. At the same time, countries that were most favorably evaluated tended to elicit considerable similarity among the stereotypes of women, men, and the general case when ratings of communality were the focus. In other words, characteristics such as family orientation, likability, and enjoyment of life were generally ascribed to everyone in a country when that country was highly regarded.

These variations suggest that the process of stereotyping by nationality is more subtle than it might first appear. Women are seen to differ from men, not only in ways consistent with pervasive gender stereotypes, but also in a manner that suggests they are believed to experience a different social context within their country. In other words, people can entertain the possibility that more than one type of immigrant might emerge from a single country, recognizing differences in the experiences and socialization people within a country might have. On the face of it, this statement seems obvious. Yet it is surprising how little attention is given to the ways in which factors such as gender, class, or social position shape assumptions about immigrants, creating different images both within and between national groups.

Cognitive Influences on Ethnic Stereotypes

Stereotypes of immigrant groups are also influenced by the context in which they are seen, once they arrive at their destination country, and by particular intersections between the viewer and the viewed. In his compilation of epithets, Allen (1983) observed that groups that were more numerous in a society were likely to garner more terms to describe them. But is it possible to find some pattern or regularity in the types of names that are used, apart from the simple function linking frequency of label to size of group?

Brian Mullen addressed this question, considering both the average valence of terms used to refer to a group and to the complexity or degree of variation among them (2001). Using Allen's (1983) original data base but limiting his sample to nineteen Western European ethnic immigrant groups,[5] Mullen tested predictions for the effects of familiarity and degree of *foreignness* and for group size. In general, the ethnophaulisms studied by Mullen can be characterized as low in complexity and negative in valence. In other words, most stereotypes of ethnic and immigrant groups are neither very positive nor very complicated. Yet within the nineteen groups, even a relatively homogeneous set such as the one he used, differences in the degree of complexity and negativity were found. Three dimensions reliably predicted the patterns of ethnic labels: the size of the immigrant group; the observer's familiarity with the group; and the degree of foreignness the group represented. With regard to the first factor, Mullen found that when a group's proportion of the total population was relatively smaller, they were described in terms that were more negative and less complex. Thus their salience as *tokens* in the country seemed to generate more simplistic representations. The second factor, *familiarity*, was indexed by Mullen and his colleagues in terms of historical coverage and the prevalence of popular music by that group in standard music collections. Here the analysis showed that less familiar groups were regarded more negatively and with less complexity. Finally, Mullen and his colleagues created an index of foreignness based on complexion, facial appearance, and language distance, using criteria established by historians and linguists in which distance is calculated from an assumed Anglo-Saxon norm. Not surprisingly, more foreign immigrant groups were characterized with greater negativity and less complexity.

Comparing the influence of these three factors, it appears that group size had the strongest effect on the complexity of judgments and that foreignness was most influential in the degree of negativity. These results point to several key factors that shape images of immigrant groups. Assuming that the size of the group is related to the likelihood that a citizen will encounter a member of it, we see that greater familiarity with a group leads to more complex representations. In social cognition terms, larger groups are less salient as groups per se, and thus people are viewed more in terms of exemplars or individually based representations—which in turn contribute to a more variable overall image (Mullen 1991, 2001). Members of small groups are more salient as a group; representations thus tend to homogenize the individuals into a single average group member.

The degree to which a group is seen as different from one's own plays a more prominent role in likability, consistent with much social psychological research on interpersonal attraction and intergroup relations. Generally, we like people who are similar to us and we are less favorable to those who are not. Thus, rather than a cognitive-perceptual basis for judgment, as is the case with group size, judgments of likability are based more heavily on affective factors that, at their foundation, rest on an evaluative distinction.

It is important to note that Mullen considered only European groups. None of those groups now dominant in the current immigration flow to the United States—such as from Asia, the Caribbean, and Latin America—were included. Surely members of these groups would score high on measures of foreignness, as calculated by Mullen with reference to an Anglo-Saxon norm, and would be less positively evaluated (as we have seen they generally are). Color-based inferences and constructions of race, so influential in interpersonal judgment, are thus inevitably a factor in the perceptions and evaluations of immigrants.

Images of immigrants can be shaped by particular characteristics of those who emigrate from a country, selectively determined samples that can vary on the basis of gender, religion, and social class. If immigrants from a country are primarily men, how will the immigrant stereotype be different than it would be if the proportions of men and women were more equivalent? How does the socioeconomic standing of a group influence the stereotypes formed? Differences in educational background and economic circumstances of the immigrant group influence their access to opportunity structures within the new country; the positions that they come to occupy—for example, as manual laborers versus entrepreneurs—in turn shape the views that citizens of the host country form even though they may be unaware of the class influence on their impressions. Consider Korean immigration to the United States, for example, a group that tends to have higher levels of education and greater financial resources than some other immigrant groups. This greater capital makes it likely that Korean immigrants will on average come to occupy different occupational niches and hence take on stereotypes associated with those occupations (for example, entrepreneurial attributes such as hard-working, ambitious, and upwardly mobile). In contrast, a group that comes with less capital, on average, generates stereotypes that, though they have their basis in stereotypes of class, become associated with ethnicity instead. Haitians in the United States are a case in point.

Historical and political conditions also play an influential role, because sympathy and resentment are engendered by the conditions of arrival. This statement applies to refugees in particular, who tend to come in large concentrated groups that attract more attention, but it can be applied to immigrants as well. Refugees from countries that have been political foes of the United States, for example, are often welcomed as strong and principled—the early Cuban immigration is a clear example. In contrast, those who come from countries less clearly defined in terms of the American agenda may be viewed with more suspicion or indifference, and are likely to be granted fewer positive traits in any subsequent characterization.

Models of Stereotypes and Intergroup Relations

In spite of their initial emphasis on the intrinsic characteristics of immigrant groups, Park and Miller (1921) acknowledged that "the definition of the situation" could play a role in the traits that immigrants have, or are perceived to have. From a social psychologist's perspective, recognizing the importance of situational factors is a fundamental tenet. Years ago, Donald Campbell and his colleagues pointed to the influence that structural features of a society, such as industrialization and poverty, can have on the character of national stereotypes, such that a country's successful production is associated with individual competence or the reverse, that poverty is associated with incompetence (Campbell 1967; Levine and Campbell 1972).

In recent years, the links between structure and stereotype have been explored further, particularly within the European context by Edwin Poppe and his colleagues, who asked secondary school students in six central and eastern European countries to judge nine European groups (Phalet and Poppe 1997; Poppe and Linssen 1999). Like Fiske and her colleagues, these investigators conceptualized stereotypes as two-dimensional. One dimension is related to perceived competence, as in the Fiske model; the second dimension is conceptualized as morality, which bears considerable similarity to the warmth dimension of Susan Fiske and her colleagues. The morality dimension carries added judgmental weight, however, with those high on the dimension seen not only as nice but also as virtuous and those low on the dimension seen as immoral. Together these dimensions yield a typology of winners and losers who are either sinful or virtuous. In their analysis, Karen Phalet and Edwin Poppe (1997) showed that members of one country can derogate those of another country in different ways. "Sinful losers" is a label that is applied to people of central and eastern Europe, such as the Turks and Gypsy minorities, who are believed to be low on both competence and morality; "sinful winners" refers to groups such as Jewish and German minorities, who are seen as more competent but no more likable or moral. Note the similarity of these findings to the placement of Turks and Germans in the U.S. analysis of national stereotypes shown in figure 4.2. In further analyses, these investigators showed that judgments of competence are heavily influenced by economic conditions, such that countries believed to be more economically powerful are also seen as more competent, echoing Campbell's earlier suggestions (1967). Judgments of morality, in contrast, were predicted by a nation's size and by the degree to which the country in question was perceived to have conflicts with the respondent's country and to generally be nationalistic. Citizens of larger countries were believed to be less moral, as were those perceived to be more nationalistic (Poppe and Linssen 1999).

The work of Poppe and his colleagues illustrates, recalling the model presented in chapter 1, the influence of macro-level features on individual beliefs. Moving to another level of analysis, we can also find evidence of meso-level influences, as represented by the more immediate relationship between groups—in this case, between the group being stereotyped and the group doing the stereotyping. We saw earlier how Fiske's stereotype content model uses the two dimensions of warmth and competence to place groups in semantic space, where the locations correspond to distinct patterns of affective judgments (Fiske et al. 2002). In an extension of this model, Fiske and her colleagues theorize that cultural stereotypes emerge from specific forms of intergroup relationships (Cuddy, Fiske, and Glick 2004). Competence, in this view, reflects a judgment of the relative status and power of another group. Greater competence is associated with those believed to be high in power and status, and less competence is associated with those seen as less powerful and lower in status. The possibility of competition is connected to judgments of warmth: we like groups that are seen as nonthreatening, while feeling some aversion to those that are seen as competitive or as having negative intentions toward us. This proposition recalls some earlier words of Isaiah Berlin, who said that "tribes hate neighbouring tribes by whom they feel threatened, and then rationalize their fears by representing them as wicked or inferior, or absurd or despicable in some way" (2001, 12).

Fiske and her colleagues predict distinct orientations toward groups that fall in one of the four quadrants (Cuddy, Fiske, and Glick 2004). For example, groups that are admired—seen as high on both warmth and competence—are likely to elicit direct help and cooperation. Referring again to figure 4.2, only the English would be so situated—certainly consistent with the favored nation status of Britain in recent U.S. history and with the positive treatment generally accorded to Anglo immigrants. As another example, some groups are seen as competent but not so warm, engendering cooperation but not necessarily active help, and possibly some negative treatment as well. The Chinese, Germans, and Japanese are so positioned in figure 4.2, suggesting recognition of their skills but some caution about their possible competitive threat.

As noted earlier, the Katz and Braly work (both the original study and the follow-ups) focused not on impressions of immigrants but rather of current citizens of those countries. Citizens who do not emigrate are useful as an indicator of the national traits that immigrants might be thought to bring with them, and can also serve as a point of comparison between the image shaped by the country's national history and politics and the conditions of entry for that country's emigrants. These comparisons would in fact be interesting to test more directly as a way of assessing the role that immediate context plays in shaping stereotypes of immigrants.

FROM IMAGES TO ACTIONS: GROUP-BASED DISCRIMINATION

One doesn't have to look far to see that orientations toward different immigrant groups are not merely words, but also play out in behavior. The quote from Akemi Matsumoto Ehrlich—"Japanese by blood, hearts and minds American, with honor unbowed bore the sting of injustice for future generations"—is inscribed on a memorial stone in Washington, D.C., dedicated to those citizens of Japanese descent who were interned during World War II. In one of the sorriest chapters of U.S. history, approximately

120,000 Japanese-Americans were placed in concentration camps for the duration of the war. Their characters were demeaned and their motives suspected, even though most of those interned were born in the United States and some even had family members fighting for the United States in the war (Nieves 2001).[6] In the wake of September 11, echoes of this earlier time can be seen in the treatment of many immigrants from Muslim countries, more than 80,000 of whom were required to register with the newly created Department of Homeland Security and approximately 13,000 of whom were scheduled for deportation (Elliott 2004).

Though perhaps more limited in scope, examples of discrimination that are significant in the lives of immigrants are all too easy to find. In New York City, Mexican immigrants working in fashionable restaurants are often limited to positions as busboys, unable to move up to the better paying and more prestigious position of waiter, and are both underpaid and subject to ethnic slurs (Greenhouse 2005).[7] In New Jersey, federal raids—typically conducted in the middle of the night—led to the deportation of numerous illegal aliens, primarily from Latin America (Knarr 2004). A recent documentary film, *Farmingdale,* tells the story of a New York community's clash with immigrants. There, on Long Island, where hundreds of primarily Latino immigrants come regularly to work in the houses and gardens of residents, two men were physically attacked by white men who attracted them with promises of work (Healy 2004).

Defining Stereotypes, Prejudice and Discrimination

Social psychologists distinguish between three types of bias: stereotypes, prejudice, and discrimination (Fiske 1998, 2004). Defined most simply, stereotypes refer to the cognitive beliefs and associations that one holds about a group; prejudice refers to the emotions and feelings that are associated with the group; and discrimination consists of the actual behaviors and actions directed toward others. Often the three processes work closely in tandem. Cognitively based stereotypes about a group, for example, such as whether they are hard workers or criminals, may be easily mapped to affective feelings about work and criminality, which in turn will predispose one to act positively or negatively toward a group member. At the same time, it is theoretically possible to have beliefs about a group that are not emotionally charged (for example, they like to eat curry or they dress in colorful clothes). Similarly, it is possible to feel negative about a group without linking it to any particular characteristics (for example, "I just don't like them") and without taking any obvious actions toward members of the group (perhaps because a target member is not readily available or often encountered). Although these dissociations among beliefs, affect, and behavior do exist, discrimination is often linked to at least a moderate degree with both stereotypes and prejudice. Moreover, we find that the affectively based prejudices that people have typically have more influence on their behavior than the cognitively based beliefs (Dovidio et al. 1996).

A key element in understanding each of these forms of bias is that they are formulated in terms of a group of people, defined in such a way as to make it possible for a person to say (sometimes idiosyncratically, to be sure) who is in the categorized group and who is not. That said, actions may be taken toward an individual who is a member of that group because it is assumed that he or she is representative of the group. This assumption of group homogeneity has several implications (Fiske 2004). First, it indicates a belief that members of the group are similar to one another and that there is relatively little variation among them, which justifies treating them as interchangeable. Second, perceivers assume that members of the group share the stereotypical attributes in question and, most often, that they have no attributes that would be inconsistent with the stereotype. With this set of assumptions in hand (or in head), it seems reasonable to act the same way toward all members of the group.

Certainly those who are initially seen as representatives of a group can present themselves in ways inconsistent with the stereotypes. In such cases, those perceiving have various reactions documented by social psychological research—a field of investigation too extensive and complex to detail here. Such evidence can be ignored, can be used as a basis for distinguishing the individual from the category, or, in rarer cases, can propel change in the stereotypic category. The main point is that assumptions of group homogeneity are almost inevitably faulty when applied to any single representative of the group.

Most often, we think of stereotyping, prejudice, and discrimination as negative. Unquestionably, many stereotypes contain negative elements, prejudice is often expressed in negative terms, and discrimination frequently results in unfavorable outcomes for the person who is a target of discrimination. Under some circumstances, however, the biases work in a positive direction. Consider the model minority stereotype, in which it is believed that members of a particular group (for example, Koreans or West Indians) possess a set of positive, valued characteristics, such as hardworking, motivated, and honest. In this case, we see a positive attitude, and often favorable action directed toward those identified as members of the group. Yet even when bias is in the positive direction, problems can result for an individual. Consider a Korean student who is, for example, only average in intelligence and motivation. If Koreans are assumed to be hardworking and motivated, then that student may be expected by others (such as teachers) to excel. Should the student not fulfill these expectations, he or she may become frustrated and anxious—a case of positive bias leading to negative outcomes.

We now realize that much of the work of stereotyping and bias operates not at a conscious level but rather at an unconscious one, where they may go unrecognized and unacknowledged. The cultural permeation of group stereotypes means that these images are part of the air we breathe, learned over years of socialization in the culture, and experienced automatically. At this point, a warehouse's worth of social psychological literature is available to document the multiple ways in which these automatic, non-conscious images and processes work to influence our actions (Dovidio and Gaertner 1993; Fiske 1998). These tendencies can be countered by con-scious efforts, given the time and opportunity for such effort. Yet because they lurk below the surface, they give durability and longevity to the often-negative group stereotypes and in turn influence many of the daily encoun-ters that immigrants have.

The Climate of Discrimination

For the immigrant who is a member of a less favored group, the social con-text is one of daily affronts and curtailed opportunities. Prejudice can be blatant, such as when a restaurant manager tells a Mexican employee, "I know how you Spanish boys are about stealing stuff" (Greenhouse 2005). Or it can be more subtle, expressed in cooler and less direct forms that might exaggerate cultural differences or trumpet traditional values (Petti-grew 1998; Pettigrew and Meertens, 1995). In surveys of the attitudes of western Europeans toward their immigrant groups (for example, Germans evaluating the Turkish minority or British evaluating West Indian immi-grants), Thomas Pettigrew and Roel Meertens (1995) observed that blatant prejudice was less readily endorsed than subtle prejudice, consistent with the idea that contemporary norms generally discourage the expression of the most overt forms of prejudice. At the same time, some noticeable dif-ferences in the expression of blatant expression existed, suggesting that the norms vary in the extent to which they are seen to be applicable to certain groups. The German expression of blatant prejudice against Turks was rel-atively high, for example, and the French were more willing to express neg-ative attitudes toward North Africans than toward Asians.

Similarly, discrimination can be direct or indirect (Pettigrew 1998). The latter is less obvious and refers to a kind of second-step process, whereby earlier decisions create conditions that have later discriminatory conse-quences. Policies regarding the rights of immigrants or guest workers, for example, may subsequently put them in a position where occupational discrimination is more likely. After an Argentinean immigrant in the United States described a social snub, he went on to say, "but that kind of thing seem minor compared to the cultural and economic obstacles of being undocumented. . . . Once you reach a certain level, you realize that the next job up is only for Americans. And even the job you have is unstable" (Javier F. 2004).

Direct discrimination is far easier to detect and can be readily observed among immigrant communities, in the United States as well as in Europe. Pettigrew observed that "in every western European nation, foreigners have far higher unemployment rates than do natives" (1998, 89). Studies in England have shown discrimination toward immigrants in areas ranging from employment and housing to banks and car rentals (Pettigrew 1998). Employment discrimination is well documented in the United States as well. Despite, or perhaps because of, the fact that more immigrants are coming to the United States with more skills and educational qualifications, "contemporary immigrants are much more likely to experience downward occupational mobility when they arrive" (Foner 2000, 90). Lack of fluency in English or the barriers of U.S. licensing requirements can sometimes be a contributing factor. At other times, the differential outcomes are more apparently based on prejudicial evaluations and biased treatment. Studies of earnings of Muslims and Arabs before and after September 11, 2001, provide a rather clear case study in which group-based discrimination seems a likely cause (Kaushal, Kaestner, and Reimers 2004). Comparing the weekly earnings of Muslim and Arab men from 1999 to 2002, Kaushal and colleagues found a statistically significant 8 percent drop after September 11. The earnings of Muslim and Arab women dropped between 4 and 6 percent during the same period, a similar but not statistically significant pattern of decline.

Discrimination is perhaps most clearly seen in objective indices of employment and education. Yet the atmosphere of discrimination is far more pervasive, as the work on unconscious bias would suggest. Moreover, it is important (if surely more difficult) to consider the total climate within an institution that may exert unequal pressures on the participants in that institution. Consider a school system, for example, in which students from several different immigrant groups participate. In one urban school observed by Susan Rosenbloom and Niobe Way (2004), classes contained students from both Asian and Latino immigrant groups. When interviewed about their experiences with discrimination, the Latino students (as well as native-born African American students) were most likely to talk about adults, such as teachers, police, and shopkeepers, as the agents of discrimination. Asian immigrants, by contrast, typically pointed to other students as sources of prejudicial statements and discriminatory treatment. A fuller analysis of the system suggested that the teachers preferred Asian students, an instance of a positive bias based on beliefs about a model minority. At the same time, students from less-favored groups resented such preferential treatment, and expressed their resentment in verbal abuse and physical harassment of the Asian students. Even more complicated patterns emerged when the investigators looked within particular ethnic groups, as for example in distinguishing children from Puerto Rico versus Dominican immigrants. Here too, both prejudice and discrimination emerged in conversation and in behavior, testifying to the multiple perspectives and layers that any particular climate can contain.

PSYCHOLOGICAL CONSEQUENCES OF PREJUDICE AND DISCRIMINATION

Stereotypes not only live in the heads of those who believe and endorse them—in this analysis, the members of a host country viewing immigrants to the country—but they are likely to become part of the life space of the immigrants as well. These beliefs about what others think of one's group— what are sometimes termed metastereotypes (Sigelman and Tuch 1997)— are often accurate and can even be exaggerated assessments of the negative images that others hold.

The phenomenon of stereotype threat, conceptualized by Claude Steele and his colleagues (Steele 1997; Steele and Aronson 1995; Steele, Spencer, and Aronson 2002), is premised on the assumption that stereotypes "in the air" become part of the reality with which a person must deal. Thus, if one's group is judged to be inferior in math, as women often are, or in general academic skills, as African Americans often are, those beliefs become part of the metastereotype, a recognition that others feel that way and a consequent anticipation that those beliefs could be relevant to how one him- or herself is judged. When a stereotype about your group is relevant to performance in a particular domain, you are likely to experience anxiety— from feeling threatened by the perceived likelihood that others think you will not succeed and fearing that you will confirm those beliefs. The impact of that threat is reduced performance, as has now been shown in scores of studies across groups varying in gender, ethnicity, and social class (Crocker, Major, and Steele 1998; Steele, Spencer, and Aronson 2002). In chapter 7 we will see how this model operates in the case of immigrants from the Caribbean. The phenomenon is potentially much broader in its applicability, however, given the negative stereotypes that are associated with many immigrant groups.

The term stigma is often used by social scientists to designate groups that have been discredited and deemed unworthy by the dominant group in a society (Crocker, Major, and Steele 1998). In current usage, stigmatization is considered a context-dependent process rather that a fixed personal characteristic. In other words, what is stigmatized depends on who is doing the naming. Earlier conceptions of fixed characteristics with inevitable negative consequences are too simplistic, in reference to both immigrants and any other groups. At the same time, for some viewers in some contexts, immigrants do represent a group that is to be devalued. Further, many of the consequences of stigmatization, which can include decreased performance, as in the stereotype threat situation, as well as problematic social interactions, are surely descriptive of the immigrant experience. As defined by Elizabeth Pinel (1999), stigma consciousness refers to the awareness that one's group is negatively valued and that one will, as a result, be likely to experience negative consequences when others recognize that group membership. Considerable research shows that immigrant groups are well aware of the ways in which they are regarded—and indeed, given the climate of discrimination that I have described, how could they not be? Studies of Mexican-Americans, for example, have found that members of the group believe that Anglos hold negative views of them (Casas, Ponterotto, and Sweeney 1987). Recall the data shown in figure 4.1 that compares immigrants and nonimmigrants in their judgments of immigrant groups, where those new to the country are in complete accord with natives on the pecking order of the various groups.

Experience with discrimination makes a person understandably wary that negative situations will reoccur. In the case of African Americans in U.S. society, Rodolfo Mendoza-Denton, Geraldine Downey, and their colleagues have explored how expectations of rejection based on ethnic group membership can undermine confidence and reduce motivation (2002). The African American students they studied varied in the degree to which they were sensitive to race-based rejection (RS-race), as assessed both by their expectations that situations were likely to be discriminatory and their anxiety about their possible treatment in such situations. Looking at students both in the short run (over a three-week period) and in the longer run (over the course of five semesters), these investigators found clear differences between students who were higher or lower on the RS-race measure. In daily functioning, students high in RS-race were less positive toward their professors and reported a lower sense of personal happiness and well-being. Over the five academic terms, students high in RS-race showed a steady decline in their grade point average, and their confidence and trust in the university administration were significantly lower.

The Mendoza-Denton study, although based on black students at an elite university rather than an immigrant population in general, nonetheless suggests some of the consequences than follow from repeated experiences with discrimination. If immigrant groups are stigmatized in similar ways, we might expect that they too will show the negative impact of these

Figure 4.3   Anxious Expectations of Race-Based Rejection Among
Immigrant Groups

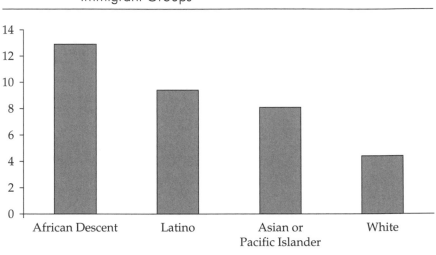

Source: Author's compilations.

experiences. Although we do not have the data to compare academic outcomes, we have collected data on the degree to which students of immigrant backgrounds (in a New York City public university) report expectations of and anxiety about rejection based on their ethnic group membership. Our study included both first- and second-generation immigrants from one of four ethnic-national groupings: African descent (primarily from the Caribbean), Latino (a majority from the Dominican Republic), Asian and Pacific Islands (including a variety of national origins), and white (primarily from eastern Europe and the former Soviet Union). Figure 4.3 shows the scores on a measure of RS-race for each of the four groups, reflecting a significant difference between the groups. Students of African descent reported the highest scores on the measure and white students showed the lowest. Latino and Asian students fell between the two extremes. It is worth noting that men and women in the sample did not differ in their scores, nor was there any difference between first- and second-generation students. Thus, the experiences surrounding discriminatory experience are remarkably similar within a particular demarcated group. Time spent in the United States does not seem to be a critical factor in one's experience with discrimination—for those subject to it, the climate sets in very quickly and becomes a constant part of lived experience.

Reaffirming the point made earlier, not all immigrants have the same experience. The color line continues to be a significant aspect of immigrant life. Historically, as Jacobson (1998) argues, "race is absolutely central to the history of European immigration and settlement [to the United States]. . . . The European immigrants' experience was decisively shaped by their entering an arena where Europeanness—that is to say, whiteness—was among the most important possessions one could lay claim to" (8). Contrast the European experience with that of Puerto Ricans who, despite territorial status within the United States, are still subject to prejudice and high residential segregation—an outcome that Massey and Denton (1993) attribute directly to their African heritage. Then, as now, "race continues to be the basis for profound inequalities and prejudices" (Foner 2000, 166). This is not to say that discrimination on the basis of perceived race is inevitable. Race is, in the view of most contemporary scientists, a social construction and not a biological reality. Yet as Foner has stated, "the awesome power of race is related to its ability to pass as a feature of the natural landscape" (2000, 142). Over the last century in the United States, and increasingly in Europe as well today, much of the variance in the prejudice and discrimination that immigrants experience can be linked to skin color and other physical markers of ethnic origin.

CHANGES IN THE STEREOTYPES OF ETHNIC GROUPS

Although the process of stereotyping is tenacious—and, indeed, testifies to a basic human tendency to categorize and find satisfying meaning— the content and the application of stereotypes to particular groups shows fluidity over time and place. As examples of historical vicissitudes, we can look to the case of Asians in general, and the Chinese and Japanese in particular. In 1882, through the provisions of the Chinese Exclusion Act, the Chinese became the first group to be specifically banned from the United States; in 1917 other Asian groups were included in the prohibition. The rationale for this policy was summarized in what we might consider an ethnophaulism on the part of the ruling federal district court: "The yellow or bronze racial color is the hallmark of Oriental despotisms" (quoted in Foner 2000, 161). The term *Oriental*, with its connotations of exoticism and evil and its assumptions of racial distinctions, continued in popular usage until the late 1960s (Yu 2001). In tandem, the perceived threats of Chinese laborers to native-born workers delayed the legitimization of Chinese immigrants until 1943—only then were they allowed to become citizens. Not until 1952 were all Asians eligible for naturalization (Foner 2000).

Even more dramatic are shifts in stereotypes that register a reaction to a specific historical moment, exemplified by the images of Japanese-Americans following the attack on Pearl Harbor. With that act, Japanese-Americans quickly became a distinct and questionable class of citizens, suspected of aiding the enemy and painted as untrustworthy. Subsequently, with the postwar rebuilding of Japan, the Japanese came to represent a completely different image, one associated with hard work, a belief in higher education, and an emphasis on economic improvement. No longer a dangerous case of Yellow Peril, Asian-Americans are now viewed as the embodiment of a supposed Confucian ideal, one that includes many of the desirable characteristics of the Protestant work ethic (Yu 2001). Whether the frame is Confucian or Protestant ethic, Asian-Americans in general, including not only Chinese and Japanese but also Vietnamese and Koreans, are often touted as a model minority, believed to excel in education and occupational pursuits. More recently, arrivals from Southeast Asia (for example, India) are also moving into the category of "good" immigrants. At the same time, although their competence is acknowledged, many of these same groups are downgraded on dimensions of warmth and sociability, leading to their rejection in interpersonal situations (see Lin et al. 2005).

One doesn't need to go back sixty years to see the impact that political events can have on group stereotypes. In the aftermath of the attack on the World Trade Center in New York City in September 2001, Arab-Americans—a group probably not well articulated in previous years—became a target of insinuation, discrimination, and stereotyping. A senate candidate in Louisiana expressed a need to look extra carefully at those "who wear diapers on their heads" (Ayres 2001). Negative references to "towel heads" and "ragheads" cropped up on various Web sites. Incidents of violence toward Muslims, and even those mistakenly identified as Muslims, such as Sikhs, were reported in the United States and in other countries as well (Elliott 2004; Bryan 2005). At the end of 2001, the FBI reported a sharp increase in hate crimes against Muslims, from twenty-eight in 2000 to 481 in 2001 (cited in Kaushal, Kaestner, and Riemers 2004). One survey reported that nearly 40 percent of people polled favored some form of internment for Arab-Americans, a chilling echo of the World War II treatment of Japanese-Americans.

Stereotype data collected in a recent national sample by Fiske and her colleagues finds that U.S. citizens view Arabs and Muslims as both unlikable and moderate to low in perceived competence (Fiske et al. 2002; Cuddy, Fiske, and Glick 2004). Thus, they seem to fall in the lower left quadrant of figure 4.2, a space previously defined in similar studies by the relatively negative but less clearly articulated images of Turks. Although we do not have data from a comparable sample of people surveyed prior to the 9/11 attacks, it is not unreasonable to assume that any change since that date has been in a negative direction.

The Princeton Quartet—the four studies of ethnic stereotypes of Princeton University students using the original Katz and Braly methods—provide an interesting baseline for looking at change in ethnic stereotypes over time. Recall that at each point—1932, 1950, 1967, and 2000—students were asked to indicate which of a set of eighty-four possible traits were characteristic of each of seven potential immigrant groups. Over the years, some rather large shifts in the content of these ethnic-national stereotypes have occurred (perhaps precipitated in part by changes in the Princeton student body, which became considerably more diversified during this period of time). In some cases, the changes can be linked to historical context, best illustrated by the changed images of both Germans and especially of the Japanese in the period following World War II. (Interestingly, although Italy was also a member of the Nazi-Fascist coalition, the stereotype of Italians was less affected than those of their coalition partners were.) Both Germans and Japanese were viewed in much more nationalistic terms in 1951 than they had been earlier; for the Japanese, this shift was accompanied by a marked decline in the attribution of traits such as intelligence and industriousness. In 1967 and 2000, these trends sharply reversed again. Now, in the aftermath of postwar rebuilding and redevelopment, people from both countries were seen as highly industrious and efficient. By 2000, intelligent, scientific, and industrious were the traits most frequently used to describe both the Germans and the Japanese. For the Japanese especially, as noted earlier, evaluative shifts were quite strong (Leslie et al. 2005).

China is another example of dramatic shifts in time, both in the content and the favorability of the ethnic-national stereotype. In the earliest Katz and Braly survey, Chinese were characterized as superstitious, sly and conservative, traits consistent with the more general Yellow Peril imagery. Steadily these earlier stereotypes eroded, to be replaced with more positive traits such as intelligence and industriousness. A belief that the Chinese value tradition remained part of the core stereotype, accompanied by an increasing belief in the importance to the Chinese of family ties. More generally, the Chinese showed the sharpest increases in rated favorability over the fifty-year span, moving from a position near the bottom of the rankings to a place near the top, along with Italians and Japanese (Leslie et al. 2005).

An example of shifts in the opposite direction is provided by the English, though it is not as extreme as the Chinese case. The image of the English appears more tempered than it once was, with declines in attributions of intelligence and sportsmanlike (perhaps related to an increase in exemplars provided by well-publicized riots on the soccer fields). Beliefs in the traditionalism and conservatism of the British remain, however, undoubtedly reflecting at least in part the continuing traditions of the monarchy. And, as shown in figure 4.2, among the seven countries studied, the English remain the sole occupants of the most favorable quadrant.

Once again, it is important to remember that these ethnic stereotypes are directed at people who live in those countries and not more specifically at immigrants from those countries. They are, as I have suggested, one influential basis for immigrant stereotypes, but they can also be modified by the more specific conditions of entrance and placement in the United States (or in whatever country of immigration we want to consider). As noted earlier, it would be interesting to explore just what shifts in ethnic stereotypes occur from point of departure to point of entry, and what factors are most influential in those changes.

The evidence that ethnic stereotypes can change over time—sometimes very dramatically, as in the case of the Chinese and Japanese—offers a strong argument for the importance of context in shaping the images that we hold. Stereotypes can last, both because they have the proverbial kernel of truth and because the particular image is one that is easily communicated and part of the common discourse (Schaller, Conway, and Tanchuk 2002). But the importance of context, whether of historical event or particular juxtapositions of host and immigrant, needs to be appreciated as a significant shaper of belief and in turn of behavior. A substantial body of research on intergroup contact offers promise for the possibility of change in negative attitudes and stereotypes toward outgroups and foreigners (Pettigrew and Tropp 2005; Pettigrew et al. 2005). The challenge for those in a host country, as they regard their new immigrants, is to be able to separate figure from ground and fiction from fact—to move beyond the simplified stereotype to the more complex realities of immigrant life.

From the perspective of the immigrant, pervasive stereotypes mean that they arrive not as neutral unknowns, but rather as exemplars of groups, whether immigrant in general or more specifically ethnic or national, about which well-entrenched beliefs often precede them. In this context, they must define, explain, and often defend themselves to those whose views may seem discrepant. Not all individuals or groups encounter the same expectations, nor do they all face exactly the same challenges. All immigrants must, however, find ways to negotiate an identity that works for them, one that somehow deals both with elements of origin as well as circumstances of the present. It is these issues of identity that I address in the following chapters.

Chapter Five | Who Am I?
The Construction of
Ethnic Identity

I became a United States citizen four years ago because of my long love affair
with New York. . . . I am a Bangladeshi woman and my last name is Rahman,
a Muslim name. . . . Before last week, I had thought of myself as a lawyer, a
feminist, a wife, a sister, a friend, a woman on the street. Now I begin to see
myself as a brown woman who bears a vague resemblance to the images of terrorists we see on television. . . . As I become identified as someone outside the
New York community, I feel myself losing the power to define myself.

—Anika Rahman (2001)

I was born in Senegal when it was part of France. I speak French, my wife is
French and I was educated in France. [But] the French don't think I'm French.

—Semou Diouf (quoted in Smith 2005)

THE TRAGEDY OF the World Trade Center destruction that prompted Anika
Rahman to feel that she had lost the power to define herself is certainly a
more dramatic confrontation with one's identity than many immigrants
experience. Semou Diouf's similar doubts arose from a less tragic but no
less political episode, a period when young French residents of African
and Arab descent set fire to cars and buildings in the immigrant suburbs
of Paris and other major cities throughout France. The statements of both
Rahman and Diouf might be considered unique in their explicit linkage to
national events in the United States and France, respectively. Yet both stories also contain many elements that are common to the experiences of all
immigrants: deciding how to conceptualize ethnic and national identity,

91

weighing possible combinations between the identity of origin and a newly claimed identity in the country to which they have moved; merging that newly formulated sense of identity with other important aspects of self; and doing all of this within a social context in which beliefs about immigrants and about one's ethnic and national group are held and conveyed. Further, Anika Rahman's story, set in the historical moment of New York City in September 2001, also exemplifies the dynamics of social identification, the sense of identity as a process that can continually be renegotiated rather than a category acquired early and maintained unchanged.

Far from being simple concepts, ethnic and national identity are rich in meaning, multidimensional and needing careful examination of the constituent parts in order to fully understand what they imply. Once the concept is taken apart, the whole can be seen more clearly, and some examples will be used to illustrate this reassembly. Adding additional complexity to the analysis, we need to address questions of multiplicity and intersectionality: how do identities combine in the lived experience of those who hold them? These issues, which focus on the structure and meaning of ethnic identity, are the topic of this chapter.

ETHNIC IDENTITY: WHAT AND WHY?

The concept of ethnic identity has a long history in social science discourse and its status has been widely debated. At times it is considered a dominant reality of American life, essential in characterizing a nation that has its roots in immigration. At other times, ethnic identity is viewed as a thing of the past, what Portes and Rumbaut, reflecting on Gans (1979), describe as the belief that ethnic identity became "an optional leisure-time form of symbolic ethnicity" (2001, 149). In the contemporary world, however, immigration trends in the United States and elsewhere have given ethnic identity a high profile, replacing notions of the "twilight of ethnicity" (Alba 1985) with ethnic identity politics.

Defining Our Terms

Some definitions are in order before proceeding. In particular, I would like to consider the concepts of ethnic identity, national identity, and social or collective identity, each of which is relevant to the analysis to follow. That of ethnic identity has its roots in sociology, most often attributed to the work of Max Weber (1921). In Weber's definition, ethnic groups are based on a belief in common descent, based on either physical characteristics or shared customs. Later definitions, as Stephen Cornell and Douglas Hartmann (1998) discuss, often shifted the temporal basis from past to present, emphasizing the languages, religion, and behaviors that groups share in their current experience. Yet with increasing work on the importance of collective memories, it seems reasonable to bring back this sense of past, as several authors do (Cornell and Hartmann 1998; Schermerhorn 1978). Also reflective of current work in psychology, most contemporary definitions of ethnic identity include some element of self-consciousness—an explicit awareness by members of the group of their groupness.

National identity often overlaps with *ethnic identity*, but the two terms are not identical. With national identity, a key element is the recognition of and allegiance to the nation-state. Nationalism may forge allegiances among ethnic groups in order to create a national image, often in reaction to some external pressures. In Finland, for example, Swedish and Russian identification and language preceded the Finnish nationalist movement and its endorsement of the Finnish language as a unifying element (Anderson 1983). In the case of the former Yugoslavia, several ethnic groups were united under a single national identity umbrella. France is another illustrative case, where the civic identity of French is designed by policy to incorporate groups of various ethnic origin, ranging from citizens of Guadeloupe and Martinique who have department status in the French political system, to immigrants from the former colonial countries of Africa, though, as recent events have shown, the ideals may not be realized in practice. Countries, such as Finland and France, or the United States and Canada, are the basis for national identities. At an expanded level, one might also consider the politically constructed European Union to be an international variation of a national identity, although its subjective status among inhabitants is still uncertain (Chryssochoou 2000).

As Stephen Cornell and Douglas Hartmann (1998) suggest, national identity is distinguished from ethnic identity because of the political agenda that is part of the former. Such agendas shift over time so that national identity, perhaps more than ethnic identity, is a process as well as a state of being (Reicher and Hopkins 2001). Another difference between ethnic and national identity, in my view, is the specificity of the physical reference point. In the case of national identity, a person can typically point to a particular geographical location as the site of the identity (though a space that, as in the case of the former Yugoslavia, may no longer be a geopolitical reality). Ethnic identity, by contrast, is defined more in terms of the people with whom one shares meanings and histories; it is not as tightly linked to a particular physical locale and often crosses national boundary lines.

If ethnic and national identity are two distinct positions, can they reside easily within the same psyche? Canadian policy, described in chapter 2, presupposes a belief that they can. In Canada, with its explicit policy of diversity, the boundaries of ethnic and national identities are clearly distinguished.

Immigrants are encouraged to maintain their ethnic identities at the same time that they endorse the civic aspects of a national identity, consistent with data that suggest peaceful coexistence. A statement by a Midwesterner, born in Latvia but resident of the United States for approximately fifty years, expresses the same belief: "As I've grown older, I recognize the fact that I can be a very strong [American] citizen and also can be Latvian—no big deal about it" (Smith, Stewart, and Winter 2004, 619). Research recently done in South Africa suggests that not only can ethnic and national identity be compatible, but that they can be mutually supportive. Thus, James Gibson (2004) found that the correlations between ethnic group identification and the importance and pride associated with being a South African were uniformly positive, arguing against the hypothesis that strong subgroup identification is incompatible with strong national identification.

Yet the lines between national and ethnic identification are not always so clear. In some cases, as when a nation has been politically stable for generations and is ethnically homogeneous as well (Sweden serves as one example here), distinctions between national and ethnic identity are minimal. A more psychologically complex example is provided in the statement of a U.S.-born, Spanish-speaking young man of Dominican heritage interviewed by Portes and Rumbaut (2001): "I'm still part Dominican. That's my nationality. If you become African American you give your nationality away" (151). Here, at the individual level of definition, distinctions between ethnic and national identity are blurred. Despite his legal status as an American, the man refers to Dominican as his national identity, a position further complicated by the reference to African American, in which ethnicity and nationality are combined.

The ambiguities between ethnic and national identity are not easily resolved. Objective definitions and subjective understandings can be contradictory. Further, the identity hyphenation so common in the United States (for example, Korean American) suggests a belief that one can simultaneously hold and blend together the ethnicity of origin and the nationality of current citizenship or residence. These complexities support my argument that the study of immigration requires a careful look at psychological as well as demographic aspects of identity categories.

The third term that I introduce here is *social identity*,[1] a concept developed by social psychologists to describe those aspects of self-concept that are based on group membership. Social identity is a general concept: both ethnic and national identities can be considered examples of a social or collective identification. The scholarly contribution of this concept is its focus on specific psychological processes and an explicit recognition of the link between the individual and the society. Social identity implies both the existence of socially defined categories—what Verkuyten (2005) calls social fact—and the subjective experience of defining oneself in terms of the available categories. It is analytically possible to separate the two aspects, as Verkuyten insists that we do. At the same time, the fundamental interdependence of the two elements of social process is, in my view, critical to recognize and theorize.

Categories are used all the time, both when describing oneself and when referring to others. Thus, one might speak of women and men; professors, lawyers, and bricklayers; Muslims, Catholics, and Jews; or Serbians, Malaysians, and Peruvians. These categories are widely available in the society and are used both by others and by the self. In adopting the term social or collective identity, one implies that the identity is shared with others who can be described in terms of a common set of characteristics. Like ethnic and national identity, social identity assumes some form of shared experience, although it is less specific as to the nature of the shared material than the other two concepts.

As used in reference to the self, social identity implies that one subjectively accepts or claims a category label as in some respects self-descriptive. This shift from recognition of the socially stated category to a personal identification with the category Maykel Verkuyten and Angela de Wolf (2002a) describe as a distinction between being and feeling. Being is simply the recognition of an ethnic label, exemplified by the statement, "it's just that you happen to be born that way. . . . You can't change that" (380), expressed by a Chinese immigrant in the Netherlands. Feeling, in contrast, refers to the inner acceptance of the category. As one participant described the difference, "on the outside I'm Chinese, but inside of me I feel Dutch" (Verkuyten and de Wolf 2002a, 382).

Other people may influence the choice of categories by which one describes oneself, as when they assign age or gender or ethnic categories based on visual cues. Yet these assignments do not determine our identification: we may or may not agree with the assignment and may or may not think of ourselves in those terms. Feeling or subjective claims refer to an inner truth that cannot be refuted by the perceptions or judgments of others. Even within a single family, where the conditions of immigration and family descent may be very similar, members can differ in their ethnic self-definitions.

The Coury family in Cleveland, Ohio, interviewed by *New York Times* reporter Lynette Clemetson, illustrates the variations that are possible ("Some Younger U.S. Arabs Reassert Ethnicity," January 11, 2004, p. 1, 14). Joseph Coury immigrated to the United States from Lebanon in 1898 at the age of twelve. Adding to the family line were relatives who immigrated to the United States in the 1980s, escaping the fighting that was taking place in Lebanon; their recent experiences in that country provided a fresh introduction to Lebanese culture for the young Joseph Coury IV. Today, Joseph Coury IV identifies himself as Lebanese-American, despite patterns of intermarriage that make him only one-quarter Lebanese by blood lines. "I have different ethnicities in me," he said, "but this is the one that feels tangible." Consistent with his claim to the label, Coury pronounces his name as it would be done in Arabic, rather than the Americanized version that his family adopted. As president of the Persian and Arab Students Association at his university, he pushed for the addition of Arabic language courses to the curriculum. At the same time, other members of this family claim different labels. Two cousins whose father immigrated to the United States call themselves Lebanese. A cousin prefers the term Arab-American, and an uncle (also with a mixed history of intermarriage) considers himself white.

Thus, the exploration of what people call themselves becomes a critical inquiry for understanding social identity. It is not merely a knowledge of label or a question of semantics. Rather these definitions of self have consequences for behavior. As in the case of Joseph Coury IV, the tangibility of Lebanese-American led him to actions at his university, involving himself with a group of like-defined people and pushing for the establishment of language courses that could make Arab culture and traditions more salient. These behaviors are not characteristic of many of his relatives, most of whom might be considered members of the same ethnic category in the eyes of others. These external assignments do not have the motivational properties that internal claims do, however, underlining the importance of understanding the processes of ethnic self-definition.

Constructing Ethnic Categories

A fascinating example of the disjunction between category labels assigned by others and social identities claimed by individuals emerged from an analysis of the U.S. census data as they relate to the Hispanic population (Navarro 2003). In the standard census forms, people were asked to identify themselves as belonging to one of five categories: white, black, Asian, American Indian, or a category that includes natives of Hawaii and the Pacific Islands. If none of these was seen as appropriate, people had options to indicate "some other race" or to select more than one racial designation. Consideration of census date over the past three decades (1980, 1990, and 2000) shows a decreasing tendency for Hispanics to identify themselves as white (from 58 percent in 1980 to 48 percent in 2000) and an increasing tendency to claim either some other race or more than one race (from 38 percent in 1980 to 49 percent in 2000). In fact, of all people who used the category "some other race" when filling out the census forms, 97 percent were Latino.

The use of Latino versus Hispanic as an ethnic category is itself a story of disjunction between labels assigned and labels chosen by people themselves. Hispanic is a term introduced by the U.S. Census Bureau in 1970, intended to be applied to all people of Spanish origin (Comas-Díaz 2001). In this regard, it made official the less formal designation of Spanish-speaking that had prevailed before (but had not been part of official census categories). By 1980, the term Hispanic was not only firmly established in the census operation but was also—as Daryl Fears reported in the *Washington Post*—widely used in a variety of government and organizational forms, including job applications and school enrollment ("Latino or Hispanics? A Debate about Identity," August 25, 2003, p. A1). With its allusion to origins in the Iberian Peninsula, the term Hispanic appeals to those who turn to Europe as a point of reference, a group which includes Cuban-Americans in south Florida. For others, however, the reference to Europe seems inappropriate. As the writer Oscar Casares wrote for *The New York Times*: "Hispanic? Where was the Mexican in me? Where was the hyphen? The word reminded me of those Mexican-Americans who preferred to say their families came from Spain, which they felt somehow increased their social status" ("Crossing the Border without Losing your Past," September 16, 2003, p. A25).

For many, the pretensions of Hispanic and the concomitant disregard for the indigenous populations of Latin America who existed prior to colonial invasions makes the term *Latino* preferable. It also allows for gender marking, that is, Latino versus Latina, which is an additional argument for it by some supporters (Shorris 1992). Reflecting these debates, the U.S. Office of Management and Budget incorporated Latino into its official definition of Hispanic for the 2000 census, defining the category as Hispanic-Latino (Marrow 2003).

Recent survey data suggest that preferences for terminology are still very much in flux. In one survey, approximately half of the people sampled (53 percent) said that both terms—Hispanic and Latino—defined them. One-third of the respondents (34 percent) preferred the term Hispanic, while a relatively small minority (13 percent) preferred Latino (Fears 2003). Beyond these more encompassing labels exist many more specific terms of self-description, often referring to a particular country or national origin. Thus, for Oscar Casares (*New York Times*, September 16, 2003, p. A25), the debate over labels is resolved by saying "I am, like my father, Mexican." Even with respect to a single country, however, the terms can differ. Consider those that have been used to refer to immigrants or sojourners from Mexico: Mexican, Mexican-American, Chicano and Chicana, and Xicano and Xicana (Comas-Díaz 2001).

Evidence for the construction and conflation of ethnic group labels can be seen in other immigrant populations as well. Consider the term Asian American. Adopted in the United States, this term has become a label of convenience to refer to people who have immigrated from anywhere in East or South Asia, including China, Vietnam, Japan, Korea, the Philippines, Cambodia, and sometimes India, Pakistan, and Bangladesh as well. In innumerable ways (such as language, political history, ethnic origins), these groups are very different from one another; and yet the external application of the label presumes some homogeneity.

Brazilian immigrants provide another example of the problems of correspondence between self-definition and categories provided by others (Marrow 2003). People in the United States often lump immigrants from Brazil into a general category of Latino or Hispanic. From the perspective of Brazilians, however, their Portuguese language and heritage excludes them from official census categories that specify Spanish culture or origin. Accordingly, in the 1990 census a majority of Brazilian immigrants, both first- and second-generation, responded to the Hispanic origin question by saying that they were not Spanish-Hispanic. At the same time, the vast majority of Brazilians identified as white when questioned on the census (Marrow 2003), a contrast to the decreasing number of Hispanics who do so. This tendency is somewhat in contrast to the only 42 percent who identified themselves as white (branco) in a 1995 racial survey in Brazil (Telles 2004). The difference reflects both the dominance of the white-black nomenclature in the United States and the alternative conceptions of race in Brazil. In Brazil, unlike the United States or South Africa, laws never existed defining racial-group existence. Instead of relying on descent (for example, one-sixteenth African ancestry), racial classification in Brazil is generally based on skin color and allows for a more continuous range of labels (Telles 2004). In fact, one of the most popular and at the same time most ambiguous is moreno, generally translated as brown but allowing for many interpretations. In the 1995 Brazilian survey, 32 percent of people considered themselves moreno, another 7 percent chose pardo (an official census category for brown), and yet another 6 percent chose moreno claro. Only 8 percent used preto or negro, which translate as black (Telles 2004). Given these patterns of racial definition, first-generation immigrants from Brazil may find it difficult to respond to the U.S. census categories. It is interesting to note, however, that second-generation Brazilian immigrants in the United States are more likely to use both categories—white and black—as self-descriptive than are first-generation immigrants, suggesting the socialization of black-white dichotomies in the United States.

Another debate over ethnic labels has recently surfaced with regard to the use of African American (Perkins 2006; Swarns 2004). Here the question is whether the label can be claimed by immigrants who were not born in the United States or whose parents emigrated to the United States (where examples include such high-profile figures as former U.S. Secretary of State Colin Powell or current Senator from Illinois Barack Obama), or whether it is the exclusive province of those whose roots go back many generations in the United States with its distinctive history of slavery. These variations are a sharp reminder that even what might seem the most straightforward aspect of identity—defining a label for a group—is far more complicated than census forms would suggest.

PARSING THE ELEMENTS OF ETHNIC IDENTITY

These discussions of labels are more than an esoteric debate about terminology. Ethnic identity—indeed, any social or collective identity—carries a whole range of meanings and assumptions about one's definition of self, about value and importance, about social networks and cultural history. It is the richness and depth of meaning associated with the concept of identity that gives it its analytical power.

This depth and range of meaning can also be a source of confusion, however. What one person means when referring to identity may be quite different from what another means. One might be thinking only about the demographic grouping, for example, whereas another might assume a particular history and ideological position. Because the concept of identity has often been called upon to bear considerable theoretical and political weight, some writers have suggested that the term be abandoned completely (Brubaker and Cooper 2000).

That is not the route that I will take. Ethnic identity is a key concept for those of us who study immigration and to eliminate it from the discourse would be, I believe, a serious mistake. Embedded within the concept of ethnic identity are critical psychological processes by which people—immigrants in particular—define and situate themselves in social, cultural, and historical contexts. Yet we do need a kind of road map to navigate the multiple meanings and implications of the concept. For this purpose, I use a framework developed by Richard Ashmore, Kay Deaux, and Tracy McLaughlin-Volpe (2004). In our analysis of collective identification, we articulated seven distinct aspects of social identity, as shown in table 5.1. Each element offers a separate facet, a unique piece to the overall concept of identity. This is not to suggest that immigrant identity comes to us in such a neat set of pieces. However, by taking the concept apart and looking at its various components, some of the conceptual confusion surrounding identity can be eliminated and points of comparison between different

Table 5.1 Elements of Ethnic Identity

Self-Categorization
Identifying oneself as a member of, or categorizing oneself in terms of, a particular
  social grouping
  "I am, like my father, Mexican." (Casares 2003)

Importance
The degree of importance of a particular group membership to the individual's
  overall self-concept
  "I am a Croat, and this means everything to me." (Timotijevic and Breakwell
2000)

Evaluation
The positive or negative attitude that a person has toward the social category in
  question. Evaluation can be further divided as being based on favorability judgments made by people about their own identities (Private regard) versus favorability judgments that one perceives others, such as the general public, to hold
  about one's social group (Public regard).
  "I feel the Serbian side much more . . . [but] I don't like the Serbian mentality."
(Timotijevic and Breakwell 2000)

Attachment and Sense of Interdependence
The emotional involvement or the degree to which the person feels at one with
  the group. Aspects of attachment include the perception of common fate with
  the ways that members of one's group are treated in society.
  "Talking to another West Indian . . . growing up, the similarities are there you
know, things like that. It's why you're West Indian. You share a common experience." (Gilkes 2004)

Social Embeddedness
The degree to which the collective identity is embedded in the person's everyday
  network of ongoing social relationships
  "In the family parties, the funerals, the baptisms, the weddings and the birthdays, our private lives continued to be Mexican." (Dublin 1993)

Behavioral Involvement
The degree to which the person engages in actions that directly implicate the ethnic identity category in question. This element can include language usage, cultural practices and political activities.
  "I . . . can't be said to be really Chinese. Because I hardly talk Chinese, and I
can't write Chinese." (Verkuyten and de Wolf 2002a)

Content and Meaning
The associations and meanings that an identity has for the person, including
  traits and dispositions associated with the category; ideological reference to
  experience, history, and position in society; and narratives about the group and
  one's place in that group.
  "I was exactly what they came up with when they designed the [Yugoslavian]
system . . . Raised to be like if somebody attacked your country from outside you
would just go . . . I think if somebody attacked the country I would have joined
the military at the time and defended the country." (Bikmen 2005)

Source: Adapted from Ashmore, Deaux, and McLaughlin-Volpe (2004).

identities, or between people holding the same identities, can be articulated more clearly.

Let me add one cautionary note before moving on. In adopting this structural analysis, I am not assuming that identity is fixed and stable over time and place. As will become much clearer in chapter 6, the view of identity proposed here is one of negotiation and variability. Certainly when talking about immigration, identity must be conceptualized in terms of change. At the same time, it is not only possible but highly useful to be able to "stop the process" for an analytic moment to look at the distinct elements of identity, a view that will allow more targeted and precise discussion of identity change.

Self-Categorization

As discussed earlier, categorization is a social fact, a set of understandings about how the world can be divided up and where people are likely to be placed within a set of available categories. These categories are socially available and widely used. In using the term self-categorization, however, we are asking for more—we require that the category label be one that the person is willing to consider self-descriptive. Acknowledging that a category label is self-descriptive does not necessarily mean that one regards that label as particularly important, or even that one considers it a positive feature. As subsequent discussion will show, importance and evaluation can be analytically separated from the process of categorization per se. Further, I will argue that it is essential to make these distinctions and that the dynamics between what is socially imposed and what is personally claimed often hinge on just these differences between category and other elements.

Census data is a prime exemplar of the use of self-categorization as the basis for defining ethnic identity. Many large-scale surveys of immigrants rely on similar categorization procedures. Kasinitz, Mollenkopf, and Waters (2002), for example, in an ambitious study of second-generation immigrants in the New York City metropolitan area, asked interviewees which one race they considered themselves to be, providing a list of fifteen options, including such possibilities as Asian-Indian, Vietnamese, and Samoan. They further asked the respondent to name their ancestry or ethnic origin, defined as the country of one's ancestors. Portes and Rumbaut (2001) used a somewhat more open-ended strategy in their survey of immigrant children in Miami/Fort Lauderdale and San Diego, asking them a question— how do you identify, that is what do you call yourself?—but also providing a set of examples, such as American, Latino, Cuban, Haitian-American. Responses were then classified as one of four types: foreign national-origin identity, for example, Cambodian; hyphenated American identity, for example, Cuban-American; American national identity; and pan-ethnic minority group identity, for example, Hispanic, black. Mary Waters (1990) probed further, first asking people to select a category from the census survey that she provided and then asking people to explain the basis for their choice.

What seems a simple categorical choice may not be all that simple for many respondents. Waters (1990) referred to the procedures of the 1980 census, in which people were asked to describe their ancestry and were permitted to give up to three responses.[2] On this task, 31 percent of the respondents reported multiple ancestry. In her own interviews, Waters observed "just how much sifting and sorting occurs *even before* [her respondents] consider the question" (23; emphasis in original). Further, as distinctions such as Chicano and Mexican-American illustrate, the choice of label is decidedly an individual statement. Much as has been the case with Americans of African descent, the choice of a label makes a statement. Thus, in the latter case, U.S. history shows a shift in usage from Negro to black to African American over the course of the past fifty years, with each term carrying distinctive meaning (Philogène 1999).

Nor, if given the opportunity, do people necessarily limit themselves to a single ethnic category. In our own research, we find increasing numbers of people who check two or more categories or who, when asked in an open-ended question, will list several ethnic and racial categories. In the 2000 census, respondents were permitted to select "one or more races" for the purpose of self-definition, an option that was taken by 2.4 percent of the population, approximately 6.8 million people (Bean and Stevens 2003). Trends in intermarriage suggest that this number will continue to rise, with one estimate suggesting that 25 percent of the population will claim multiple ethnic category membership by the time of the 2050 U.S. census (Bean and Stevens 2003). Further the Bean and Stevens analysis shows that the tendency toward multiracial identification varies across groups, and is most common among those with Latino or Asian backgrounds and less common when ancestry is primarily white or black. At the same time, almost half of the Hispanic respondents rejected all racial categories provided, and many preferred the category "some other race" from those provided. Often they added a more specific label such as Mayan or mestizo (Navarro 2003). Geography influences the patterns as well. Perhaps not surprisingly, Hawaii leads the list of multiracial identification; it is followed by states that have high immigrant populations, such as California, New York, and Texas. Multiracial claims are least common in states such as Maine, which has very little ethnic diversity, and Mississippi, where black-white distinctions have been prominent.

Finally, in recognition of the dynamics of social identification, it should be noted that self-categorization may change over time. In their longitudinal study of the children of immigrants, for example, Portes and Rumbaut (2001) assessed ethnic identity in 1992 and again in 1995–1996. Over half of their respondents reported a change in ethnic identification from one time to the next. Perhaps most interesting, for those who believe in the melting pot model of ethnic assimilation, these authors observed changes away from an American identity and toward pan-ethnic or immigrant identities. In sum, categorization may be the simplest element of identity, in terms of its definition—but in functional operation, it is far more complex.

Importance

As Waters (1990) noted in launching her in-depth interview study of ethnic identification, categories on their own "reveal neither the strength or the extent of ethnic identification" (10). Although two people may both acknowledge or claim an ethnic group membership, the importance that they attach to that membership can vary widely, from being central to their sense of self to being an incidental fact of ancestry. The significance of ethnicity is clear in the words of Eva Hoffman, as she describes how "the country of my childhood lives within me with a primacy that is a form of love. It lives within me despite my knowledge of our marginality" (Hoffman 1989, 74). Contrast this fervent endorsement with the Chinese immigrant in the Netherlands who says with certainty, "I absolutely don't feel Chinese" (Verkuyten and de Wolf 2002a, 387).

The term *importance* denotes the extent to which an identity is significant for the self-concept; other terms in the literature that carry similar meaning include centrality, prominence, and strength (Ashmore, Deaux, and McLaughlin-Volpe 2004). This feature of ethnic identity often captures divergences between the opinions of others and the claims of self. Both sides may agree that Chinese, for example, is an appropriate label for description. Yet though the observer may assume that all who fit that label have an equivalent investment in the group, individuals can vary widely in the degree to which they consider their Chinese-ness important to their sense of self. At one extreme, a person may approach "disidentification" (Steele 1997; Verkuyten 2005), in which so little importance is accorded to the identity category that it becomes almost absent from the self-repertoire, even though others might continue to use the label. As a counterexample, a person can accord high importance to an identity that is not obvious, or even accepted, by another. A gay or lesbian, for example, might highly value their sexual orientation, yet that identity could be unknown or unaccepted by others. Similarly, the popular Brazilian label moreno is unrecognized and unused by most who live outside South America.

In her work on ethnic identification, Waters (1990) asked people directly about the importance of their ethnic identification: for example, "would you say that being ___ is important to you?" Answers to this question included the following statement by a sixty-year-old man: "Now definitely as I get older, it gets more important. It is important to have a sense of identity as you get older. To know who you are" (46). For this man, ethnic identification has apparently increased over time. In contrast, Herbert Gans's (1979) concept of symbolic ethnicity assumes that ethnic identity declines in importance over time, perhaps not within the individual's lifetime, but certainly across generations. Gans (1979) suggests that for many people in the United States, ethnicity has become detached, exercised only as occasional cultural rituals or practices rather than being a central part of one's life. Thus, an American of Italian heritage might enjoy eating pasta and celebrate Columbus Day without linking those experiences to other central aspects of self. Although positively regarded, the identity is considered to be relatively unimportant.

For understanding behaviors related to identity, importance is critical. Simply knowing the category into which someone can be placed, either by assignment of others or as a self-affirmed census category, is probably of limited value in predicting or understanding the choices that a person, whether immigrant or native-born, will make from an array of possible paths.

Evaluation

Evaluation refers to the valence associated with an identity—how positively or negatively it is regarded. Often it is assumed that people hold their ethnic or national identity in high regard ("I'm proud to be an American") with little questioning. Eva Hoffman, describing a conversation with a Russian artist, says: "He felt convinced that Russia was the greatest—really the only—country in the world. . . . It was such a pride" (1989, 74). Yet others may waiver or even reject their ethnic and national identification, finding it a source of shame or limitation. Many Serbian immigrants, for example, have difficulty dealing with the implications of the Yugoslav conflict for their self-definition. Consider the man who moved from Kosovo to London, as he described his condition to Lada Timotijevic and Glynis Breakwell (2000): "I feel more like a Serb, and I feel the Serbian side much more . . . [but] I don't like the Serbian mentality."

This illustrates the need to distinguish importance from evaluation when talking about ethnic identity (Ashmore et al. 2004; Verkuyten 2005).

A person can feel that an identity is central and important, as the Serbian respondent did, yet be ashamed or embarrassed by the designation because of events or experiences associated with it. Alternatively, one can feel very good about an ethnic identity, without seeing it as particularly important to an overall concept of self. I personally feel very positive about my (50 percent) Finnish heritage, for example, but it does not figure prominently in any accounting of my significant identities. As a perhaps more common example, many people celebrate their Irish heritage on St. Patrick's Day, no matter how tenuous the connections may be, yet think little of that part of themselves the rest of the year. Gans's (1979) notion of symbolic ethnicity fits well here.

Another important distinction with regard to evaluation is the difference between evaluations by the self and evaluations by others (Ashmore, Deaux, and McLaughlin-Volpe 2004). Within the social psychological literature, these two perspectives are sometimes termed *private* and *public regard*, respectively (Luhtanen and Crocker 1992; Sellers et al. 1998). Traditionally, theorists assumed that these two forms of evaluation must coincide. Thus, in the metaphor of a looking glass (Cooley 1902) or the social mirror (Winnicott 1971), people are thought to see themselves as others see them. Such a theory seems unproblematic (if not always supported) when the views of others are positive. If society views immigrants from India as a model minority, for example, then incorporating this external evaluation of the ethnic group into the self-concept would seem easy to do (though an individual's own experience with failing to meet this imposed standard can certainly cause personal difficulty).

When a group is seen in more negative light, however—viewed as undesirable in some respects or stigmatized—then these theories of reflected appraisal suggest more unpleasant consequences for the focal group. As we have seen in preceding chapters, immigrant groups are frequently the target of negative ascription. The Chinese in the late nineteenth and early twentieth century, the Irish and the Italians in the twentieth century; more recently, Mexicans and Haitians—each of these groups has frequently been characterized in unfavorable terms by people and press in the United States. In their study of the children of recently arrived immigrants in Boston and San Francisco, Suárez-Orozco and Suárez-Orozco (2001) asked children to complete the sentence, "Most Americans think [people from my country] are ___." Coding the answers in terms of their evaluative status (positive, neutral, or negative), the investigators found that two thirds of the children completed this sentence with unfavorable words, such as "bad," "stupid," "garbage," and "useless." Negative associations were strongest for the Dominican (82 percent), Haitian (80 percent), and Mexican (75 percent) children. Only among the Chinese were fewer than half of the responses negative (47 percent), but positivity was still rare (19 percent positive and 32 percent neutral comments).

Are these negative evaluations by others accepted and internalized by members of the targeted group? Research suggests not—or at least not always. Groups who are stigmatized by the society at large do not necessarily incorporate those negative views into their self-concept, as Jennifer Crocker and Brenda Major (1989) have shown. Rather, people are able to develop a set of coping strategies or an alternative set of mirrors that can buffer them from the negative evaluations of others. Questioning students in the United States who were either Euro American, African American, or Asian American, Crocker and her colleagues (1994) found that though whites and Asians showed a strong correspondence between their views of themselves and their perceptions of how others viewed their group ($rs = +.50$ and $+.59$, respectively), there was no relationship between these two measures for African Americans ($r = .02$). In their case, where the public perception was believed to be more negative, members of the group seem to have simply ignored the "looking glass" and based their evaluations on other sources. Who these other sources are has not been fully explored, but it seems likely that ingroup support becomes a more powerful reference group for those who are devalued by the dominant groups in a society.

Pride can be an important aspect of ethnic identity. Yet, as is clear from the data described here, positive evaluations are not mandatory. Ethnic identity can entail negative as well as positive feelings, both when viewed from one's own perspective of experience and history or when reflected from the appraisals of others. Often it is the negative evaluation associated with ethnic or national identity that will push a person toward claiming an alternative identity—issues that I will discuss later.

Attachment and Sense of Interdependence

In *Lost in Translation*, Eva Hoffman describes a conversation that began in a debate about Barry Goldwater's political position and evolved into an analysis of her Polish identity. Responding to a friend's claim that dignity requires self-sufficiency, the young Eva Hoffman asked, " 'But why shouldn't people help each other?' I ask ... There's no common word for 'self-sufficiency' in Polish, and it sounds to me like a comfortless condition, a harsh and artificial ideal" (1989, 176). Further, in responding to her friend's claim that dependency is bad for the character, Hoffman argued, "but we're all dependent on each other." It is interesting to speculate how this particular belief in attachment might have been influenced by the political structures of Communism in the Poland that Hoffman left in 1959. The more direct issue here, however, is to see attachment as a key element of ethnic identity.

As defined by Ashmore, Deaux, and McLaughlin-Volpe (2004), attachment and interdependence refer to the affective involvement that people feel toward members of their group and the degree to which their own fate is believed to be intertwined with the fate of others in the group. For the immigrant, this interdependence is typically based first on family, often including extended relationships that involve a network of relatives. Maintenance of the ethnic identity of origin can depend critically on the maintenance of these networks; when links with the family become frayed, other aspects of identity often diminish in importance as well. Richard Rodriguez (1982), in his autobiographical account of growing up, illustrates this process of distancing, so different in character from the account of Eva Hoffman. As he begins to feel American and seeks to distance himself from his Spanish heritage, Rodriguez comments that "the special feeling of closeness at home was diminished by then. Gone was the desperate, urgent, intense feeling of being at home. . . . We remained a loving family, but one greatly changed. No longer so close" (1982, 22–23).

A sense of common fate extends beyond the boundaries of known families to a belief that one's outcomes are in some way linked to the outcomes of others who share an ethnic identity. In research conducted in Los Angeles, Lawrence Bobo and Michael Johnson (2000) found that a sense of common fate based on racial-ethnic group identity was evident in most groups, though stronger in some than others. African American groups scored particularly high on a measure of common fate, for example. Among Asian groups, Koreans were stronger than Chinese and Japanese; among Latino groups, those with Central American ancestry expressed more common fate than Mexicans did.

These kinds of connections are what make social identities social. The identity is based on more than one's positive feelings about group membership, as would be represented in the individual self-concept. Rather, attachment and interdependence extend the boundaries of the self to encompass others, so that one shares both pleasure and pain.

Social Embeddedness

Closely related but conceptually distinguishable from interdependence is the notion of social embeddedness. Whereas interdependence and attachment emphasize the perceptions and feelings that people have about their ethnic group, social embeddedness refers to the actual relationships and social networks that support and sustain the identity (Ashmore et al. 2004). Within these networks, people carry out their daily interactions, and others within the network know one in terms of the particular identity. A Latvian immigrant in the Midwest described her world: "We went to a Latvian church, we had a Latvian bakery, we had a Latvian gas station owner, we had Latvian beauticians, a Latvian doctor. You know, you tended to stay together and help one another" (Smith, Stewart, and Winter 2004, 626). This embeddedness in a culture involves particular behaviors, which I will consider shortly. Perhaps more significantly, however, it defines a context and a frame in which a person operates and negotiates identity concerns.

For the immigrant these networks have always been important in both practical and symbolic ways. Oscar Handlin (1951), in his classic account of what he called the uprooted, described the institutions that allowed immigrants to gather together, maintaining ties to the country of origin in the case of the church and creating institutions to deal with the problems faced in the new country, in the case of mutual aid societies. As Handlin described the role of the church in immigrant life, he claimed that "the more thorough the separation from the other aspects of the old life, the greater was the hold of the religion that alone survived the transfer" (117). Through their involvement in the church, whether the Catholic church of the Irish and the Italians or the Lutheran church of Germans and Finns, immigrants were able to relate to others who shared their culture of origin—in many cases, people who came from the same villages. Mutual aid societies developed to supplement what the church could offer. Often the initial impetus for these societies was a need to arrange proper burials for those who died; later their functions expanded to include a variety of charitable activities that could benefit members of the immigrant community. A similar sense of social embeddedness is reflected in the words of Ernesto Galarza, a Mexican immigrant who later became an economist and labor organizer: "In the family parties, the funerals, the baptisms, the weddings and the birthdays, our private lives continued to be Mexican" (Dublin 1993, 233).

William Thomas and Florian Znaniecki's (1918/1920) work on Polish peasants in the early part of the twentieth century also revealed the importance of social networks and, more specifically, of networks that as closely as possible supported the identity of origin. When relocating in the United States, the Polish immigrants typically developed workmen's groups, which were located first in boardinghouses. In doing so, they showed a clear preference for Polish immigrants over other immigrants, for people from the same town in Poland over people from other towns, and for relatives over friends. As Kay Deaux and Daniela Martin (2003) have discussed, such networks are often essential for an identity to be maintained. They provide a context in which a person has easy access to others who are similar and who can validate one's identity and membership in the group. In the case of the Polish peasant, establishing a group of people who were not only Polish but who were also relatives or from a common town (or both) allowed immigrants to maintain well-established identities as Polish even in a new country. The relevance of these networks to ethnic identity was also shown by Patricia Gurin and her colleagues (Gurin, Hurtado, and Peng 1994) in a study contrasting Mexicanos, those born in Mexico, with Chicanos, those born in the United States. The meanings associated with the two identities differed, as did the pattern of interpersonal contacts. Mexicanos had more contact with other persons of Mexican descent, and Chicanos were more strongly involved with both Anglos and members of other ethnic minority groups.

For an immigrant who wants to maintain a particular identity, as the Polish peasants Thomas and Znaniecki described seemingly did, finding supportive networks is critical. Although studying Latino college students rather than immigrants per se, Kathleen Ethier and Kay Deaux (1990, 1994) described a process they termed "remooring." For those Latino students whose identity was important to them, it was essential that they find supportive networks of other Latinos amidst the foreign territory of an Ivy League campus. Joining Latino organizations and making friends with other Latinos allowed them to reconnect their identity to the immediate context, substituting a network on campus for the family and neighborhood that had supported their ethnic identity in the past. By the end of the students' first year in college, the strength of their ethnic identity bore no direct relationship to their cultural background but instead was related significantly to the current Latino context. In a similar demonstration of the relevance of context, Tom Postmes and Nyla Branscombe (2002) found that African Americans who lived in more highly segregated environments perceived more support from blacks and identified more strongly as African American. In contrast, those who lived in more integrated environments were less strongly identified as African American. A parallel case can be made for immigrants. To the extent that community and residential segregation exist, identification with the country of origin should be stronger than when ethnic enclaves are less pronounced.

Ethnic enclaves are often common in urban areas, as each immigrant group establishes a foothold in a different part of the city. Particularly in the case of Spanish-speaking immigrants, as Massey (1995) observes, the current trend is not for these enclaves to diminish as the original residents merge with the larger community, but rather for Spanish neighborhoods to thrive and expand. Because nearly 40 percent of new immigrants to the United States are Spanish speaking, they can easily find compatriot communities where they can continue to speak their native language and to engage in the cultural practices of their homeland.

At the same time, the large urban centers of the country, such as New York City, provide an opportunity for immigrants from different countries to have contact with each other (Kasinitz, Mollenkopf, and Waters 2002).

As a consequence, though immigrants may have relatively little contact with native whites or blacks, they often have considerable contact with members of other ethnic groups, particularly among the second generation. Kasinitz and his colleagues argue that for these immigrants, an identification as a New Yorker takes precedence over both ethnicity and American as a categorical label, reflecting the social networks in which they are most likely to participate.

Behavioral Involvement

Behavioral involvement—what Verkuyten and de Wolf (2002a) call "doing" ethnicity—includes a wide range of activities in which people engage and that attest to their identification with their ethnic group. These activities can range from celebrative parades to food preferences, from the language spoken in the home and with friends to the political groups that one supports. It is in fact difficult to think about ethnic identity without referring to examples of behavioral involvement. As a Croatian in London described himself to Timotijevic and Breakwell (2000): "I am a Croat, and this means everything to me: it is the place you were born, the food you eat, the music you listen, it is your roots" (364).

Writing about early twentieth century immigrants, Oscar Handlin claimed that "the event that excited the greatest enthusiasm was the parade, a procession which enabled the group to display before the whole world the evidence of its solidarity, which enabled the individual to demonstrate that he belonged, was a part of a whole" (1951, 177). Moving forward to twenty-first-century New York City, one finds dozens of annual parade days, each celebrating a particular immigrant group in the city. Probably the largest of these is the West Indian, which annually attracts more than a million people to Brooklyn for a day of parade, food, and music. Although smaller in numbers, no less enthusiastic participants in parades celebrating the cultures of Puerto Rico, Brazil, and of course the Irish on St. Patrick's Day testify to the importance of behavioral display for the affirmation of an ethnic identity.

Only 15 percent of the white immigrants sampled by Richard Alba (1990) reported no experience with ethnic-oriented activities, from a list that included eating ethnic foods, attending ethnic festivals, and discussing one's ethnic background with a friend. Even among the native-born white sample in Alba's study, only a quarter of the respondents reported no behaviors related to their ethnic background, and another quarter reported six or more such behaviors. Leading the list was eating ethnic food, reported by 47 percent of the native-born whites. Alba found that the behavioral expression of ethnicity was most often associated with other indicators of ethnic identity, such as subjective importance and an ethnically consistent family background. Further, he stressed the mutual influence of cultural expression and subjective importance upon each other, as increases in one domain typically lead to increases in the other.

In taking this position, Alba would seem to be arguing against the symbolic ethnicity position of Herbert Gans (1979, 1992, 1994). As defined by Gans, symbolic ethnicity "is intended mainly for the purpose of feeling or being identified with a particular ethnicity, but without either participating in an existing ethnic organization (formal or informal) or practicing an ongoing ethnic culture" (1994, 578). Thus, activities such as cultural celebrations, ethnic media, and ethnic foods and fashions are considered "free from affiliation with ethnic groups and ethnic cultures" (Gans 1992, 44). (Affiliation, in this case, presumably refers to the traditional sociological measures of institutional and spatial integration; would it be equally true for friendship patterns and informal networks?) For Gans, then, indices of behavioral involvement can exist apart from most of the other elements of identity I am discussing here, with the possible exception of some rudimentary form of categorization in an ethnic group.

In contrast, Richard Alba (1999) has argued that any subjective claim to an ethnic identity must be accompanied by actions, termed here behavioral involvement, to be valid. For me, the answer to this debate is slightly different. Rather than making assumptions as to whether behavioral involvement is independent of subjective identification or whether it necessarily follows such identification, I suggest that both patterns can occur. For some, ethnic identification is broadly based, including most of the elements that I identify in table 5.1. For others, a narrower path may be defined, and the limited involvement suggested by the term symbolic ethnicity will be an appropriate descriptor. The critical and revealing issue then becomes one of specifying the conditions under which one or the other of these patterns will hold—and in doing so, to be better able to predict the future course of a person's actions and engagements.

One of the most debated aspects of ethnic identity, here classified as a form of behavioral involvement, is language usage. Although participation in a parade honoring another country is often viewed as harmless entertainment (or even an occasion for a nonethnic to join, as in the popularized St. Patrick's Day celebrations), language usage is much more controversial, often viewed as a critical yardstick of ethnic and national allegiance. Thus, the straight-line assimilation models implicitly assume that immigrants who do not speak English when they arrive will learn to do so, and then will shift to the exclusive use of English (Bean and Stevens 2003). Theodore Roosevelt, the ardent fan of Zangwill's *Melting Pot*, voiced this position early on: "We have room for but one language here, and that is the English language, for we intend to see that the crucible turns out people as Americans, and not as dwellers of a polyglot boarding house" (quoted in Portes and Rumbaut 2001, 113). Seemingly true to that declaration, "the United States is unique in the rate at which other languages have been abandoned in favor of English" (Portes and Schauffler 1996, 11).

The United States has never made English language an explicit criterion for admittance, although immigration policies were sometimes developed with the intention of favoring those emigrating from English-speaking countries (see chapter 2). At the same time, Anglophonic expectations have always been strong and were made explicit in a 1994 statement by the U.S. Commission on Immigration reform: "Immigration carries with it obligations to embrace the common core of the American civic culture, to become able to communicate—to the extent possible—in English with other citizens and residents" (quoted in Bean and Stevens 2003, 168). At a more local level, English-only campaigns have frequently been mounted and sometimes successfully enacted in state referenda. Even when passed, however, the laws are often not put into practice in the face of clear needs for multiple languages in schools and service organizations, as well as the countervailing forces of global commerce that produce multilingual labels and instructions for so many products that enter everyone's household.

Many have argued that ethnic identity is largely maintained through language usage (Giles 1977; Gumperz 1982). Speaking a language other than English "is assumed to attest to an attachment to a culturally defined group" (Bean and Stevens 2003, 143), and observers often make stark we versus they judgments on the basis of language cues. Even English, when spoken in an accent not common in the United States, can serve as a marker of foreign origin. On the other side of the coin, not being able to speak the language of one's heritage group often results in exclusion from that group. As Kay Deaux and Kathleen Ethier (1998) heard in their interviews with Latino students, students who were not fluent in Spanish believed that other Latinos at the university would not accept them and would actually discriminate against them. Similarly, in a study of Korean-American immigrants, one respondent recalled a visit to Seoul, when "the natives looked down on us because a lot of us couldn't speak Korean . . . they were basically saying, 'you're so stupid' " (Kibria 2002, 305).

Whether language is a necessary component of ethnic identity can be debated, but there is no question that it is often a central element. Eva Hoffman, referring both to language and the associated culture, has said that "they constitute us in a way of which we perhaps remain unconscious" (1999, 48). Similar sentiments are expressed by a Croatian immigrant to London who, while acknowledging the multiplicity of language usage, puts emphasis on the language of origin: "You can speak I don't know how many languages, but you will create a masterpiece in a language you dream in; we only love in one language" (Timotijevic and Breakwell 2000, 365). More pointedly, a Latino immigrant in Florida said: "To a lot of us bilingual South Floridians, Spanish is the language of love and war. It's just the way things are. Punto" (Portes and Rumbaut 2001, 122). Conversely, an immigrant in the Netherlands considers his lack of facility in Chinese as evidence that he does not hold that identity: "That's also why I'm so very Dutch and can't be said to be really Chinese. Because I hardly talk Chinese, and I can't write Chinese" (Verkuyten and de Wolf 2002a, 385).

The use of language as an element of identity may be important in distinguishing between those who would, for example, call themselves Korean versus those who would use a hyphenated form such as Korean-American. But I suspect even that attempt at specificity may be overly simplistic. Immigrant groups differ, for example, in the frequency with which the parents speak a non-English language with their children (Portes and Rumbaut 2001). To cite just a few of the statistics reported by Portes and Rumbaut, 99 percent of Cambodian parents speak a language other than English with their children, compared to 54 percent of Japanese and only 12 percent of immigrants from the Middle East and Africa. Portes and Schauffler (1996) found that girls were more likely to retain the language of their parents than were boys—a result reminiscent of the findings of Ethier and Deaux (1990), where Latina college students reported stronger identification with their ethnic group and accorded greater importance to their role as a daughter than did the Latino students.

Generational shifts are often observed in language usage. In a recent study of Vietnamese immigrants, 49 percent of the 1.5 generation, defined in this study as respondents who came to the United States when they were between the ages of six and thirteen, reported proficiency in speaking Vietnamese as compared to only 11 percent of the second generation, defined in this study as either born in the United States or as having immigrated before they were five years old with at least one Vietnamese parent (Espiritu and Tran 2003). Yet though generational shift is both theorized and observed, in itself generation cannot fully explain the patterns of language usage. If a grandparent lives in the home, for example, middle-school students are more likely to be able to speak the language of the country of origin (Pérez 1996).

The latter findings suggest the kinds of relationships that may exist between different elements of ethnic identity. Speaking with family members in the language of origin can facilitate a sense of interdependence and attachment that also characterize identity, just as the inability to communicate with one's parents in that language can weaken the links. Consider the statement of a twenty-two-year-old Vietnamese immigrant who did not have facility in the language of origin: "There are times when me and my dad would drive in a car and there's nothing to talk about because there is that language barrier. I can't find the right words in Vietnamese, and he can't find the right words in English" (Espiritu and Tran 2003, 385). More critical in his depiction of language and family, Richard Rodriguez recalled "the fierce power Spanish had for many people I met at home. . . . They seemed to think that Spanish was the only language we could use, that Spanish alone permitted our close association" (1982, 30).

The experience of Rodriguez notwithstanding, the increasing numbers of Spanish-speaking immigrants in the United States provide a context in which the continuing use of the language of origin may be far more common than it has been for other immigrant groups. As of the 2000 census, almost 13 million people in the United States reported speaking Spanish at home (Bean and Stevens 2003). Unlike immigrants from Asia, another leading geographic region for current immigration to the United States but one in which a diversity of languages are contained within the pan-ethnic rubric, immigrants from the many countries of Central America, South America, and some of the Caribbean islands share a language, though with varied regional accents (Bean and Stevens 2003; López 1999). These numbers provide the conditions for a kind of demographic concentration that can facilitate maintaining one's original language without necessarily impeding the learning of English (Portes and Schauffler 1996). Fluency in the native language also allows people to maintain ties with their country of origin, providing the basis for the development of what are being called transnational identities (to be discussed later). As just one example here, Rumbaut (2003) finds that the frequency of sending remittances back to the country of origin is significantly correlated with fluency in that language.

As so much evidence shows, language is an important element of ethnic identity. But as the research also shows, tendencies to retain the language of origin are complexly determined, influenced by demographics and contexts as much as being a simple individual indicator of ethnic loyalty. Further, the research on language usage makes it very difficult to sustain a simple straight-line assimilation model, in which ethnic identity is abandoned as a new national identity is acquired. Questions of hyphenation and combination become central to the analysis of ethnic identity—issues to which I will return shortly.

Content and Meaning

It is a "myth that there is always a single valid definition for any given identity," Stephen Reicher and Nick Hopkins (2001, ix) asserted, in a statement that can surely be applied to the analysis of ethnic identity. The quantitative markers that we often use to define identity—for example, what is the category label, what is the rated importance of being a member of that category, what evaluation is placed on membership, and what concrete behaviors are engaged in as an expression of the identity—each suggest some common metric by which members of a group can be scaled and represented. Yet the felt essence or "guts" of an identity often means much more than these simple metrics can convey. Further, a multitude of meanings, associations, and cultural practices can be contained within a single category. The reality of this statement is evident when one thinks, for example, about the category Hispanic or Latino. As Massey (1993) commented, "Hispanics share no common historical memory and do not comprise a single, coherent, community. . . . Saying that someone is Hispanic or Latino reveals little or nothing about likely attitudes, behaviors, beliefs, race, religion, class, or legal situation in the United States" (454). Less obvious, perhaps, but equally true are the variations within any ethnic category. In the case of African American identity, for example, the work of both William Cross (1991; Foster 2004; Vandiver et al. 2002) and Robert Sellers (Sellers et al. 1997; Sellers et al. 1998), together with their colleagues, demonstrates the multiple meaning constellations within a single ethnic category of native-born Americans. Expanding coverage to include immigrants from Africa and the Caribbean who have adopted the African American label reveals much more extensive variations in meaning (Perkins 2006).

The semantic content of an identity can take a number of forms, including simple traits or characteristics associated with the category, ideological positions implied by category membership, and narrative and collective memories that link present category membership to past events (Ashmore, Deaux, and McLaughlin-Volpe 2004). Some of these content forms can be tapped by quantitative measures, such as a trait ascription task or the endorsement of provided ideological statements. Other forms, particularly narrative and collective memories, require the investigator to use more qualitative methods of data collection, such as extended interviews or text analysis.

Traits   As discussed in chapter 4, group stereotypes abound in the area of ethnicity. Not only are these stereotypic beliefs held by others, but often they become part of a person's own view of his or her ethnic group, a shorthand way of defining the group membership. Within some theoretical frameworks, such as social psychology's self-categorization theory (Turner 1999; Turner et al. 1987), the process of what is termed self-stereotyping is almost automatic, as a group member sees him- or herself as like, and in many respects indistinguishable from, all the other members of the category. For self-categorization theory, however, this identification with the category's stereotyped traits is a transitory process, coming into play when the category is salient and being mostly irrelevant when other categories are in focus.

In describing her shifting ethnic identity, the Polish immigrant writer Eva Hoffman relied on traits and behaviors to illustrate the nature of the change. "My mother says I'm becoming English," she said. " This hurts me, because I know she means I'm becoming cold. . . . I'm learning to be less demonstrative. . . . I'm more careful about what I say, how loud I laugh, whether I give vent to grief. The storminess of emotion prevailing in our family is in excess of the normal here" (1989, 146–47). Sometimes these descriptions are very similar to what an outside observer would say when asked to describe a particular ethnic group. In the work of Henry and Bankston (2001) on Louisiana Cajuns, for example, contemporary Cajuns described themselves in terms highly similar to those others used. Both insiders and outsiders referred to history, to occupational patterns, and to language. As Jacques Henry and Carl Bankston explain, "Cajuns are mostly defined by what they do and where they live, both by themselves and by others" (1035).

In other cases, the appropriation of traits is more selective, focusing on some aspects of the common group description and ignoring or denying others. One might expect people to incorporate the positive features of a group stereotype and to ignore the less flattering elements. Yet, as the description of Hoffman shows, such a prediction is probably too simplistic. It might be useful to think more in terms of core and peripheral characteristics, as Jean-Claude Abric theorized (2001) in the context of social representation theory. By this analysis, one would focus on those stereotypic features of the category that are most central, most consensual, and most resistant to change. These would be the traits without which the category would lose its meaning, both to the self and to others. Peripheral elements, in contrast, could be optional and more personal, shaped by circumstances and particular experiences. These could be traits that are shared with some but not necessarily all members of the larger ethnic group. Together, the traits would be a way of linking oneself to other members of the group, without taking on the identical stamp that self-categorization theory posits.

Ideological Positions   Particularly in the case of national identities, ideological material—what Patricia Gurin and Aloen Townsend (1986) refer to as group consciousness—is part of the identity content. As they define it, group consciousness "refers to the member's ideology about the group's position in society" (1986, 139) and can include components of collective discontent over a group's relative power and resources, the appraised legitimacy of the existing stratification system, and a belief in collective action (Ashmore, Deaux, and McLaughlin-Volpe 2004).

Analysts of African American identity have taken the lead in exploring the various ideological positions contained within an ethnic rubric. Robert Sellers and various colleagues (Sellers et al. 1997; Sellers et al. 1998), as one example, have isolated four ideological positions endorsed by African Americans: nationalist, oppressed minority, assimilation, and humanist. In each case, the assessment of the ideological position draws on various domains of activity, including political and economic development, cultural and social activities, and perceptions of the relationship between one's own group and the dominant group. William Cross (1991), Kenneth Foster (2004), and Beverly Vandiver et al. (2002) have most recently focused on three positions: assimilated, Afrocentric, and multicultural. These programs of research attempt to identify distinct meaning systems within the more general category of African American.

The former Yugoslavia offered a conceptual space for Nida Bikmen (2005) to examine the different ideological positions held by those who had emigrated from that war-torn site. Her interviews with refugees in the United States pointed to two distinct ideological belief systems, which she characterized in the phrases "we all lived together" versus "we knew they would do this." The first emphasizes unity among the three ethnic groups and the endorsement of a superordinate identity as Bosnian. The second represents a much less sanguine view, recalling past attacks and suspicions that were not forgotten and indeed were refueled under the nationalist leadership of Milosevic. These differing positions, based on experiences in the former Yugoslavia, continue to provide a basis for the immigrants to define their ethnic identity, even now that they are removed from the contested site. Bikmen's work attests to the importance of collective memory in the constitution of ethnic identity, as well as illustrating the intimate links between ideological position and collective memory.

Collective Memory   Collective memory "is the active past that forms our identities" (Olick and Robbins 1998). A concept developed by the sociologist Maurice Halbwachs, who was a student of Durkheim, collective memory emphasizes the social construction process, whereby events of the past are interpreted and retold in the present, providing a shared basis of understanding for the current members of a collective. Religiously based identities are a prime example of the use of collective memory to define an identity. In Halbwachs's words, "we can ... say of every religion that it reproduces in more or less symbolic forms the history of migrations and fusions of races and tribes, of great events, wars, establishments, discoveries, and reforms that we can find at the origin of the societies that practice them" (Halbwachs 1992, 84). Consider the Jewish Passover seder as a prime example. But even for less formally defined groups, collective memories are constructed and influence the functioning of the group. Indeed, it has been said that "there are as many collective memories as there are groups and institutions in a society" (Coser 1992, 22).

Collective memories of a group can refer to rituals, holidays, political events, and the histories of one's ancestors. In its active construction, however, collective memory also needs to be conceptualized as an ongoing process that takes place in a contemporary context. The present surroundings, current events, and even the interpretations of other groups with whom members interact can shape the form and content of collective memory (Lyons 1996). These interpretations often serve to justify the actions of one's own group and to cast aspersions on those of another (Doosje and Branscombe 2003). Moreover, collective memories have future implications as well as past and present bases. In adopting a particular version of history, members of a collective also commit to a future agenda in a way that will be consistent with the values and the implications of their memory (Rosenzweig and Thelen 1998).

Immigrant stories are rich with these kinds of memories, which provide a link between past histories and current circumstances. Through stories and songs, through rituals and photographs, ethnic identity is defined, redefined, and transmitted from old to young. The nuances and layers of this material are a far remove from the simple question of categorical label, where this analysis of ethnic identity began. But it is an appropriate place to reach in our journey to understand the full meaning of ethnic identification.

COMPLICATING THE ANALYSIS: ISSUES OF MULTIPLICITY AND INTERSECTIONALITY

In breaking the concept of identity into a set of constituent parts, I make the concept more complicated and multifaceted than is often the case. Some commentators are untroubled by a simple yes-no version of ethnic identity—either you are or you aren't. Many of us doing research in this field, however, have found the simplicity of that approach a dead end, a strategy that fails to appreciate the variations and meanings that seem inevitably a part of ethnic identity. Thus I suggest and develop here the strategy of multiple elements of identity that can be charted and combined in various ways.

Would that we could stop there—but even this more complicated story of identity is still too simple. I have treated ethnic identity as if it existed in isolation from other aspects of the self. In reality, however, ethnic identity both merges and conflicts with other identities that are important to the self. These combinations are well illustrated in the words of Anika Rahman, where images of ethnicity, gender, religion, and occupation tumble around in her thoughts.

Conceptions of Multiplicity

The idea of multiple identity, as it plays out in the field of immigration, takes two distinct forms, which I am terming within-category and between-category multiplicity. In the first, the two identities in question are within the same domain. Thus, in what might be considered the prototypical case for immigrants, an identity associated with the country of origin confronts the possibilities of a different American (or Canadian or French or other national) identity. The issue here is two potentially competing ethnic and national identities that need to be negotiated in some fashion.

Terms such as bicultural and multicultural, as well as biracial and multiracial, signal a concern with this form of multiplicity. The central question raised in discussions of this within-category multiplicity is whether a person can maintain both identities, that is, whether the two (or more) identities are inherently conflicting or whether some form of resolution between the two can be attained.

A second form of multiplicity, suggested by Rahman's description of herself as a Bangladeshi woman who is also a lawyer, a feminist, a friend, and so on, is concerned with combinations that represent different categories of identification. As proponents of intersectionality have argued, social identities do not neatly partition themselves, but instead create points of intersection at which, for example, both gender and ethnicity define the experience. Thus, the Dominicana and the Dominicano immigrant will not necessarily experience their ethnicity and nationality in the same way. Nor are they likely to have identical experiences in the country to which they immigrate, creating different profiles of what an American identity might be. A similar argument can be made for social class. To be an upper-class Cuban immigrant who emigrated when Fidel Castro first came to power in Cuba is different from being a lower-class Cuban who came to the United States in the 1980 Mariel period (the marielitos). In this form of between-category multiplicity, one is less likely to ask which of the two (or more) identities should be maintained. Rather it is assumed, either implicitly or explicitly, that most people have multiple identities that are relevant to different domains of their life. The possibilities of conflict between norms and values associated with one category and those associated with another category can become an issue, at which point this form of multiplicity bears a resemblance to the within-category debates. More important in the between-category form of multiplicity, however, are questions as to how membership in one identity category shapes and changes the meanings and experiences associated with another category. In other words, the analysis of immigrant experience becomes both more dynamic and more complicated when this form of multiplicity is acknowledged.

I'll return to a comparison of these two forms of multiplicity and what they imply in terms of the identity elements that have been reviewed. First, however, let me describe in more detail the ways in which these forms of multiplicity are being addressed in contemporary immigration research.

Multiplicity with Ethnic-National Categories

Discussions of immigration almost inevitably raise the question of how the immigrant deals with the dual ethnic-national identities that are available—one based in the country of origin and another offered by the country of immigration. The potential dissonance created by participation in two cultures is reflected in the early writings of both Robert Park (1928), a pivotal figure in the sociology of immigration, and in the work of the African American scholar W. E. B. Du Bois (1903/1976). Park introduced the concept of marginal man, describing a person who is "living and sharing intimately in the cultural life and traditions of two distinct peoples, never quite willing to break . . . with his past and his traditions, and not quite accepted . . . in the new society in which he now sought to find a place" (1928, 892). Similarly, Du Bois, in offering the notion of "double consciousness" as experienced by the American black, described how "one ever feels his two-ness—an American, a Negro; two souls, two thoughts, two unreconciled strivings; two warring ideals in one dark body" (1903/1976, 9). In a more contemporary vein, Gloria Anzaldua describes a mestiza who "copes by developing a tolerance for contradiction, a tolerance for ambiguity," who "learns to be Indian in Mexican culture; to be Mexican from an Anglo point of view" (Anzaldua, quoted in Verkuyten 2005, 149).

Traditional theories of assimilation (to be discussed in more detail in chapter 6) assumed that the immigrant would move from one national identity to the other over some reasonable course of time. More recently, this straight-line model has yielded to more complicated frameworks that often begin with the assumption that both identities can continue to be salient. The simplest form of this assumed multiplicity is seen in the hyphenated terms so common in the United States, such as Mexican-American, Korean-American, or Italian-American. These terms suggest a relatively easy combination of an ethnic identity that is maintained with a newly acquired national identity—though the actual meanings associated with

Figure 5.1   Berry's Model of Acculturation

		Maintaining Cultural Identity?	
		Yes	No
	Yes	Integration	Assimilation
Developing Relationships with Host Country Group?			
	No	Separation	Marginalization

Source: Adapted from Berry (1990).

these terms are much more variable than this simple characterization suggests.[3]

Perhaps the best-known version of this combination framework is John Berry's acculturation model (1980, 1990, 1992, 2001), which I introduced briefly in chapter 3.[4] As a total framework, Berry's model recognizes the broader domains of demography, economics, and politics as well as social psychological factors such as acculturation and intergroup relations (Berry 2001). In practice, however, the emphasis of this model has been on the combinations defined by two contrasting orientations—first, the extent to which a person wants to maintain the cultural identity of origin, and second, the extent to which a person wants to interact with members of the host society. It is assumed that these two dimensions are independent, such that a person could adopt both or neither, as well as one or the other. The result of this bidimensional analysis is a typology, represented here in figure 5.1, that characterizes four acculturation strategies.[5] Two of the cells—separation and assimilation—represent cases in which only a single identity is maintained, rather than any form of combination. The integration cell represents the additive case, where both origin and host are combined.

A more recent version of an additive model is the work of Benet-Martínez and her colleagues on what they call *bicultural identity integration* (2002; Benet-Martínez and Haritatos 2002). They define this concept as the degree to which people "perceive their dual cultural identities as compatible and integrated" versus "oppositional and difficult to integrate" (Benet-Martínez et al. 2002, 496). Conceptually, both those who see themselves in hyphenated terms and those who offer a more fused identity definition can be considered high in bicultural identity integration (Benet-Martínez and

Haritatos 2002). In their initial work, the basis for classifying someone as high or low in bicultural identity integration consisted of a single scaled response to a short vignette.[6] Subsequently, these researchers developed a multi-item scale that tapped two distinct components of their theorized concept, *cultural conflict* and *cultural distance.* The first of these deals with perceptions that two cultural orientations are either in conflict or are compatible; the second attempts to get at the idea of separation versus hyphenation or fusion. The empirical work of Verónica Benet-Martínez and her colleagues shows that these two measures are to some degree conceptually distinct. Interestingly, while an endorsement of some form of fusion increases with more time in the United States (at least in their sample of individuals, primarily undergraduate or graduate students, born in a Chinese country and currently living in a college town in the Midwest), perceptions of cultural conflict are unrelated to length of time in the country. More generally, the authors suggest that their measure of cultural conflict may be primarily tapping affective aspects of the bicultural experience, while their distance measure is more oriented toward cognitive and linguistic aspects. Perhaps the latter domain is more predictably part of the socialization of immigrants, while affective experiences have a more variable occurrence.

Several investigators approach the question of bicultural identity from a developmental perspective, emphasizing the process of construction and formation of a multiple identity. (Phinney and Alipuria forthcoming; Smith, Stewart, and Winter 2004). Within these developmental frameworks, achievement of a bicultural identity is seen to be the satisfactory accomplishment of both a search and exploration process and a commitment to the resultant identity state. Several investigators find it useful to divide the bicultural identity category into two subtypes, which they refer to as "blended" versus "alternating" (Phinney and Devich-Navarro 1997; Smith, Stewart, and Winter 2004). In the former, people do not report any sharp separation between the two identities; in the latter, the reported experience is one in which identity expression varies markedly according to the setting.

Teresa LaFromboise, Hardin Coleman, and Jenifer Gerton (1993) have also analyzed the phenomenon of biculturalism. Their emphasis is less on static identities and more on the acquisition and exercise of skills, a process they term *cultural competence.* In their comparison of fusion (blending) and alternation models, they argue for the second, in which a person gains competence in two cultures rather than being forced to abandon one or to sacrifice some elements from both. Ying-yi Hong and her colleagues (Hong, Roisman, and Chen 2006) offer a model of cultural attachment, which considers how people can develop independent links and emotional ties to two cultures. Her work also shows how people can readily switch between cultural frames when prompted by situational cues (Hong et al. 2000; No and Hong 2004).

This shift from descriptions of static identity combinations to models that emphasize dynamic process and contextual change is becoming more common in social psychological thought. Taking the assumption of change a step further, Shaun Wiley (2005) uses discourse analysis to probe the use of different strategies of ethnic identification in a sample of Mexican and Dominican second-generation immigrants. He identifies three forms of bicultural identification, in addition to a fourth version of complete separation of the two cultures. In one bicultural strategy, which Wiley termed blended, people combined the two cultures, albeit in fairly abstract terms. In the two other forms of bicultural identification, people talked of alternating identities, either to achieve congruence with the situation they were in (for example, feeling most Dominican when with their family) or as an experience of contrast from the setting (for example, feeling most Mexican when at all-American parties). Important from the perspective of discourse analysis is the assumption that identities are actively engaged in social contexts. What emerges on which occasions thus depends as much on the context of discourse as on the predispositions of the speakers.

Transnationalism

The increasingly popular concept of *transnationalism*, a term originating in political science, international relations, anthropology, and sociology (Levitt and Waters 2002), offers another take on the question of multiplicity within ethnic and national categories. First used by those in international relations to describe nongovernmental activities that cross national boundaries, the term then was appropriated by anthropologists to describe "the ways in which connections to collectivities constituted across space seem to override identities grounded in fixed, bounded locations" (Levitt and Waters 2002, 7). In its original use, transnationalism referred more to general process than to specific experience, and more to geographical sites than to individual psyches. More recently, however, with increased attention from other social scientists, studies of transnational migration have begun to focus on individual experience and the implications of activities for immigrant self-definition (Levitt and Waters 2002; Upegui-Hernandez 2005).

In debates about transnationalism, both explicit and implicit analyses frequently emerge. At the explicit level, the focus is on the specific activities that might define transnationalism, such as trips back to the country of origin, remittances sent, and voting in the elections of one's home country. Implicit in these discussions, and often the basis of perceived threats and derogation, are questions as to whether a person can maintain an identification with the country of origin without being disloyal to the country of residence. Using concepts introduced earlier as elements of identification, these questions center on aspects of categorization, importance, and evaluation of the two identities and hypotheses as to whether conflict is inherent in multiplicity.

From my perspective, referring back to the framework for analyzing identity presented in table 5.1, these issues could be profitably addressed by using a more differentiated approach that would consider each element in turn. Not only does such an approach allow us to distinguish between different features of the transnational experience, it also shifts the focus to the lived experience and assessments of the person and allows us to examine the differences that exist between people in this regard. In so doing, we shift from the assumptions of observers to the actualities of the actor in determining whether conflict or discomfort exists in the dual identification.

At the simple level of categorization, for example, one might define the transnational in terms of citizenship, to the extent that dual citizenship is a possibility. Applying this criterion to Ewa Morawska's (2004) recent study of Polish immigrants in Philadelphia, 90 percent of the immigrants in her sample would be considered transnational, in that they retained Polish citizenship while holding an American passport. "This is my natural right, I was born Polish," one respondent said (Morawska 2004, 1383). Further examination of the elements of identification in this sample reveal the more nuanced aspects of transnationalism. In this group, for example, the majority of the respondents eschewed formal Polish-American organizations in the United States but developed strong informal ties with people of Polish origin. They also made annual visits to Poland and regular phone calls to homes, and nearly half entertained the possibility of moving back to Poland. Contrast these findings with a sample of Russian Jewish immigrants that Morawska (2004) also investigated, in which greater involvement in local ethnic establishments combined with the majority's belief that they would never return to the former Soviet Union. Other examples of transnational patterns are seen in immigrants from the Caribbean, Mexico, and other Latin American countries. Here behavioral involvement, as indexed at the personal level by the sending of remittances or at the political level by voting in national elections in the country of origin, which is a major activity in communities such as the Dominican immigrants in New York City, is often extensive.

I am suggesting that the understanding of transnationalism can benefit from consideration of the elements of ethnic identification, as a means of analysis and comparison of what is much more than a simple category of transnationals. Such an analysis, as it is pursued, needs to be interpreted in the context of the many social, economic, and political conditions that

Morawska (2004) has outlined, considering the potential influence of factors characteristic of both sending and receiving countries, as well as the social and physical distance between them. The further question of whether transnationalism is good, either for a country or for an individual, remains to be answered pending these more multidimensional analyses.

Multiplicity Between Categories

Some forty years ago, Milton Gordon said he hoped for a society "in which one may say with equal pride and without internal disquietude at the juxtaposition: 'I am a Jew, or a Catholic, or a Protestant, or a Negro, or an Indian, or an Oriental, or a Puerto Rican'; 'I am an American'; and 'I am a man' " (1964, 265). This statement suggests a parallel positioning of one's social identities, such that they coexist on equal terms but with no particular relationship to one another. Contemporary scholars challenge that assumption, however, arguing that the way one views the world reflects the particular intersection of one's social category memberships (Crenshaw 1995). Thus, being a Latina versus a Latino would mean not only different understandings of gender, but would also entail different definitions of ethnicity, each shaped by gender in distinctive ways.

An example of gendered definitions of ethnicity is found in a sample of Latina, primarily Dominican, women who had immigrated to New York City (Diaz, Martin, and Deaux 1999). These women were asked to describe themselves as women, as ethnics (for example, Latina, Hispanic, Dominican), and then as ethnic women. They offered very different characteristics in each case. Questions about nationality elicited words that would probably be shared by men of the same ethnicity (for example, references to cultural heritage, language, and pride in country). Gender was described in terms that emphasized the biological possibilities of womanhood, and in particular motherhood. In describing the conjoint category of, for example, a Dominican woman, the women in this study offered positive dispositional characteristics, such as strength, intelligence, self-sufficiency, and passion—traits that rarely emerged from either single category label. In addition, this intersectional location was the site for descriptions of prejudice and discrimination, enacted by both American citizens and Hispanic men. Thus, quite clearly in these data, the intersection proved to be greater than the sum of its constituent categories.

Religion also provides fertile ground for examining the interplay of identities. Consider the case of Russian immigrants, approximately 75 percent of whom are estimated to be Jewish in the Philadelphia area from which Morawska (2004) drew her sample of Russian Jewish immigrants. In her interviews nationality, ethnicity, and religion were intertwined. Decisions to emigrate were influenced in large part by religious discrimination, and experiences of becoming American were often expressed in terms of new meanings associated with being Jewish. Another example of the mix of ethnicity, nationality, and religion is found in a study of Polish Tatars, reported by Verkuyten (2005). Members of this minority group in Poland descend from the Mongols of Genghis Khan; they now live in the national state of Poland and are practicing Muslims within a state that is primarily Roman Catholic. Verkuyten describes the different narratives that constitute each of these identities and the fusions that allow the various narratives to coexist, both with each other and in the framework of the larger national context.

Work by Patricia Ruiz-Navarro (2004, 2005) illustrates the interplay of ethnic, religious, and political identities among Mexican immigrants in New York City. In her study of the celebration of the Virgin of Guadalupe, she shows how religious affiliation shapes the meaning of being a Mexican immigrant in the United States, a definition that is further intertwined with political action for changes in the immigration laws that affect undocumented Mexicans. Rumbaut (2002) has found positive associations between the frequency of religious attendance and the practice of sending remittances to the country of origin, suggesting that ethnic loyalty is supported at least in part by religious identity.

The importance of class to identity is also easily demonstrated, particularly if one considers how different the immigration experience is, for example, between a Mexican agricultural worker and a Hong Kong businessman or, in a more direct comparison, between the professionals who left Cuba in the early 1960s when Castro came to power and those who came later in the 1970s, no less educated on average than the Cuban community then established in Florida, but less likely to be professional (Arboleya 1996).

Ruminations on Identity and Multiplicity

In each of the examples presented, we see evidence of what Verkuyten has called "the messier categories of social life" (2005, 178). To acknowledge multiplicity of identity surely complicates the task of those who try to analyze the immigrant experience. Yet these issues of multiplicity and hybridity are inevitable in their emergence and rich in their implications, and we must address them if we are to move our understanding forward.

I have suggested that two types of multiplicity exist—one between identities that potentially exist in the same domain, often represented in hyphenated forms that identify both origin and destination (for example, Mexican-American), and a second that speaks to the intersections between different types of identity, such as gender and religion and ethnicity, that establish unique positionality. The value of maintaining this distinction between the two types of multiplicity depends on the degree to which we can establish different processes or factors at work. Although our knowledge here is rudimentary, I see some grounds for making the distinction.

When two identities from the same domain are being considered, the question of potential conflict inevitably comes to mind. From the outsider's perspective, this questioning can range in form from genuine perplexity (for example, how is it possible to be both Norwegian and American) to certainty ("once an Irish, always an Irish") to accusations of disloyalty (for example, the assumption that those of Japanese descent would be likely traitors during World War II). From an insider's perspective, the issue of conflicting loyalties is often more nuanced, as the models of biculturalism, cultural competence, and cultural frame-switching suggest. Evidence from these theoretical and empirical explorations argue for a model of identity, such as the one offered in this chapter, that considers multiple elements of identification that may or may not covary with one another. Thus, one might look for variations in the degree to which ethnic identities were important or in the forms of behavioral involvement that were carried out. The different focus of the two questions could easily lead to different answers with regard to conflict or reconciliation between identities, and produce different patterns between groups and among individuals. A particularly productive line of research, I suspect, would be a consideration of possible variations in social embeddedness of the two identities and the ways in which social networks are differentially constructed to support each identity. The frequent observation that second-generation children must operate between the traditional definitions of the family and the newly introduced norms of American peers and school groups is just one example of how immigrants resolve potential conflicts between different ethnic identities, finding bases to support each identity without necessarily combining the two.

Multiplicity defined as an intersection of categorically different identities raises other issues. Assumptions of conflict are not immediately apparent in this case, and indeed, it is often taken for granted that people have multiple categories of membership that exist independently of one another. The obligation of researchers in this case is to question that assumption of insularity. Gender, for example, though long ignored in studies of immigration (Pessar 2003), almost certainly determines many of the interactions and opportunity structures that an immigrant encounters. Whether the domain is social practice, occupational niche, or economic consequence, gender and ethnicity have an interactive effect. From the perspective of the immigrant, these experiences shape the ways in which identity is defined. From a research perspective, analysis of the importance of these intersections is likely to be more informed by narrative accounts from the convergent space than by simple ratings of the comparative importance of each identity category taken individually. Here, too, a more detailed look at social networks and behavioral commitments, considered as representations of intersectional space, could also prove useful.

In neither form of multiplicity can we assume a static resolution. Indeed, one of the key aspects of identification from a social psychological perspective is its fluidity and the dynamic possibilities of expression and change. In the next chapter I will try to deal with these dynamic issues more directly, moving the focus from a structural analysis of identity categories to the dynamics of identity negotiation. In this analysis, both the diverse characteristics of immigrants and the variable opportunities and barriers are considered in tandem, defining the multifaceted world of immigrant experience.

Chapter Six | Negotiating Identity: Beyond Assimilation Models

"A man who thinks of himself as belonging to a particular national group in America has not yet become an American."

—Woodrow Wilson (1915, quoted in Gordon 1964, 101)

"The old folk knew then they would not come to belong, not through their own experience nor though their offspring. The only adjustment they had been able to make to life in the United States had been one that involved the separateness of their group, one that increased their awareness of the differences between themselves and the rest of the society. In that adjustment they had always suffered from the consciousness they were strangers."

—Oscar Handlin (1951, 285)

THE DEBATE THAT surrounds assimilation has nearly a hundred years of U.S. history to support its assertions. Woodrow Wilson states the creed of the melting pot, contending that all should give up their particular origins to become a part of the homogenized American identity. Oscar Handlin, by contrast, speaks from the view of the immigrant who is either not prepared or not able to erase the distinctions that separate foreign-born from native. Attempting to encompass these positions, from the perspective of the social sciences, is the broadly conceived model of assimilation. First associated with Robert Park and the Chicago school of sociology in the early part of the twentieth century, assimilation theory has had remarkable longevity as the guiding framework for studying immigration in the United States. Indeed, as Charles Hirschman declares, "assimilation has historically been one of the foundational and far-reaching concepts in American social science" (1999, 129). Yet in the same analysis he notes that "there are few words in contemporary academic social science that arouse more negative valence than *assimilation*" (1999, 128, emphasis in original).

The debates surrounding assimilation are one part of the story that I want to tell in this chapter. Assimilation theory makes a set of assumptions about the *process* of immigration, a process in which one moves steadily or not so steadily from identification with one's country of origin to assimilation as a member of the new country, which is, in most of the work with this theory, the United States. Assimilation theory says much less, however, about the experience of immigration from the perspective of the immigrants themselves. The conditions that define these insider experiences are the site of needed theorizing by psychologists.

Equally important to consider, from the perspective of a social psychologist, are the variations in this experience that make one immigrant story different from another. Consider the story of Bharati Mukherjee, who immigrated to the United States from India with her sister—"two Calcutta-born women from identical backgrounds with the same Cambridge-tested accent, the same convent education, who have been in the United States for over thirty-five years" (Mukherjee 1999, 76). Yet while her sister lives in Detroit, where she met and married an Indian student, where she wears saris, cooks traditional Indian food, and plans to retire to India in a few years, Mukherjee married an American of Canadian parentage, has lived in both the United States and Canada, eats and dresses in what she terms "an amalgam of the places I've lived" and can "not imagine returning to India for other than family visits and relaxed vacations" (1999, 76). Mukherjee asks "which one of us is the freak?" Put less judgmentally, we might ask whose experience of immigration is more typical and why do these two sisters differ so much?

As I mentioned in chapter 5, I believe we must consider issues of ethnic identity and assimilation in a dynamic context, as a confluence between the individual and the circumstances that are worked out and negotiated in an ongoing process. This chapter is about those processes that affect and ultimately define the immigrant experience. In developing a preliminary framework for understanding that experience, I ask three simple questions. What does the immigrant bring to the process? What does the immigrant confront? What does the immigrant do? To answer these questions and to suggest a basis for future theoretical work, I reintroduce some of the concepts discussed earlier, including stereotypes, ethnic identity, and social hierarchy. Here those concepts will, in a sense, be put in motion, drawn together in a more dynamic and interwoven account. Before embarking on this analysis, however, some review of classical assimilation theory is needed in order to understand what assumptions have been made and what questions have been left unanswered in earlier, less psychological accounts.

BASIC MODELS OF ASSIMILATION:
THE MELTING POT IN THEORY

In a classic text by Park and Burgess published in 1921, assimilation was defined as "a process of interpenetration and fusion in which persons and groups acquire the memories, sentiments, and attitudes of other persons and groups and, by sharing their experience and history, are incorporated with them in a common cultural life" (1921/1969, 735). In 1930, Park added to this basic definition the experiences of prejudice and discrimination that an immigrant might experience. Assimilation, he suggested, implies that a person is "able to find a place in the community on the basis of his individual merits without invidious or qualifying reference to his racial origin or to his cultural heritage" (Park 1930, 281). These two deceptively simple assertions lie at the basis of several decades of analysis and debate on assimilation theory.

It is interesting to note the psychological and even individual emphasis of the original Park and Burgess definition insofar as it points to the central role of memories, sentiments, and intergroup attitudes. Yet despite the seeming importance of internal cognitions to the experience of assimilation, subsequent generations of social scientists looked to more external indicators as proxies for these internal experiences—typically, to measures of economic status, occupational attainment, housing and school segregation, and intermarriage (see Alba and Nee 1999; Hirschman 1983). Not only do these external indices say little about memories, sentiments, and attitudes, but they are also considered primarily at the level of the group, suggesting that assimilation should be assessed by comparing the outcomes of one group (the immigrant) to another group (the host country norm, which in the case of the United States is typically defined as white native-born U.S. citizens).

Some forty years after Park and his colleagues introduced the concept, Gordon (1964) proposed a more nuanced analysis, arguing that a multidimensional conceptualization was necessary to understand the assimilation process. In his alternative to a singular notion of assimilation, Gordon outlined seven separate dimensions of assimilation, as shown in table 6.1.

From Gordon's perspective, these various dimensions were semiindependent, though with some regularities and interplay. Cultural assimilation (which includes the ability to use English) was posited to occur first, but it might or might not be accompanied by other types of assimilation. Once structural assimilation (the integration of institutions and networks) occurred, however, Gordon argued that all other forms of assimilation would "naturally follow" (1964, 81). Further, Gordon made the one-way street assumption about assimilation that was to characterize most subsequent

Table 6.1   Dimensions of Assimilation

Type of Assimilation	Process
Cultural or behavioral assimilation	Change of cultural patterns to those of host society
Structural assimilation	Large-scale entrance into institutions and social networks
Marital assimilation	Large-scale intermarriage
Identificational assimilation	Development of host identity, replacing identity of origin
Attitude receptional assimilation	Absence of prejudice
Behavior receptional assimilation	Absence of discrimination
Civic assimilation	Absence of value and power conflict; no challenges to normative stance

Source: Adapted from Gordon (1964).

work, in defining identificational assimilation as the development of a host identity that would replace the identity of origin. This unidirectional movement was not inherent in the original Park and Burgess definition, which referred to "interpenetration," an idea that was for the most part lost in later theoretical and empirical analyses.

In positing a multidimensional concept of assimilation, Gordon was able to deal, at least in part, with some of the troubling inconsistencies that had plagued earlier investigators when they discussed the ways in which immigrants adjusted to their new country. At the same time, his scheme was more a descriptive taxonomy and less a theoretical guide as to how and when the various processes might causally link (Alba and Nee 1999; Hirschman et al. 1999). Further, though relatively few have questioned the relevance of any of the dimensions proposed by Gordon, the dimensions have not received equal attention from subsequent generations of researchers. Measures of structural and marital assimilation, both easily measured at the group level with large-scale census tracts, are typically taken as indices of assimilation. Measures of prejudice and discrimination, which require some shift in perspective to include host as well as immigrant target, have been more often the subject of general discussion than of careful analysis. Civic assimilation has also not attracted much empirical work outside of simple accountings of voting behavior. Psychological measures of individual identification have only recently begun to emerge in immigration discussions (see, for example, Portes and Rumbaut 2001). Thus the empirical base needed to test Gordon's theoretical framework is lacking.

A specific focus on the course of change was added to the assimilation model with the introduction of the term *straight-line assimilation* (Gans 1973; Sandberg 1973). Generation is assumed to drive the assimilation process, such that each generation will move further from the condition existing at point of immigrant entry and closer to a wholly assimilated state. For the most part, those working with the concept of straight-line assimilation have not turned to Gordon's multidimensional model, but rather have used either a more global concept of assimilation or have focused on a single index, such as residential segregation or intermarriage rates.

Before considering some of the alternatives to the basic assimilation canon (Alba and Nee 1999), I should note that the hypothesized final stage of assimilation itself is not unambiguous. At least two interpretations of end-state assimilation have been proposed, typically going under the names of "Anglo-conformity" and "melting pot" (Gordon 1964; Greeley 1974). In the former, all of the movement is assumed to be by the immigrant group moving toward the host group which, at the time these models were formulated, was heavily an Anglo norm. The second variation, the melting pot model, assumes some bidirectional influence (as did Park and Burgess), such that both immigrant and host groups acculturate in some degree to each other. Contemporary definitions of assimilation often finesse this choice. Alba and Nee (1999), for example, define assimilation as "the decline, and at its endpoint the disappearance, of an ethnic and racial distinction and the cultural and social differences that express it" and go on to say that "by intent, our definition is agnostic about whether the changes wrought by assimilation are one-sided or mutual" (159). At the same time, however, the focus of empirical investigation is rarely on the host community, except insofar as it is considered a standard against which the progress of the immigrant group is measured. Moreover, it is really quite difficult to devise an appropriate test for such global concepts of assimilation, given the problems inherent in defining the identity status of the host country (particularly a multiethnic society such as the United States) and in devising acceptable measures of assimilation.

RECONSIDERING ASSIMILATION THEORY 1

Despite the sustained prominence of assimilation theory, some voices and events have challenged its premises. In the late 1960s and 1970s, what is sometimes called the revival of ethnicity school (Greeley 1974; Hirschman 1983) put forth the argument that ethnicity continued to be important in the United States and was a fundamental axis for social and political action. This affirmation of ethnic pluralism (Bean and Stevens 2003), in contrast to a melting pot notion of homogeneity, coincided with and indeed was influenced by the increased activity for civil rights on the part of many different groups in the United States. This period also includes the 1965 changes in immigration policy that sharply altered the distribution of immigrants, away from European predominance to a more diverse ethnic make-up. Both of these forces presumably influenced social scientific theorizing about assimilation and its alternatives.

In a counterargument, Herbert Gans (1979, 1992, 1994) continued to support an assimilation model while offering some variations on the simple straight line. One variation he called the bumpy line theory of acculturation. This model acknowledges that there is heterogeneity in the process and that the straight line of assimilation has "no predictable end" (1992, 44). The bumps in this process are "various kinds of adaptations to changing circumstances" (1992, 44). They can be the result of conditions encountered in the society, such as discrimination, or they can represent different strategies or resources (that is, human capital) that an immigrant group brings to bear (and presumably, the interaction between these factors, as changed conditions make it necessary for later generations to develop strategies different from those that may have worked for earlier generations). As an example of environmental constraints, Gans (1992) points to "involuntary ethnicity" by which a group's nonassimilation may be prolonged because of ethnic labeling by others. Whether this is simply a bump in the normative road, or in fact represents a different path, is debatable, as I and others will argue.

As discussed, symbolic ethnicity is another concept that Gans (1979, 1992, 1994) offered to account for observed variations in ethnic adaptation while preserving the essence of straight-line assimilation theory. Symbolic ethnicity suggests that people can assimilate to the host country in most respects, while maintaining some interest in selected cultural practices such as food and celebrations. This symbolic form of ethnicity can, Gans contends, "have a long lifespan" (1992, 45). Indeed, he suggests that later generations may come back from being wholly American to seek a symbolic ethnic identity, if it is "pleasurable and cost-free" (1994, 588).

Despite these attempts to preserve assimilation theory, the variability of actual immigrant experience and the changed demographic patterns of immigration have led many to question the basic assumptions that shape the general theory. Marcelo Suárez-Orozco (2002) characterized three of the problems with the terms *clean break, homogeneity,* and *progress.* Clean break refers to the assumption that a person definitively leaves the country of origin and takes up residence, citizenship, and identity in the new country. As Foner (2000) has argued, the line between old and new was never drawn so sharply, and thus the clean break may never have existed in pure form. More evident in recent times, however, with the advances in communication and transportation, are the continuing links that maintain between the two locations. Patterns of transnationalism, as discussed in chapter 5, reflect a continuing movement, both physical and psychological, that is not acknowledged in traditional models of assimilation.

Suárez-Orozco's second critique targets the assumption of homogeneity: "To assume that immigrants today are joining a homogeneous society dominated by the white middle-class European American Protestant ethos . . . may no longer be useful" (2002, 27). Rather, today's immigrants come as representatives of a far more diverse set of cultures than did earlier generations, and they arrive in a society that is itself far more diverse. As a consequence, the immigrant experience seems to many observers to be much more heterogeneous than ever before. Further, as Suárez-Orozco notes in his third critique, the assumption of inevitable progress needs to be questioned as well. Not all immigrant groups become wiser, healthier, and richer with longer residency in the United States. In fact, increasing numbers of studies of second-generation immigrants show just the opposite—poorer physical and psychological health, higher infant mortality, declining academic achievement, and higher criminal institutionalization with longer residency in the United States (Rumbaut 1999; Suárez-Orozco 2002).

These seeming anomalies and obvious divergences from a straight-line assimilation model have led sociologists to develop what is termed a segmented assimilation model (Portes and Zhou 1993; Zhou 1999). Responding particularly to the contested issues of homogeneity and universal progress, these theorists posit three alternative patterns of immigrant adaptation: upward mobility and assimilation to the host norms; downward mobility and integration with the underclass; and economic achievement coupled with the maintenance of ethnic community and values. The first of these is obviously the classic straight-line assimilation model, which is most likely to apply to those immigrants who come with some social capital and who more closely approximate the Anglo-European norm in appearance and culture. The second pattern, what some have termed the ethnic disadvantage model (Bean and Stevens 2003), is the seeming inverse of the American dream—a path that takes steps downward on the socioeconomic ladder. Groups that follow this path are those who are more likely to face race-based discrimination and those who come with fewer skills and less education, both of which limit the opportunity structures that they encounter. The third path in the model of segmented assimilation, sometimes termed adhesive assimilation (Hurh and Kim 1984), is yet another variation on the traditional theme. Here upward economic mobility is possible while cultural norms are maintained, perhaps exemplifying an ideal of cultural diversity rather than a melting pot.

As a theoretical framework, the model of segmented assimilation is stimulating a great deal of research and debate about factors that might account

Table 6.2   Model of Incorporation

	Skin Lighter	Skin Darker
High SES	Symbolic ethnicity	Selective assimilation
Middle SES	Straight-line assimilation	Bumpy-line assimilation
Low SES	Straight-line assimilation	Reactive ethnicity

Source: Bean and Stevens (2003).

for different paths taken by immigrants. Even the term itself is being questioned: Bean and Stevens, to take one example, use the term *incorporation* to refer to "the broader processes by which new groups establish relationships with host societies" (2003, 95), of which assimilation can be one mode. Analyzing which particular mode of incorporation will be the most likely experience for any particular immigrant group, they point to the influence of two factors: socioeconomic status and skin color. In their model of incorporation, which is presented in table 6.2, the resources represented by socioeconomic status provide or limit the opportunities that a particular immigrant group is likely to have. At the same time, the likelihood of discrimination and prejudicial treatment, linked to skin color, constrain those opportunities for those of darker skin (a factor represented as dichotomous in the Bean and Stevens figure, but which is certainly assumed to be a continuous variable). For those who are lighter in skin and have considerable economic resources, ethnicity can be more symbolic, in the ways that Gans suggested. In contrast, Bean and Stevens propose that those who have darker skins and limited resources are more likely to accept and assert their ethnic identity in reaction to the limited opportunities and external barriers they experience.

Other analyses point to social networks as an explanatory factor in assimilation patterns. The work of Min Zhou and Carl Bankston (1998) in the Vietnamese immigrant community is one example, in which the authors attempt to explain differences within a single immigrant group, as opposed to differences between ethnic groups. They find that while some young Vietnamese stick with the ethnic communities established by their immigrant parents, benefiting from its social structures and family support system, others choose the more Americanized route that often leads to downward mobility and criminal behavior. To interpret their findings, they propose a model of ethnic social relations, in which social networks and cultural identification become key factors in predicting which path of assimilation is followed.

I find these developments in sociological theories of assimilation very welcome. Not only do the newer models give recognition to the considerable variation that exists in contemporary immigrant patterns of incorporation, they also open the door to a broader consideration of the social and psychological issues that are relevant to the immigrant experience. To the Suárez-Orozco (2002) critiques of past models of assimilation (clean break, homogeneity, and progress), let me add a trio of my own concerns: level of analysis, contextual influence, and dynamic process. These issues help to define the social psychological frame of analysis I am advocating.

Level of Analysis

It is not surprising that traditional assimilation theory, emerging from the discipline of sociology, uses groups as the principal unit of analysis. Thus, as noted earlier, the outcomes of greatest interest include such group-level indicators as residential segregation, employment patterns, and intermarriage rates. The emphasis on group patterns is not, however, mandated by assimilation models. Park and Burgess, for example, specifically referred to "persons and groups" in their original definition. Similarly, in describing the concept of symbolic ethnicity, Gans (1979, 1992, 1994) shifted from assimilation at the level of group patterns to symbolic ethnicity at the level of individual practices, and from designation of ethnic group by assignment to selection of ethnic identity by choice. For Gans, this distinction was a way to hold on to straight-line models of assimilation while acknowledging that, once outside of traditional demographic criteria, the meaning of assimilation is both contentious and uncertain. It is not necessarily clear, however, that symbolic ethnicity is wholly an individual-level phenomenon, unlinked to social networks, cultural history, and current contexts. Nor is it clear that assimilation, as traditionally conceived, did not depend on the mental representations and behaviors of individuals—witness Park's original definition that included reference to memories, sentiments, attitudes, experiences, and history.

In their recent analysis of assimilation theory, Richard Alba and Victor Nee (2003) explicitly address the issue of level of analysis, offering a framework that draws both on the methodological individualism of Weber, which directs attention to the agency and choice of individual actors, and the methodological holism of Durkheim, which brings conceptions of cultural beliefs and opportunity structures into consideration. They suggest that in looking for causes, one needs to consider a variety of processes and mechanisms that generate assimilative patterns. A key element of their analysis is the concept of boundaries, that is, "a categorical distinction that members of a society recognize . . . and that affects their mental orientation and actions toward one another" (2003, 59). Applying a level of analysis framework to this concept, I suggest a distinction between what Alba and

Nee call boundary crossing and boundary blurring. The former refers to an individual-level action, by which a person moves from one group to another—passing or assimilating to the dominant culture. The latter suggests a societal level change, in which the boundary itself is less used or relied upon by groups in general. This distinction is captured within social identity theory (Tajfel 1981) by the alternative strategies of individual social mobility versus collective action directed at changes in the social hierarchy.

Recognition of a distinction between individual and group level of analysis is an important first step. What remains to be fully explored, however, is exactly what is going on at the individual level. Many of the processes that are assumed to take place as immigrants do or do not assimilate to a new culture need to be considered at the level of individual experience. Thus, between the categories of immigrant definition (for example, ethnicity, nationality, generation) and the outcomes of interest (for example, education, employment), a myriad of actions and interactions, thoughts and feelings occur that shape the eventual outcomes. It is at this level of analysis that much work is needed.

The treatment of generation in the study of assimilation is a good example of why a more psychological level of analysis is needed. Gans (1973) gave generation a central role in the immigration story when he introduced the concept of straight-line assimilation. Accordingly, the theoretical position that each generation would show more assimilation than the previous generation to the host country norm was translated into a methodological paradigm, in which generation become a key variable for analysis. Generational analysis has energetically continued and can be seen as a bedrock in contemporary work, evidenced by a flood of recent book titles: *The New Second Generation* (Portes 1996); *Legacies: The Story of the Immigrant Second Generation* (Portes and Rumbaut 2001); *Ethnicities: Children of Immigrants in America* (Rumbaut and Portes 2001); and *The Changing Face of Home: The Transnational Lives of the Second Generation* (Levitt and Waters 2002). The need for such analyses becomes clear as the continuing flow of immigrants to the United States, begun in the 1960s, now produces sets of people within the same ethnic group who do not have the same experiences or confront the same situations. But can the differences in experience be captured by the simple distinction between those who are born in another country and those who are born in the United States?

Some years ago demographers recognized problems in considering all who are born in the United States as equivalent when they introduced the concept of a 1.5 generation (Rumbaut 1976). This group, typically defined as foreign-born children who immigrated to the United States before they were twelve years old, was created to allow special attention to children who, though technically first-generation immigrants, nonetheless experienced most of their adolescence and high-school level education in the United States. But even this three-category system (generations 1, 1.5, and 2) has been found wanting. Rumbaut (2004) more recently proposed a finer set of gradations broken down by life stages. In this new typology he defines seven distinct periods of first-generation immigration, ranging from those who arrive in early childhood (between the ages of zero and five) to those who arrive in late adulthood (fifty-five years and older). Within the second generation of immigrants, he also makes a distinction according to whether one or both parents were foreign-born. Rumbaut (2004) provides data to support the utility of these distinctions, finding differences in domains such as educational attainment, language proficiency, and encounters with the criminal justice system. Important in the interpretation of these data are noticeable differences according to national origin, whereby the average age of immigrants from one country can be significantly younger or older than those from another country. As an example, immigrants from Mexico and Guatemala tend to be younger and immigrants from Russia and China have typically been older. These variations suggest that we have a great deal more to learn about the socialization experiences of immigrants across various life stages, both as a group phenomenon and at the level of individual action and interaction.

Context and Variability

In shifting to the individual level of experience, we also need to examine more carefully the conditions that surround and define the immigrant's experience. These contexts vary tremendously, from the geographical differences of being in a large city or small town to variations in the interpersonal situations a person encounters. Context is also defined by those who co-occupy the arrival destination. In describing contemporary New York City, for example, Kasinitz, Mollenkopf, and Waters (2002) use the term "majority minority city" to highlight the fact that current immigrants to the city are most likely to be interacting with other minority and immigrant groups. Numerically, there are more people in New York City who are members of non-Anglo ethnic groups than there are Anglos. Some cities on the West Coast of the United States are similar in this regard. Thus, earlier models of "immigrant group meets white host" are really inappropriate in characterizing the day-to-day experience of many of today's immigrants, especially those who come to the major gateway cities such as New York and Los Angeles. At the same time, traditionally more homogenous areas of the United States have also experienced dramatic growth in immigrant populations during the past ten to fifteen years, creating a myriad of conditions and immigrant-host profiles (Singer 2004).[1] Surely this is a productive area of study in the years to come.

Opportunity structures available to immigrants differ widely, depending on a variety of factors that include the labor market conditions at the particular site of immigration, the presence or absence of co-ethnic communities and local government policies (Singer 2004, 2005). These external factors must then be considered in conjunction with the characteristics and skills that the immigrants themselves bring, including their knowledge of the host language. Differences in opportunity are compounded by differences in attitudes of citizens of the host country. Gordon (1964) recognized the importance of context when he included "attitude receptional assimilation" and "behavior receptional assimilation" in his taxonomy, both concepts pointing to the fact that the exercise of prejudice and discrimination on the part of host country residents can affect the assimilation process of the immigrant. In chapter 3, I discussed much of the evidence showing biased attitudes and behaviors toward immigrants.

Further, as described in chapter 4, these biases are not randomly distributed. Rather, some groups are far more likely to be the recipients of negative reactions than other groups are, a condition that is one of the underlying assumptions of table 6.2. Such attitudinal differences create different climates and different expectations, again calling on us to do a finer-grained analysis of the immigrant experience.

The Dynamics of Ongoing Processes

A further limitation of models of assimilation is the sometimes explicit and often implicit assumption that there is an end point—that assimilation is a movement, at whatever rate, from a known starting point to a definable end point. Not all would make this claim. Gans (1992), for example, has said that the line has no predictable end. Alba and Nee (1999, 2003), who included the phrase "and at its endpoint the disappearance" in their 1999 definition of assimilation, dropped that phrase four years later, saying only that assimilation is "the decline of an ethnic distinction" (2003, 11). I would certainly be among those who suggest an ongoing process rather than a specifiable end point, as well as one that is not necessarily unidirectional. That is, on some occasions, as Portes and Rumbaut (2001) also suggest, a process of reactive ethnicity can shift assimilation into a reverse gear.

But the issue is more complicated than whether there is a specifiable end point. Following from the arguments that an individual level of analysis is needed and that context and variability must be considered is the need to look at ongoing process—at processes that not only can be charted at the level of group movement across time, but that also require a more focused consideration of fluctuations in individual lives. As discussed in chapter 5, the phenomenon of transnationalism is an additional element in this analysis. Indeed, as Morawska (2004) has argued, transnationalism and assimilation must be considered in conjunction with one another, a position with which I am in total agreement.

Thus, from this evolving perspective, the emphasis is less on the static definition of a person's move toward or away from an assimilative state, and more on the active process of identity negotiation, as it is carried out in daily interactions and variable contexts. We shift the emphasis from assimilation as a state of being to identity negotiation as an act of doing. To quote the Uruguayan essayist Eduardo Galeano, "identity is no museum piece sitting stock-still in a display case, but rather the endlessly astonishing synthesis of the contradictions of every day life" (1991, 124–25).

A FRAMEWORK FOR STUDYING IDENTITY NEGOTIATION

The concerns just expressed led me to consider new ways to think about immigration as it is experienced by the individual immigrant in a particular set of circumstances, and to try to identify the social psychological processes that are common to many immigrants. Rather than focus on a single ethnic group, a particular historical period, or an invariant sequence of events, I want to develop a framework that can be applicable to all immigrant experiences. I begin this analysis with three basic questions: What does the immigrant bring to the situation? What does the immigrant encounter? What does the immigrant do? In choosing this language, I emphasize the active process of immigrant work. Rather than an exercise in categorization, this view of immigration focuses on what the immigrant brings, confronts, and does, acting as an agent in each case but necessarily dealing within a particular context that will influence the course of events.

Each of the questions subsumes a variety of concepts and processes, as shown in figure 6.1, some of which have received considerable attention and others of which have only recently been identified. In the remainder of this chapter, I elaborate on each of the questions.

What Does the Immigrant Bring?

Questions about the characteristics that immigrants bring with them are heavily shaped by disciplinary stance, resulting in a focus that resides at particular levels of analysis. Much of the work emanating from demography and sociology, for example, targets particular categories of group membership, such as ethnicity and gender. Here the question, at least initially, is

Figure 6.1   Key Questions for Identity Process Analysis

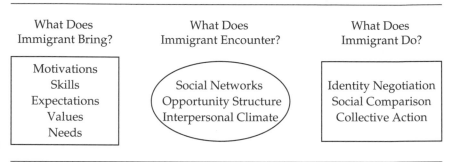

What Does Immigrant Bring?	What Does Immigrant Encounter?	What Does Immigrant Do?
Motivations Skills Expectations Values Needs	Social Networks Opportunity Structure Interpersonal Climate	Identity Negotiation Social Comparison Collective Action

Source: Author's compilations.

who the immigrants are—where they come from and where they go. Thus, in the case of Latino immigrants, we know that more than half are from Mexico, and that others come from Puerto Rico, Cuba, the Dominican Republic and, increasingly, from countries in Central and South America such as Colombia, Guatemala, and Ecuador (Saenz 2004). In terms of destination, Latino immigrants traditionally have been concentrated in California, New York, Texas, and Florida (Portes 1998; Waldinger and Lee 2001), but recent migration patterns are much more diverse, including sharp increases in the numbers of Latinos throughout the southeastern United States (Saenz 2004). Similarly, one can chart the paths of Asian immigrants, documenting separate tracks for immigrants from China, the Philippines, Korea, or Vietnam (Waldinger and Lee 2001). Gender patterns of immigrants have also been documented, both past and present (Foner 2000; Hondagneu-Sotelo 2003; Pessar 1999). In interaction with nationality, differences in the male-female ratio of immigrants can be charted as well, showing substantial divergences between countries such as the Philippines (more women) and Mexico (more men).

Social and demographic analyses focus not only on who the immigrants are, but what skills and experience they bring with them. Consistent with an emphasis on outcomes such as educational attainment and occupational placement, demographic analyses record education levels, job skills, and English-language proficiency (López 1999; Massey 1999; Raijman and Tienda 1999; Waldinger 2001). Again, these patterns are broken down by demographic categories, so that one can focus specifically on the skills of, for example, Filipino nurses (Choy 2000) or high tech workers from India and Mexico who work in the Silicon Valley (Alarcón 2000).

Demographic analyses are useful in establishing general patterns and associations between who a person is, what marketable skills a person brings, and outcomes such as education and occupation that have social consequences and social policy implications. To a psychologist, however, more is needed—specifically, a different set of answers to the question of "what does the immigrant bring?" As categories of membership, nationality and gender can be considered rough markers for a variety of psychological experiences and social conditions. Feminist scholars (Hondagneu-Sotelo 2003; Pessar 1999) have shown that gender is part and parcel of the social fabric of a country and a people, woven into the institutions as well as shaping the course of family transactions. Gender not only defines who one is, but also affects the opportunities one has, the assumptions one makes, and the treatment one receives from others. So too does ethnicity come with social psychological attachments. Ethnic groups differ in their values, their religious practices, and their family structures, and encounter different situations when they immigrate to another country.

Recognition of these complex constellations has led many investigators, particularly in anthropology, to more intensive, qualitative interviews with particular groups of immigrants in an attempt to understand what they bring and what they experience. For example, Prema Kurien (1999) conducted an ethnography of Hindu Indian organizations in southern California, exploring the ways in which gender norms, as expressed in the transported culture, religion, and male-dominated organizations, shaped the experiences of the women in the community. In another study, Jennifer Hirsch (2000) interviewed two generations of Mexican women, half of whom still lived in Mexico and half of whom had immigrated to the United States. Through comparisons of both geography and generation, Hirsch was able to tell a story about values and practices in the old country and in the new that illustrated both maintenance and change. Ethnographic analyses such as these provide a holistic and often compelling picture, showing the ways in which the interplay of institutions and structures in a community shape the experiences of those who reside within (Morawska 2003).

For the psychologist, however—at least for this psychologist—something more is still needed. That something consists of a more intensive look at the working mind of the individual. From this perspective, answers to "what does the immigrant bring?" require consideration of motives, values, and expectations. Understanding the immigrant experience from this perspective brings a greater sense of agency to the story, helping us to see how people make choices and take actions within their contexts. Further, it gives us a way to make distinctions among members of the same ethnic or national group, allowing us to explore difference as well as similarity in the experiences of members of a definable group or category.

The importance of this perspective is not unrecognized. Massey, for example, in listing elements that he believes are essential to a satisfactory theoretical account of international migration, includes "motivations, goals, and aspirations of the people" (1999, 50). Yet, though recognized, the models of motivation developed to date are fairly simplistic, often relying on a simple push-pull hypothesis. By this analysis, typically resting on economic factors, immigrants are motivated to leave one country because of the insufficient resources there and to go to another country because of its relatively greater resources. As Massey, Durand, and Malone (2002) point out, however, it is not necessarily the very poorest nations that are most likely to be the source of immigration. Rather, they argue, using Mexico as an example, that some degree of economic development is needed in the country of origin, creating an instability that then promotes immigration.

As just described, push-pull is a group-level model, offering hypotheses about which countries are more or less likely to be a source of sending or receiving immigrant populations. The same general thinking can be applied at an individual level of analysis, hypothesizing that those people who have the fewest resources are mostly likely to immigrate. Certainly the opportunity to earn more money is paramount for many immigrants, and is often coupled with intentions to send money back to families in the home country (Sládková 2005). For some, the pull of economic benefit is primary but time-limited. Interviewing people in Honduras who were planning to emigrate to the United States, Jana Sládková found that many expressed intentions to return to their home country in two to five years, assuming that they would have gained adequate money in that period of time to improve their life in Honduras. Although it is certainly true that many immigrants make their decisions based on a need to increase resources, the push-pull model as defined by financial need has limited utility as a predictor of individual decisions to emigrate. And indeed, in countries such as Canada where immigration policy is tilted in favor of those with occupational skills and economic resources, a simple deficit resource model would not be viable.

An alternative psychologically based push hypothesis suggests that people who choose to immigrate are in some ways better or stronger. Throughout the literature on immigration, we find expressions of the belief that immigrants have higher aspirations and achievement orientation, have greater ego strength, and are more effective in pursuing goals than others who do not immigrate. (In chapter 7 we will see how this form of explanation has often been invoked in comparing West Indian immigrants to native-born African Americans, without any real empirical support.) Although the popularity of this immigrant profile is considerable, empirical support is often nonexistent. Some recent data, however, support the belief that a personality pattern of immigrants can be specified. In studies of college students in central and eastern Europe and Russia, Bonka Boneva and Irene Frieze (2001) found that both achievement motivation and power motivation were associated with students' stated desire to emigrate. Also associated with likelihood of emigration were a constellation of values—specifically, a greater centrality for work and a lower centrality for family. The latter finding seems somewhat surprising, given the importance of family networks and social capital in the immigrant experience. One suspects that a sample of college students who think they might want to emigrate has some specific characteristics that would make one cautious about generalizing these results too hastily. Further, it is important to remember that the decision to immigrate is often a group negotiation, to which more than one individual contributes and with which not all members agree with equal enthusiasm. Indeed, there is no reason to assume that second-generation immigrants show anything other than the normal range of motivation, unless some more sophisticated models of family socialization are developed.

Further complexity is added to the question of personality profiles by the work of Eugene Tartakovsky and Shalom Schwartz (2001), who studied the motives of Russian Jews who chose to emigrate to Israel, Germany, or the United States.[2] They isolated three distinct motives for the decision to emigrate, each of which rests on a different set of core values. Self-development motivation is associated with a positive attitude toward change and disregard for traditional values and forms. Preservation motivation is almost the opposite, with its emphasis on conservation of values and a resistance to novelty and challenge. The third is materialism, associated with the promotion of self and a lack of concern for the collective interest. Not only did the Russian Jews in this sample differ in their motivational profiles, but their motivational priorities were associated with varying choices of country. Those for whom preservation and tradition were of primary concern chose to go to Israel, where they might assume that their religious identities would be best supported. In contrast, those motivated by self-development or materialism preferred Germany or the United States.

In this work we see the interplay of person and situation that is so central to a social psychological analysis. Even before officially becoming "immigrants," the Russians in this study differed in their basic value structure, and their choice of where to go was influenced accordingly. Further, these varying immigrants would come to their newly chosen country with different expectations, shaped by their motives and values. Expectations was also a focus for Eleanor Murphy and Ramaswami Mahalingam (2003), who asked West Indian immigrants in the United States to assess the degree to which the outcomes that they experienced matched the expectations that they had before coming. Of particular interest is the variation that the authors found, depending on the domain in question. Expectations were best satisfied in the realm of education and school life, and most discrepant in the area of political and racial matters. In general, as might be expected, these immigrants reported more life satisfaction when expectations had been met.

Some of the values and motivations that immigrants bring with them are best studied in the context of the family. A primary value for most immigrant parents, for example, is the importance of school achievement for their children (Fuligni 1998; Suárez-Orozco and Suárez-Orozco 1995). These values can be internalized by their children, though there is variation in this regard. Possibly influencing the relationship is the degree to which the children have a sense of family obligation. Fuligni and his colleagues (Fuligni, Tseng, and Lam 1999) have found that Asian and Latino adolescents in general have a stronger sense of family obligation than do students of European background. Further variations exist within these broad ethnic categories. Among Asian groups, for example, Filipino youth were the strongest endorsers of values such as giving assistance to one's family, having respect for the family, and being obligated to provide help in the future. Interestingly, the endorsement of these values did not differ by generation, suggesting that cultural values persist even in the face of increased contact with potentially divergent norms.

Clearly, answers to the question of "what does the immigrant bring?" are numerous and often complex. Many of the findings reported here represent only initial steps in what promises to be a long road of discovery. It is already evident, however, that a more psychologically based set of questions promise considerable yield. It is also evident that the answers resulting from this perspective are likely to be understood best in terms of interactions and conditional probabilities rather than of simple categorical truths. These contingencies are shaped significantly by the specific context that the immigrant encounters—the focus of my second framework question.

What Does the Immigrant Encounter?

When immigrants arrive at their country and city of destination, they enter a physical, social and psychological space defined by an entirely new set of parameters.[3] The physical setting presents what is often a very different climate and what is almost certainly a new physical context. Some features, such as ATM machines and subway cards, may be unexceptional for those who come from urban environments; other aspects of the new terrain may seem familiar to those who have had access to television coverage. Yet even with these recognizable elements, it is a different world for the new immigrant. Features of the physical space that define new experiences are outside of my realm of expertise, though I think that there are many fascinating questions for geographers and environmental psychologists to pose.

My analysis focuses on three particularly social aspects of the new space: community and social networks, opportunity structures, and interpersonal climate.

Community and Social Networks   The communities that immigrants enter, even within the same country, can be psychologically quite different from one immigrant group to another. When Thomas and Znaniecki (1918/1920) studied the immigration of Polish peasants to the United States in the early twentieth century, they concluded that "it is the Polish-American society, not American society, that constitutes the social milieu into which the immigrant who comes from Poland becomes incorporated and to whose standards and institutions he must adapt himself" (vol. 2, 1469–70). Then as now, ethnic enclaves are established that bring with them institutions, from stores to churches, that define the character of ethnic life.

Traditionally, immigrants moved to the largest cities in a country; in the United States, cities such as Chicago, New York, and San Francisco have always been home to the newly arrived (Singer 2004; Waldinger and Lee 2001). Within the United States, however, immigrant patterns have been gradually changing. Although large cities such as Miami and Los Angeles have grown as immigrant destinations since World War II, contemporary immigration patterns are much less constrained by state or urban center. Some of the sharpest increases in immigrant populations are now located in places such as Raleigh-Durham, North Carolina; Austin, Texas; and Salt Lake City, Utah (Singer 2004). Even within the traditional metropolitan areas, immigrants are now more likely to live in suburbs than in cities (Singer 2004).

Both for reasons of choice and chance, different immigrant groups end up in different geographical locales. Miami, for example, was the original destination of choice for nearby Cuban immigrants, but since has become a center for people from throughout the Caribbean and Latin America. Chinese immigrants are distributed fairly equally between New York and San Francisco, and to a slightly lesser extent Los Angeles; Filipinos are most numerous in Los Angeles and San Francisco (Waldinger and Lee 2001). In today's picture, however, the sites of immigration are less predictable. For example, there is a sizable Dominican community in Reading, Pennsylvania; Venezuelan and Colombian immigrants in Nebraska; Mexicans in the Eastern Shore area of Delaware, Maryland, and Virginia; and Latinos and Somalis in Minnesota. These diverging patterns challenge early understandings of immigrant communities, which were based primarily on the flow to gateway cities, and require us to think more carefully about the community and climate that immigrants enter.

As Massey (1995) has pointed out, today's immigration picture differs from that of the past in some crucial ways that relate both to policy and to economics. In what he terms a state of "perpetual immigration," the continuing inflow of immigrant groups shifts the balance from a process of gradual assimilation to one in which ethnic enclaves can maintain both their language and way of life. Particularly in the case of immigrants from Spanish-speaking countries, who constitute approximately 40 percent of all immigrants, communities within communities are established and maintain a cultural distinctiveness for their residents. As Massey notes, the development of large communities of Spanish speakers will lead to "lowering the economic and social costs of not speaking English while raising the benefits of speaking Spanish" (1995, 647). Thus, the community becomes not a step to integration into the mainstream culture, but rather a goal in itself.

Developments in modern communication technology facilitate this pattern. In major American cities, dozens of foreign-language channels broadcast exclusively in a single language, ranging from the higher-profile Spanish stations to the less well-known channels for Korean, Russian, Vietnamese, and Portuguese. It is quite possible for a Korean immigrant in New York, for example, "to live comfortably, enjoying Korean food, going to Korean churches, working in Korean businesses and now seeing Korean television" (Berger 2004). Thus the site of immigration provides not only a physical place, but also a social network that allows a person either to preserve the identity of origin or to develop an effective bicultural identity, with very little pressure, in many cases, to move toward assimilation.

New York City may provide a somewhat unique experience for immigrants. As Roger Waldinger and Jennifer Lee (2001) observe, the immigrant population of New York is far more diverse than any other city in the United States (but exceeded in its diversity profile by Toronto). New York is, in fact, what Kasinitz, Mollenkopf, and Waters (2002) have termed a "majority minority" city, in which 60 percent of the population are either first- or second-generation immigrants. As a consequence, these authors argue, the predominant interactions that immigrants have are not with the so-called core of white Americans, whose existence may be stronger as representation than reality, but rather with other immigrant groups. This pattern of interaction is thought to create a new interpersonal and intergroup dynamic, one that the authors suggests leads to an emergent identity as a New Yorker, distinct from both the ethnic group of origin and what is seen as a nonaccessible white identity as an American. Whether this identity as a New Yorker actually replaces or even supersedes other less situationally grounded identities is a question that awaits further research. Nonetheless, the claim for this unique definition is a clear example of the influence of community context on the identity negotiation process.

Opportunity Structures   A second aspect of context that the immigrant confronts concerns institutions and the associated barriers or opportunities that they present. For the first-generation immigrant living in an ethnic enclave, opportunities may be most plentiful within the neighborhood institutions, from banks to stores to churches. The work of Kenneth Wilson and Alejandro Portes (1980), based on Cuban immigrants in Miami, suggested that working for someone in one's own ethnic group can be more lucrative than work in a comparable position for an Anglo employer. However, recent and more ethnically diverse analyses in New York by Kasinitz and his colleagues show that immigrants who work in co-ethnic enterprises typically make less than those working in the broader, more diverse economy (Kasinitz et al. 2005). Their data also suggest that second-generation immigrants typically move away from the ethnic enclave for their employment.

Certainly the choice of destination is not a random one for the immigrant; it is influenced not only by the promise of social networks, which can be translated into social capital, but also by the knowledge that certain job markets appropriate for one's level of education and skills exist. For the migrant from a rural area with low education, employment might mean working in a poultry or meat-processing factory in a rural area of the Southeast or the Midwest, or a low-paying job in the delis and restaurant kitchens of urban centers. For the college-educated immigrant with computer skills, it could mean the technology firms of Silicon Valley. The concentration of people from particular immigrant groups in particular jobs is not solely dependent on the skills of the immigrant, however. Occupational niches for immigrants are often more arbitrary and accidental, as the successful entry of earlier immigrants at a particular site or in a particular job category paves the way, both through the social networks of the immigrant groups and through the expectations of employers who, finding success with some members of the group are prone to form stereotypic expectations of subsequent members of the group (Waldinger and Der-Martirosian 2001).

Language facility in English is a related factor that shapes the opportunity structure available to the immigrant. Obviously language is an element of what people bring, but the utility of the language is a question of person-environment fit. Immigrants from the West Indies, as will be described in chapter 7, are often believed to have more favorable opportunities than many other immigrant groups because English is their first language, and thus they can presumably move more easily into the service sector and into health care positions in which English is essential. In contrast, Spanish-English bilingualism is an advantage in Miami, where the relatively privileged Cuban immigrant community has raised the capital of speaking Spanish in an otherwise Anglophone country (Golash-Boza 2005). In general, however, immigrants to the United States who do not speak English fluently have severely restricted job opportunities, often limited to low-paying, less desirable, and temporary positions.

Gender is another major factor determining the opportunity structure that is available. As Waldinger (2001) notes, immigrant women are at the highest risk for unemployment, and the data suggest that even women who come to the United States with high levels of education are less able than men to use that background to get to higher status positions (Waldinger and Gilbertson 1994). At the same time, some occupations are more open to women than to men, often because of the prevalence of gender (or gender × racial) stereotypes. Child care is an obvious case in which women, rather than men, are sought out by employers. There are less obvious examples as well. Consider the Silicon Valley supervisor in charge of hiring workers for assembly jobs who claimed three things were necessary to be hired in his workforce—to be "small, foreign, and female"—and who went on to say that "these little foreign gals are grateful to be hired . . . no matter what" (Hossfeld, as cited in Pessar 1999, 63). These examples of female preference need to be set against the gender-linked male positions, however, and the overall balance suggests a less favorable context for women (Pessar 1999).

Essential to an understanding of the contexts in which immigrants must navigate is a consideration of family structure (Pessar 1999, 2003). In terms of employment opportunities, the composition of the family and assumptions about the distribution of responsibilities within the family are critical issues (for example, who is responsible for child care if there are children? Which members of the family, including children, are assumed to have financial responsibilities?). The family structure as it exists in the new country can be quite different from that established in the home country. In some cases, the character of the family structure is shaped by patterns of migration, such as when one member of the family comes alone, establishes a way of life, and is joined later by a spouse or other family members. In other cases, differences in earnings or labor force participation influence the family structure and division of labor. Still another influence is the visibility of alternative models of family structure that can challenge traditional patriarchal assumptions. These patterns are complex and somewhat outside the scope of this book (for more detailed analysis, see Pessar 1999; Hondagneu-Sotelo 2003). Yet they serve as important reminders of the critical role that contextual factors play in the immigrant experience.

Ethnic group, and the assumptions of race that accompany those categories, is another factor that shapes the context in which the immigrant experience is played out. There can be no doubt that race has an impact on the occupational, residential, and educational opportunities that immigrants experience. Immigrants are well aware of this discrimination, as exemplified by the second-generation respondents in a Portes and Rumbaut (2001) study, 87 percent of whom agreed that racial discrimination affects economic opportunities in the United States. But it is at the level of individual experience that the workings of discrimination can be seen most clearly, and it is that element of the context—what the immigrant directly confronts—that I want to deal with most fully.

Interpersonal Climate   The psychological climate for immigrants can be chilly. As the evidence presented in chapters 3 and 4 attests, many immigrant groups are the target of both negative attitudes and specific discriminatory practice. Immigrants, not surprisingly, are aware of this treatment. Survey data in Los Angeles showed that 46 percent of the Hispanics who were polled said that members of their ethnic group were always or frequently discriminated against (Sears et al. 1999). Asians in this sample were less likely to feel that way, with only 15 percent believing that discrimination was constant or frequent. Yet in other studies, Asians also have reported being the target of discrimination. A Cambodian immigrant in Minnesota, for example, told of eggs being thrown at his car with people yelling "Gook go home!" (Fennelly 2004). I suspect that few if any immigrants have not experienced some forms of discrimination. In fact, discrimination may be anticipated, part of the package that a move to the United States will bring (Sládková 2005).

In their study of second-generation immigrants in the greater New York area, Kasinitz, Mollenkopf, and Waters (2002) asked respondents whether they had ever experienced discrimination in each of a series of locations and situations, for example, work, school, or from the police. Table 6.3 shows their findings for six groups of immigrants, with figures for native-born blacks and native-born whites presented for comparison purposes. As the figures show, West Indians report the greatest experience of discrimination, generally equivalent to the figures for native-born blacks in the United States. Chinese and Russian Jewish immigrants generally had the fewest reports of prejudicial treatment, and the Latino groups—from South America, Dominican Republic, and Puerto Rico—were generally midway between these two extremes. Location made a difference, however, with the black and Latino groups being more likely to experience prejudice in public spaces, including encounters with the police, and the Chinese more likely to experience it in the school, more so than any other group.

The specific form that discrimination takes can vary, from general policies toward a category of membership to more individualized treatment. One example of the former is the condition of "driving while black," in which a person is stopped by the police simply because of appearance. An

Table 6.3   Immigrant Experiences of Prejudice (Percentage Who Report Experiencing at Each Location)

	At Work	Shops, Restaurants	From Police	At School	Looking for Work
Chinese	14	41	13	25	12
Colombia, Ecuador, Peru	20	41	22	17	17
Dominican	19	37	25	14	20
Puerto Rican	26	40	22	15	22
Russian Jew	8	12	8	11	9
West Indian	30	57	35	17	26
Native black	35	55	34	15	33
Native white	14	15	6	9	6

Source: Kasinitz, Mollenkopf, and Waters (2002).

article by Albert Raboteau for a New Jersey newspaper illustrates a type of language-based discrimination that immigrants may face, not because they cannot speak English but simply because they sometimes speak in a language other than English. "*No habla Espanol* at the Mercer County Geriatric Center," the article in the *Trenton Times* begins, and goes on to describe the formal warning that one worker received for speaking Spanish on the job ("When Speaking Spanish is Taboo," April 8, 2004, p. A1). The claim of the employer was that by speaking in a language other than English, the worker was indicating disrespect for residents of the center, causing insult, and leading them to feel excluded. This same belief that immigrants, by speaking in a language other than English, are themselves the cause of any discriminatory treatment, is reflected in comments reported by Fennelly as well. As one participant in her Minnesota focus groups said, "if somebody's speaking Spanish or Somalian or whatever . . . you're not gonna join in. So they're kind of creating their own isolation once again there" (2004, 12).

It is important to note that discriminatory treatment does not come only from whites. In the Kasinitz, Mollenkopf, and Waters (2002) study, the majority of Chinese immigrants who reported discrimination at school pointed to African Americans as the source of the treatment. Even within the same general ethnic group, biases by one regionally defined group (for example, immigrants from mainland China) toward another (for example, immigrants from Hong Kong and southern China) have been found (Taryn Tang, personal communication, February 2005). Thus, as immigrant groups come in contact with one another, a condition that a majority-minority city makes highly likely, groups that are jockeying with one another for position and status may create a climate in which new forms of discrimination emerge. It is also possible, however, as Susan Meiklejohn (2004) has proposed, that highly multiethnic communities may be the site for new forms of cooperation and for identities that transcend single ethnic labels. These intergroup dynamics are an important area for future study.

As discrimination is experienced, it affects the immigrant's sense of ethnic identification. Portes and Rumbaut (2001) found that second-generation Mexican immigrants in California, who might be thought to be in a process of moving toward an American identity, in fact reacted against things American as their experiences with discrimination became more numerous. As the authors state in reviewing their findings, "groups subjected to extreme discrimination and derogation of their national origins are likely to embrace them ever more fiercely; those received more favorably shift to American identities with greater speed and less pain" (2001, 187). In contrast, Almeida Toribio (2004) suggests that contemporary Dominican youth, rather than develop a so-called reactive identity in response to discrimination, instead create more inclusive ethnic identities that are less adversarially based than those of their parents—a suggestion consistent with the transcendence postulation of Meiklejohn. These observations lead to my third question, which shifts the focus directly to the ways in which immigrants deal with the situations they confront.

What Does the Immigrant Do?

In some accounts (ones in which the realities of transnationalism and dual citizenship are ignored), immigration is presented as a simple transition from one status to another: before you were a citizen of country X and now you are a citizen of country Y (with the point of "now" varying in the accounts, from time of entry through green card to citizenship). Primarily, these accounts assume that psychological processes (to the extent that psychological processes are considered at all) are in accord with the geographical and political markers. That is, not only is one physically in a new country with new legal status, but psychologically one has shifted from one state to another as well.

My assumptions are quite different. I view the immigrant as an active agent who, in the face of varying situations and experiences, negotiates and adapts to changing circumstances—some of which can be marked by the officially documented transition points, but most of which depend on more variable psychosocial events. In this view, not all immigrants can be expected to follow the same path, both because they bring different experiences and capital with them (as outlined in the first question) and because they encounter different situations (question number two). Further, any individual immigrant or any particular ethnic group will face different challenges and situations at different times, requiring us not to limit our attention to a single transition point but rather to be attuned to the developing processes in the immigrant experience.

In addressing the question "what does the immigrant do?" I look at two domains of activity. First are the ways in which the individual defines and negotiates a personal sense of self and identity in changed circumstances. Second are the ways in which people engage in actions with others in ways that affect both individual person and social group.

Negotiation of Self and Identity   Changes in ethnic identification and the meanings that surround that identity can be conceptualized in a number of ways. In the most elementary models, some writers have assumed a sudden and absolute shift, much like turning a switch from one position to another. Yesterday I was Polish, today I am American. Although few social scientists would seriously posit such a simplistic model, it is still possible to find evidence of that kind of thinking in social and political commentary, either phrased as a positive comment ("they have become real Americans") or in the negative commentary of someone such as Samuel Huntington, who decries what he sees as the resistance of Mexican immigrants to turn that switch. "As their numbers increase," Huntington writes, "Mexican-Americans feel increasingly comfortable with their own culture and often contemptuous of American culture" (2004, 254).[4]

More common than the quick switch theory is the idea of gradual movement from the identity of origin to identification with the host country, epitomized by assimilation models. In the original formulation by Gordon (1964), one can mark different stages along the way, but the result is often assumed to be a predictable constant. An alternative perspective, and one that has become more common in recent years, is the recognition that different end points exist. Within sociology, the theory of segmented assimilation represents such a model, with its designation of three distinct outcomes for immigrant identity (Portes and Zhou 1993; Zhou 1999). Yet even these models that predict gradual assimilation and that allow different end points, largely as a function of ethnic group, may not be up to dealing with the variations that are becoming increasingly apparent in recent studies of immigrant groups. Sears and his colleagues, for example, conducted a longitudinal study of college students at UCLA, a group that might be thought to be prime candidates for assimilation because of their already-proven educational qualifications in the American system and their presumed immersion in a multicultural college environment (Sears et al. 2003). Yet these investigators found relatively little change in the ethnic identities of either the Asian or Latino students over a four-year period. Rather than shift to American or to some form of pan-ethnic identity, these students continued to identify with their ethnic group of origin. This preservation tendency was somewhat stronger for the Asian students than for the Latino students. Further, the latter group, as was true in the Portes and Rumbaut (2001) work, showed more evidence of developing "reactive identities" in response to perceived discrimination that they experienced.

As was also true in work by Ethier and Deaux (1994), conducted with Latino students in Ivy League universities, the UCLA students who came in with the strongest ethnic identification left with even stronger ones four years later. Those with relatively weaker Latino identification when they entered college showed further declines, particularly during their first year. The college campus may provide and even proclaim a multicultural environment. Yet within this environment, it is possible to create an "ecological niche" that is supportive, not necessarily of assimilation to a melting pot, but rather of sustaining an ethnic identification. Having friends of one's ethnicity is an important part of this support system (Ethier and Deaux 1994; Sears et al. 2003), and having friends is of course evidence of the agency people exercise in creating their social environments (see also Deaux and Martin 2003).

Stability of identity is not always the rule, however, and college students may not be the most representative sample for studies of identity change in immigrants. Students, by virtue of their participation in the English-dominant higher education system, have already demonstrated a high degree of acculturation and may have experienced substantial identity reconfiguration before being assessed by researchers. In contrast, other studies attest to the significant impact of contextual change, as defined by geographic mobility or political shifts, on levels and forms of ethnic and national identification.

Although not a study of immigrants, South Africa provides a vivid example of identity being influenced by a change in political structures (Gibson 2004; Jung 2000). During the era of apartheid, South Africans were strictly divided into four so-called racial groups: white, African, colored, and Indian. The definitions for these categories were contrived and even fatuous. Consider the following definition of a white person: "someone who in appearance is obviously a White person and who is not generally accepted as a Coloured person, or who is generally accepted as a White person and is not obviously in appearance not a White person." Or of a colored person as someone "who is not a White or a Black person" (Jung 2000, 12). The dominance of this color coding was accompanied by a relatively low endorsement of the national identity of South African. Even in 1996, two years after the first democratic elections that brought the African National Congress to power, fewer than 40 percent of South Africans considered the national identity to be one of their own primary identities. Five years later, more than 50 percent did, with the increase particularly striking among Africans (from 35 percent to 48 percent) and Asians (from 53 percent to 75 percent) (Gibson, 2004). Further, as Jung's analysis of post-apartheid South Africa shows, what she terms ethnically mediated political identities—such as Zulu, Afrikaner, and Coloured—are constructed and reconstructed in accord with the changing political and social context. As such, these identities "are more multiple, fluid, heterogeneous, permeable, and indeterminate than is normally assumed" (Jung 2000, 262).

The shift in geographical context that characterizes immigration, particularly as it becomes a social site where the attitudes of others have influence, has a demonstrated effect on ethnic identification. An example of this influence is provided in the work of Jain and Forest (2004), who studied the changing identification of first- and second-generation Indian Jains through surveys and interviews conducted both in Mumbai, India, and in the United States. In India, the Jains identify primarily as a religious group with some similarities to Hinduism; there their religious beliefs make them distinctive from other groups of Indians. In the United States, however, where the Indian population is small relative to the total citizenry, Jains are viewed by others in terms of their ethnicity and are grouped with all others who share that ethnic and national background. For the Jains themselves, Indian comes to replace Jain as the basis for their identification. This prioritizing of ethnicity over religion was evidenced in patterns of friendship and of intermarriage, where the immigrant Jains indicated a preference for non–Jain Indians over non–Indian Jains. Distinctions between Jainism and Hinduism that were forcefully maintained by those living in India became much less important in a country in which the labeling by others and perceived distinctiveness of self had changed. Consistent with Brewer's theory of optimal distinctiveness (Brewer 1991), needs for inclusiveness and differentiation will shift when the relative distinctiveness of one's group within the social context changes.

How immigrants deal with contextual changes needs to be considered at both the individual and the group levels, as the work of Ankica Kosic et al. (2004) illustrates. These investigators considered how individual differences in the need for cognitive closure, defined as a preference for definite answers rather than uncertainty (Kruglanski 1989), interacted with the social networks established by Croatian and Polish immigrants to Italy, separate samples, in both of which women were the majority. For those immigrants whose needs for cognitive closure were high, their degree of acculturation to Italy depended on the company they kept—it was stronger if their social networks were more Italian, and weaker if their networks were more Croatian or Polish. When individual needs for cognitive closure were weak, the social network had less influence, particularly when both communities were readily available. Thus, in classic social psychological fashion, we find that not only context but also the interplay of person and context account for some of the variance in people's attitudes and behaviors.

At a more dynamic level, the expression of ethnic identity can fluctuate as circumstances change. People who have experienced life in more than one culture have a broad repertoire on which to draw, relevant to the concept of biculturalism discussed in chapter 5. Even seemingly subtle changes in a situation can alter the stance that a person takes. Verkuyten and de Wolf (2002b), for example, set up experimental situations in which either an intragroup or intergroup orientation was stressed for their participants, who were Chinese immigrants living in the Netherlands. Perhaps not surprisingly, the value of maintaining a Chinese heritage was expressed more strongly by the immigrants when an intragroup orientation was emphasized. Further, using the fourfold typology of Berry (as described in chapter 5), Verkuyten and de Wolf found shifts in the preferred acculturation position of their participants, with more people describing themselves as separatists when an intragroup orientation was established versus as assimilationists when the orientation was intergroup. (It should be noted, however, that the majority in both conditions endorsed an integration-assimilation position, and in equal proportions.) These results tell us two things: First, some combination of origin and present seems to be the norm; and second, circumstances can alter the position that a person adopts from a range of possibilities. Work on what is called cultural frame switching also shows that those who are bicultural, defined as having "internalized two cultures to the extent that both cultures are alive inside of them" (Hong et al. 2000, 710), will shift their behavior in accord with situational primes. Thus, the presentation of American images (for example, the American flag or a portrait of Abraham Lincoln) versus Chinese images (for example, a Chinese dragon or a photo of the Great Wall) will lead bicultural Chinese students to put lesser (when primed by American images) or greater (when primed by Chinese images) weight on external explanations for events, in accord with cultural differences in attribution that have been established in other work (Markus and Kitayama 1991; Nisbett 2003).

Selective use of behavior to convey one or another ethnic identification is not limited to laboratory demonstrations. Those who are bilingual often use language to establish an identity position. Dominican immigrants to the United States, for example, though often phenotypically black, are likely to prefer other ethnic identifications (Levitt, cited in Toribio 2004). Language is a way to convey this identity choice to others, as illustrated by a thirty-year-old female Dominican immigrant: "Sure, you're Hispanic, but you're considered black. . . . When you talk, they can tell" (Toribio 2004, 5). In another anecdote, a seventy-year-old Dominican woman, after practicing English earlier in the day that she was going to the Social Security office, later says "Buenos dias" to two Anglo-Americans passing through the office so that "they wouldn't think that I am one of those people from here" (10).

As these various examples illustrate, the process of identity negotiation and self-definition is far more complicated and variable than simple models of assimilation suggest. Immigrant identity is a position that is developed, maintained or changed, and expressed in particular contexts. Given stable contexts (for example, in a community or social network), the identity too may be relatively stable. Thus, the Chinese immigrant who moves to a primarily Chinese neighborhood, works in a Chinese restaurant, and socializes exclusively with other Chinese workers may show little alteration of identity. Yet as the UCLA and Ivy League student studies have shown, transition to a new environment does not necessarily mean that an immigrant will forsake old identities and take on new assimilated forms. Indeed, in some cases such environments lead to a strengthening of the original ethnic identity.

We still have much to learn about the pressures in an environment that elicit identity shifts, and about the functions that identities serve for those who either change or maintain their basis of identification. What is quite clear, however, is that identity negotiation is a dynamic and agentic process that calls for theoretical models able to incorporate concepts of change as well as stability of both person and circumstances.

Social Comparison   People's views of society, and their place within that society, are shaped by processes of social comparison. We determine how well our group is doing by looking to the position of other groups relative to our own. This process of social comparison has been well documented within social psychology and is a basic tenet of social identity theory, which describes the consequences of comparison for self-esteem and for intergroup conflict. The choice of a comparison group is critical. Comparison with a group that is worse off can provide some comfort, just as comparison with a group that is better off can cause dissatisfaction and a desire for change. For immigrants to the United States, the dominant white majority provides a readily available point of comparison. Indeed, notions of the American dream assume that those newly arrived will see the position of the dominant group as a goal to strive for, acting as an incentive for individual achievement. However, group-level comparisons may not always be so felicitous. In comparing their group to whites, both African Americans and Latinos, for example, rate themselves as disadvantaged (Tropp and Wright 1999). These trends were magnified for those who identified more strongly with their ethnic group, again testifying to the critical role that ethnic identification plays in social processes. When these same respondents were asked to compare themselves to other minorities, the results were somewhat more complex. Although both Latinos and African Americans saw themselves as more disadvantaged relative to whites than to other minorities, African Americans were more likely than Latinos to also see themselves as disadvantaged relative to other minority groups.

Within immigrant communities, particularly in urban areas that are home to many different immigrant groups, numerous opportunities for comparison are possible. From the point of view of whites, it is typical to see all Latino groups as representative of a single category (Huddy and Virtanen 1995). For Cuban-Americans, Mexican-Americans, Dominicans, and Puerto Ricans, however, the distinctions between groups are important. These distinctions allow members of a particular Latino group to be much more specific in choosing their comparison group, often finding both upward and downward comparisons by which to evaluate their own progress.

Social comparison processes can be quite complex and multidimensional. An illustration outside the immediate area of immigration is provided in a study by Xenia Chryssochoou (2000), who asked people from Greece and from France to compare their countries to other national groups—specifically, Germany, Portugal, Turkey, and the United States. Three dimensions of comparison were specified: cultural, economic, and political. Her results attest to the complexity of the comparison process. French participants, for example, saw their country as superior to all others on the cultural dimension but inferior to the United States and Germany in economic terms. Greeks also regarded themselves highly in cultural terms, superior to all but the French, but inferior to all but Turkey in economic terms. From the perspective of social comparison theory, this multiplicity allows people to construct relatively fine-grained images of their group—selecting, for example, a group that is doing slightly better if the objective is to set a goal for achievement, or selecting a group that is doing somewhat worse if the purpose is to feel better about one's current state. For the immigrant, comparisons with conditions in the home country often provide the basis for the latter type of comparison process. Particularly in the case of immigrants from the Caribbean and from Mexico, many of whom send substantial sums of money back to their families, perceiving that one is doing better financially here than one would be doing there becomes a force in sustaining the new life. As one Mexican immigrant reported to Patricia Ruiz-Navarro (2005), "Para mi es una vida diferente a la de Mexico. Y, tengo más oportunidades acá para ser alguien, para educarme (For me, it is a different life than that in Mexico. Here I have more opportunities to be someone, to educate myself").

Which groups one is most likely to use as comparison points depends in part on the general demographics of the city and country and then on the more specific demographics of residential neighborhood, school, and place of work. Groups that are readily available in one's daily life space are likely to be used as points of reference. Beyond that, however, exposure to other groups in a media-saturated world such as ours is in a sense unlimited (though highly biased in availability and content). Social comparison can create individual motivation for taking action to alter unfavorable contrasts, particularly when embedded in a more collective analysis of ideology and possibilities of change.

Political Ideology and Collective Action   Often the immigrant story is told in individual terms, a Horatio Alger–like scenario in which a person, or perhaps a family, emigrates to find a new life. Yet as the attitudinal and stereotype data presented in chapters 3 and 4 attest, immigrants are also viewed in terms of their ethnic and religious group memberships. From the perspective of the immigrant, these group memberships can also be important, serving to define experience as a collective phenomenon rather than individual phenomena. These group-based perspectives form the basis of political attitudes and willingness to take collective action.

David Sears and his colleagues (2003), in their longitudinal study of Asian and Latino immigrant students at UCLA, looked at the relationship between ethnic identification and political attitudes when the students were at the end of their fourth year in college. Among both Asian and Latino groups, strength of ethnic identification predicted the likelihood of political activism, including willingness to demonstrate and to sign a petition on behalf of the ethnic group. Similarly, highly identified members of both groups were more likely to perceive prejudice and discrimination against their group and to believe that minorities receive unfair treatment. For both Asian and Latinos (but more strongly for the Latinos), ethnic identity was also correlated with certain issues of public policy, including favoring greater diversity on campus and supporting more liberal immigration policies at the federal level. Among Latinos, opposition to English as the official language and support for more government aid to minorities were also associated with strength of ethnic identification. These findings, for the most part similar in the two immigrant groups, suggest that commonalities often exist between key concepts such as ethnic identification and political activism. At the same time, the specific issues of concern to Latinos were somewhat different, indicating the need to look at distinctive group patterns as well.

Evidence for group variation was also found in a recent study in which we compared immigrant and nonimmigrant groups of whites, blacks, and Latinos on their endorsement of two political ideologies that are relevant to the U.S. social system (Deaux et al. 2006). The first of these ideologies, belief in cultural diversity, emphasizes the value that different groups bring to a setting and the belief that each group will be respected and treated fairly—an ideology that Frederickson (1999) calls "the best hope for a just and cohesive society." Presumably all immigrants who come to the United States or other countries would share some of these beliefs, seeing their new country as a place where they and their group can succeed.

A second political ideology, explored by Sidanius and Pratto (1999), among others, is an acceptance and endorsement of social hierarchies. This perspective reflects the belief that groups are not inherently equal and that some rank ordering within a society is necessary and justifiable. Not surprisingly, people higher in status (for example, whites and men) are more likely to endorse this ideological position than are those lower in status. In our study, comparing first-generation immigrants to people born in the United States, we might anticipate that native-borns would be more likely to endorse a hierarchy than immigrants, who enter with what is often assumed to be a lower status relative to those who are already citizens of the country.

To study differences in these beliefs, we made comparisons between four groups, all of whom were students at the City University of New York:[5] black and Latinos born in the United States, whites born in the United States, black and Latino immigrants, and white immigrants.[6] Table 6.4 shows the mean scores for each group on the two measures of ideology—social diversity and social inequality. Both immigrant status and the color line were related to political attitudes. We had expected all immigrant groups to be positive in their views of social diversity, and indeed the mean scores were consistent with this expectation (means for each group averaged 5 on a 7-point scale). However, there are some notable differences between groups. Blacks and Latinos, whether immigrant or native-born, are more likely to endorse social diversity than whites are, and the white immigrant group is least likely to do so.[7]

Acceptance of social inequality, as shown in table 6.4, was not terribly high for any of the groups. Again, however, there were differences as a function of race-ethnicity. Black and Latino groups were less likely to support social inequality, and white immigrant groups were the most likely to do so. Thus, on both ideological measures immigrant status does not mark a uniform position, but rather is shaped by ethnicity and race. Black and Latino immigrants identified more strongly with their ethnic group, and from that position, were more likely to endorse diversity and to withhold

Table 6.4   Endorsement of Diversity and Inequality

	White U.S.-Born (n=113)	White Immigrants (n=90)	Black-Latino U.S.-Born (n=114)	Black-Latino Immigrants (n=93)
Social diversity	5.18 (.99)	4.98 (.73)	5.30 (.71)	5.33 (.87)
Social inequality	2.32 (1.19)	2.56 (.90)	2.15 (.86)	1.94 (.80)

Source: Adapted from Deaux et al. (2006) data.
Note: Ratings on a 1 to 7 scale; numbers in parentheses are standard deviations.

support for status inequalities. White immigrants in our sample were the least likely to favor diversity and the most likely to accept inequality in the system—not only in comparison to other immigrant groups, but even (though not significantly so) in comparison to native-born whites.

It may be the relative privilege of white immigrants in a society that still operates from a basis of race that leads them to be less supportive of diversity and more accepting of inequality. For the white immigrant, prospects of integration into the prevailing hierarchy, anchored at the top by whites, are obviously greater than they are for immigrants of color. White immigrants frequently assume that they can pass, achieving social mobility by merging with the dominant group.[8] The success of this strategy depends on the permeability of boundaries between groups, a concept developed within the framework of social identity theory. In the main, this is an individual strategy, in which a person succeeds on his or her own merit with little reflection on the group as a whole.

For black and Latino immigrants, boundaries are less permeable, as race and discrimination contrive to limit the access of these immigrants to higher positions in the status hierarchy. From their perspective, beliefs in cultural diversity become more important and status inequality is less acceptable. Working with one's group in some form of collective action is more likely to be a choice. As Alba and Nee (2003) explain, "when discriminatory barriers block an individualistic pattern of social mobility, assimilation, when it occurs, depends on collectivist strategies" (45). Indeed, as shown in figure 6.2, black and Latino respondents in our study were far more likely than whites to endorse collective action, regardless of immigration status.

Canadian data also support the conclusion that groups who are at a greater social disadvantage are more likely to favor collective action

Figure 6.2   Orientation to Collective Action

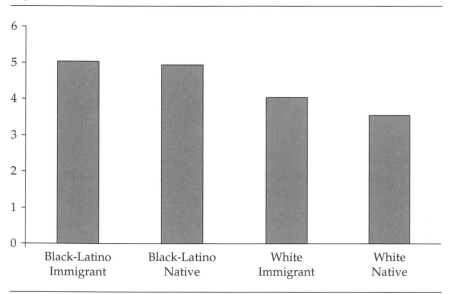

Source: Adapted from Deaux et al. (2006) data.

(LaLonde and Cameron 1993). First-generation immigrants from the Caribbean, China, Greece, and Italy, who on the average were forty-seven years old when tested, and their children, all of whom were enrolled in college and most of whom were second-generation immigrants, completed a questionnaire assessing collective orientation. This scale, the same one we used in our study, includes items such as: "I feel that there should be a stronger representation of my ethnic group in the political sector" and "I would lobby the government to improve the position of my ethnic group." Within the Canadian context, immigrants from China and the Caribbean are considered at a greater social disadvantage than those from European countries such as Italy and Greece. Accordingly, it is consistent to find that immigrants from the Caribbean and China were more likely to endorse collective action than immigrants from Italy and Greece. Another interesting aspect of these data was the generation difference. Overall, first-generation parents were more likely than their (second-generation) children to endorse collective action (paralleling a difference in strength of ethnic identification as well), suggesting that the group concerns of those who first come to a country may dissipate with their children, who have been more successful at incorporation on an individual basis. Also interesting is the fact that this

Figure 6.3   Influence of Ideology and Identification: U.S.-Born Whites

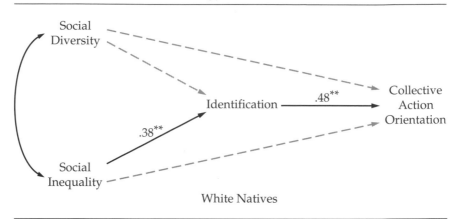

White Natives

Source: Deaux et al. (2006). Permission granted by Blackwell Publishing.
Note: Structural model for U.S.-born whites (n = 113) with standardized coefficients shown. Significant paths (* p < .05, **p < .01) are represented by solid arrows and nonsignificant paths are represented by dashed arrows.

parent-child difference was greatest in the Italian sample, reflecting the greater ease with which second-generation Italian immigrants are able to pass into the larger society, compared to what might be considered the more ethnically distinctive groups from China, Greece, and the Caribbean.

Further analysis of our own data shows some interesting patterns among the variables of ideology, ethnic identification, and orientation toward collective action. As a general rule, strength of ethnic identification mediated the relationship between ideology and orientation toward collective action. However, the pattern of this relationship differed by race/ethnicity, as well as by immigrant status, as illustrated in figures 6.3 through 6.6. Among those who were born in the United States, the critical predictor was endorsement of social inequality. The direction of this relationship was diametrically opposite for the two groups, however. For U.S.-born whites, acceptance of social inequality was positively associated with group identification and, in turn, with orientation toward collective action. In contrast, the relationship was negative for U.S.-born blacks and Latinos: that is, less willingness to accept social inequality is associated with stronger group identification, which in turn propels an orientation toward collective action. Members of each native-born group are showing a similar concern with having their group be in a favorable position, but the nature of the motivation depends on the group's current status. Among the higher status white group, preserving their position in a self-serving hierarchy is the

Figure 6.4   Influence of Ideology and Identification: White Immigrants

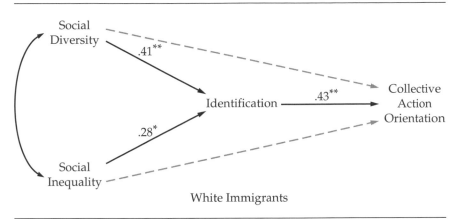

White Immigrants

Source: Deaux et al. (2006). Permission granted by Blackwell Publishing.
Note: Structural model for white immigrants (n = 90) with standardized coefficients shown. Significant paths (* p < .05, **p < .01) are represented by solid arrows and nonsignificant paths are represented by dashed arrows.

Figure 6.5   Influence of Ideology and Identification: U.S.-Born Blacks and Latinos

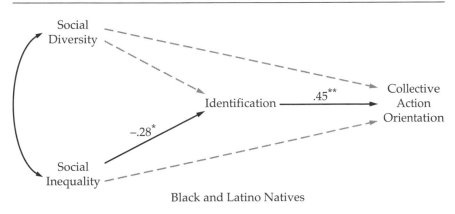

Black and Latino Natives

Source: Deaux et al. (2006). Permission granted by Blackwell Publishing.
Note: Structural model for U.S.-born blacks and Latinos (n = 114) with standardized coefficients shown. Significant paths (* p < .05, **p < .01) are represented by solid arrows and nonsignificant paths are represented by dashed arrows.

Figure 6.6   Influence of Ideology and Identification: Black and
Latino Immigrants

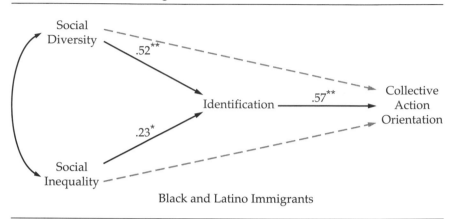

Black and Latino Immigrants

Source: Deaux et al. (2006). Permission granted by Blackwell Publishing.
Note: Structural model for black and Latino immigrants (n = 93) with standardized
coefficients shown. Significant paths (* p < .05, **p < .01) are represented by solid arrows
and nonsignificant paths are represented by dashed arrows.

motivation for group activity. When group status is lower, as it is for the
blacks and Latinos, it is the refusal to accept inequality that motivates
group action.

Among immigrant groups, beliefs in social diversity, rather than social
inequality, motivate collective action. In the case of white immigrant groups
(see figure 6.5), social diversity predicts ethnic group identification, which
in turn is related to collective orientation. The same pattern is generally true
for the black and Latino immigrants (see figure 6.6). Thus, even though the
absolute level of endorsement of social diversity differs for white and black
or Latino immigrants, with the former less favorable, the pattern of relationship between the variables is similar. In other words, though white
immigrants may be less likely to endorse social diversity, when they do so
it creates the same tendencies toward collective action, similarly mediated
by the strength of their ethnic identification.[9]

The difference between immigrants and native-borns observed in these
data suggests a different ideological basis for those who are newly arrived
versus those who are well settled. Belief in the virtues of pluralism may be
a positive draw for immigrants, particularly for those who see themselves
as divergent from a primarily white norm. For this latter group, blacks and
Latinos in the present case, it is a sense of possibility that encourages group
action. We could think of the ideology of cultural diversity as being a pull

factor—but a pull that loses some of its force in the context of status realities, to be overtaken by the push of status inequality. For native-born whites, blacks, and Latinos, it is the realities of a status hierarchy and the positions they experience within this hierarchy that foster collective action. In the case of blacks and Latinos, however, actions are presumably oriented toward countering or altering the hierarchy, whereas whites act collectively to preserve it.

SUMMARY

My analysis of how immigrants negotiate their position has been framed in terms of three key questions: what do immigrants bring to the situation, what do they encounter, and what do they do? In themselves, these questions clearly do not constitute a comprehensive theory of immigrant negotiation. The paths are not specified and the arrows are not drawn in figure 6.2, acknowledging the preliminary state of this effort. The questions do, however, provide some initial markers for what a theory needs to consider and what kinds of relationships might be explored. As these psychological models evolve, they must be further embedded in the broader social context discussed in earlier chapters. It is this conjunction of levels of analysis, from macro to micro, that represents the most exciting possibilities for future research.

Chapter Seven | Putting It All Together: West Indian Immigrants

I have to say, Joe, you're a sight made me rub my eyes. A coloured man in a British uniform. You're British, you say?

—Levy (2004, 131)

Race was important [in Jamaica] but not on a day to day basis. The difference I find is that when you get to America, you have to start thinking about race when you walk into the store.

—Vickerman (1999, 95)

Before I came here I used to be Jamaican. But now I'm West Indian.

—Waters (1999a, 57)

Look 'ere, missus. I am Guyanese and will be to the day I die. Even though me grow up in America, I know what I am.

—Butterfield (2004, 294)

I HAVE OFFERED a framework for the psychological analysis of immigration. Beginning with the broad stage of policies and demography and then moving to the more focused interpersonal conditions of stereotypes and discrimination, I have tried to depict the social-political space in which immigrants move. Throughout, I have drawn examples from a variety of ethnic and national groups, circumstances and histories, to exemplify the processes that are at work.

Figure 7.1   Elements of an Immigration Analysis as Applied to
Afro-Caribbeans

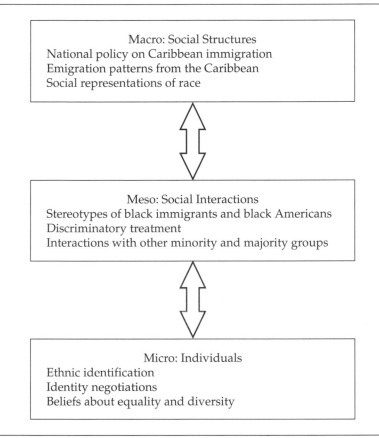

Source: Adapted from Pettigrew (1997).

Here I sharpen the focus to a particular group of immigrants, namely black immigrants from the Caribbean, using the previously introduced framework to describe various levels of analysis (see figure 7.1). Although I make reference to historical patterns of Caribbean immigration, my analysis is based primarily on the contemporary case. Similarly, though I make some comparisons with Great Britain and Canada, the focus is primarily on immigration to the United States, the majority of which, even further narrowing the lens, is to New York City.

Through this analysis of a particular case of immigration, it is possible to see more clearly the kinds of interrelationships that exist between immigrants and their context, as well as the dynamics of the immigrant experience—one in which both person and environment (a classic Lewinian formula) must be considered conjointly. These dynamics will not operate in the same way for all immigrant groups—but by focusing on a particular case, the character and complexities of the process should be illuminated.

IMMIGRATION POLICY AND DEMOGRAPHIC PATTERNS

West Indian migration to the United States can be divided into three periods that correspond to those defined in chapter 2: 1900 to 1924, 1924 to 1965, and 1965 to the present (Kasinitz 1992). Immigration from the Caribbean began around 1900. By the early 1920s, somewhere between 5,000 and 8,000 immigrants were arriving in the United States from that region each year. By the time of the 1930 census, the proportion of first- and second-generation black immigrants to the total population of blacks in the United States was approximately 1.5 percent (Kasinitz 1992). In New York City at that time, West Indians accounted for 25 percent of the city's black population (Kasinitz 2001).

Black immigration rose much more slowly between 1930 and 1965, as did immigration overall. One reason was the Immigration Act of 1924 (see chapter 2). Although the quota system that was part of that legislation did not set quotas for the Western Hemisphere (Isbister 1996), the overall cap on immigration dampened Caribbean immigration as well. Subsequently, the economic depression made the United States a less attractive destination and, in fact, from 1932 to 1937 more West Indian immigrants returned to the Caribbean than entered the United States (Kasinitz 1992; Massey 1995). Some continued to migrate to the United States, however, many using British passports to allow them to come in under the British quota, but this colonial loophole was eliminated in a 1952 act of Congress (DeLaet 2000). One consequence was a shift in Caribbean immigration patterns, such that many Caribbean people chose to emigrate to Great Britain, where the war had created labor shortages that immigration could resolve (Kasinitz 1992). Others began to move to Canada, which in 1955 lifted its ban on "coloured or partly coloured persons" (Gilkes 2004).

In the mid-1960s, these patterns changed again, in large part as a result of legislative changes in both the United States and Britain. In Britain, a 1962 law put sharp restrictions on immigration, and in the United States, as discussed in chapter 2, the 1965 Hart-Celler Immigration Reform Act flung open doors that had previously been only narrowly ajar. With regard to immigration from the Western Hemisphere, a limit of 120,000 was set with no quotas per country, in contrast to the policy for the Eastern Hemisphere, which set an upper limit of 170,000 and a cap of 20,000 on any individual country. As Dean Rusk (1965, 144) said in testimony when the immigration bill was being debated in Congress, they wanted to make it "clear to all concerned that there are no second-class countries in the Hemisphere family," a reference to an unintended consequence of earlier legislation that had limited Jamaica and Trinidad-Tobago to a hundred immigrants per year (Kasinitz 1992). Since the passage of the 1965 Immigration Reform Act, immigration to the United States from the Caribbean has continued to grow, most often to New York City, home in the late 1990s to approximately a half a million West Indian immigrants (Foner 2005). Other areas in the United States have also experienced a rise in Caribbean immigration. Approximately 25 percent of Jamaican immigrants now live in South Florida, for example (Foner 2005). By comparison, in 2001 only 10 percent of London's population was black, approximately half of whom were Caribbean immigrants—a substantial number, but also a decrease from a decade previously (Foner 2005).[1]

Comparisons between the United States and Britain are useful because they show the intricate interrelationships between policy, demographics, and the more social context of immigration (Foner 1998a, 1998b, 2005). Differences between the two countries can be charted in the characteristics of the resident population, the characteristics of the immigrant population, and the geographic distance between home and host country, all of which have shaped the West Indian immigrant experience.[2] In the United States, with its greater ethnic diversity and resident African American community, black immigrants are far less noticeable and tend to blend into established residentially segregated neighborhoods. In fact, one team of researchers found that all of the Jamaican immigrants they interviewed lived in non-white neighborhoods (Thompson and Bauer 2003). In contrast, the absence of a substantial black population in Britain has meant that Caribbean immigrants are less segregated in the community (Foner 2005). Perhaps as a consequence, the black-white intermarriage rate is significantly higher in Britain than in the United States (Foner 2005).

The immigrant flow to the two countries has differed in important ways as well, a consequence of both policy and historical timing. In terms of absolute level, as already suggested, the two countries differ, with the peak of Caribbean immigration to Britain occurring in the 1950s, the flow to the United States continuing today. Gender differences are apparent in the population figures as well. In Britain it was more common for men to migrate first and to bring family members later. In the United States, where immigrant visas (green cards) were needed, the greater availability of jobs for women as domestic workers created a different pattern. In the early part of the twentieth century, the ratio of women to men was roughly equal

(Watkins-Owens 2001). By the end of the century, women outnumbered men in the West Indian immigrant pool by a ratio of approximately 5:4 (Foner 2000), with women often coming first and then sponsoring the move of their family members. Class differences also emerge in comparisons of England and the United States. A higher percentage of West Indian immigrants to the United States come from professional and managerial backgrounds; in contrast, Britain has had a higher percentage of manual laborers, in part a response to the specific needs of the country in the postwar period (Foner 2004).

A third difference concerns the forms of transnationalism, as discussed in earlier chapters. Certainly electronic communication and the greater availability of telephone service in the countries of the Caribbean have made contact between immigrants and their friends and families at home much easier for immigrants in either country. Yet the sheer proximity of the United States to the Caribbean, particularly evident in the growing West Indian community in Florida, facilitated by cheap air fares and shared television programming, makes the experience for immigrants to the United States somewhat different from those who emigrate to England. They can be transnational, with one foot firmly in each country, much more easily than can immigrants in Great Britain. As a consequence, Foner (1998a) found that Jamaicans in New York were much less likely to talk about moving back to the Caribbean than Jamaicans in London were, precisely because they could feel that they were partly there already. Foner also found that Jamaicans in New York often talked about living part of the time in each country after they retired, an alternative never voiced by the London immigrants she interviewed.

Other conditions of history and demography can impact on the social climate for immigration, even within a single country. Foner (1998a) contrasts the reception for Haitian immigrants to Miami versus New York. Because the former arrived primarily as refugees ("boat people"), creating an image of poverty that was combined with threats of disease, including both tuberculosis and AIDS, their reception was far more negative than the less dramatic move of Haitians to New York, where they blended fairly easily into other immigrant groups of color. In summary, policies and demographics are not "dry" concepts remote from day-to-day experience, but rather are critical features of the social context—a context in which race plays a major role.

VIEWING AFRO-CARIBBEAN IMMIGRANTS

As the preceding paragraph suggests, immigrants arrive not as blank slates but instead often pre-defined, their images constructed from various beliefs held by residents of the host country. In the case of Afro-Caribbean immigrants, two sets of beliefs in particular are important: social representations of race, and specific group-based stereotypes. Social representations of race were discussed earlier (see chapter 2), as were general attitudes of citizens of the United States that implicate the color line. How do West Indian immigrants fit into this picture? Are they viewed by members of the host country (and in particular, by the traditionally white majority within the country) as "generic" blacks, or are there more specific beliefs associated with them as representatives of their country of origin? From some vantage points, it seems that black immigrants are simply another example of black, indistinguishable from African Americans who go back many generations. For example, a Guyanese immigrant interviewed by Waters was asked, "Do you think white people know the difference between Caribbean Negroes and African-American Negroes?" The respondent said no. "I think they classify them all as the same. They don't really want to know, you know" (1999a, 168).

At the same time, there is ample evidence to suggest that many whites do make a distinction, particularly when a direct comparison is being made between the Caribbean immigrant and the native African American. Almost inevitably, this comparison is one that disadvantages the latter group. Witness this often-referenced statement by Nathan Glazer and Daniel Patrick Moynihan: "The ethos of the West Indians, in contrast to that of the Southern Negro, emphasized saving, hard work, investment and education" (1964, 35). Elaborating further, these authors claimed that "the West Indians' most striking difference from the Southern Negroes was their greater application to business, education, buying homes, and in general advancing themselves" (35).

More than thirty years later, the same partiality toward West Indian immigrants emerged in interviews that Mary Waters (1999a, 1999b) conducted in a food-service company in New York, where she reported that "all of the managers had a clear preference for the immigrant blacks over the natives" (1999a, 211). "If I had one position and if it was a West Indian versus an American black, I'd go with the West Indian" (1999a, 211), said one of the managers she interviewed. He went on to cite what he saw as the reliability and willingness of West Indians to do the necessary job. Among the stereotypes that white employers used to support their preference were stated beliefs that West Indian workers are ambitious and hardworking, where African American workers are lazy, troublesome, and lacking both discipline and a work ethnic (Waters 1999a, 1999b). Elaborating on the sense of entitlement that employers frequently attributed to African Americans, one employer offered the following comments when asked what difference he saw between West Indians and African Americans:

"The willingness to work for a living . . . as compared to American blacks. The willingness to be helpful. The chip isn't on the shoulder that you may get from an American black because they're black . . . this is terrible, but I think American blacks sometimes think that they're owed something instead of working for it" (Waters 1999a, 173–74).

These statements reflect the belief that there is something inherently different between African Americans and West Indians—that either their biology or their culture predisposes them to show strikingly different characteristics. From a less dispositional and more social psychological frame of reference, we can consider some other explanations for the perceived differences. Both context and perceiver bias are candidates here. The importance of context is well illustrated in a partially autobiographical piece by Malcolm Gladwell (1996). As he described his early life in Canada, where a native-born group of blacks did not exist in any significant numbers, Jamaicans and other West Indians were viewed as dissolute youth, welfare queens, and gangsters. Far from a model majority, they were seen as the root of crime problems in Toronto. As Gladwell (1996, 81) writes,

> the West Indians were the first significant brush with blackness that white, smug, comfortable Torontonians had ever had. They had no bad blacks to contrast with the newcomers. . . . What has happened to Jamaicans in Toronto is proof that what has happened to Jamaicans here [in the United States] is not the end of racism . . . but an accident of history and geography.

Thus, the traits ascribed to West Indians in one context (Canada) are diametrically opposed to those ascribed to West Indian immigrants in another context, a function at least in part of the different reference groups to whom they are being compared. In a recent comparison of West Indian immigrants in New York City and Toronto, Gilkes (2004) also found that the immigrants to Canada were more stressed by experiences of racism and discrimination than were those who had moved to the United States.

The somewhat arbitrary character of the West Indian stereotype is also revealed in an experimental study (Eberhardt and Deaux 2000), which found that differences in evaluations of West Indians and African Americans emerged even when all substantive differences between representatives of the two groups were eliminated. In a scripted interview situation, a black man in his twenties was applying for a position in merchandising. In the videos prepared for the study, the same man was shown in two separate versions of the interview. In one case, he spoke with a Caribbean accent, with which, as a second-generation immigrant, he was familiar. In the other version, he spoke standard American English. The differences in the two conditions were quite subtle—so subtle that I had doubts whether the experimental manipulation of accent would be effective. But it was, in a striking demonstration of what has been termed "accent prestige theory" (Giles 1970; Giles and Powesland 1975). When speaking with a West Indian accent, the applicant was rated as having done significantly better than when he spoke in a standard American dialect. As a Caribbean, he was seen as having better interpersonal skills, performing better in the interview, and was given a more positive overall evaluation. In strong trends, notable given the small sample size in this preliminary study, he was also viewed as having more qualities related to job success and was predicted to have better relations with management. Thus, by using an experimental methodology, we can say with some confidence that discrimination is "real"—that, controlling for all other factors, people judge a West Indian applicant more favorably than the same person when he is thought to be African American.[3]

This study relies on accent as the basis for distinguishing between West Indians and African Americans, and indeed accent serves as an important marker for those wanting to make distinctions between the two groups. As evidence of the utility of this strategy, consider the case of Jamaican-born writer Claude McKay, who was arrested in a café frequented by African-Americans in the early part of the twentieth century and was brought in front of a judge to face sentencing. As soon as he spoke, his case was immediately dismissed by the judge, who recalled his own pleasant vacation in Jamaica (Waters 1999a). As a consequence of this experience, McKay assiduously cultivated his native accent, developing a survival strategy that successive generations of West Indian immigrants have found advantageous.

Although direct comparisons between native-born African Americans and West Indian immigrants often show more favorable attitudes toward the West Indian, it is also true that many people in the United States do not have a clear image of immigrants from the Caribbean or from Africa. Teceta Thomas (2004) asked three groups of students (white Americans, black Americans, and black immigrants) at two West Coast universities to list cultural stereotypes about black Americans and black immigrants. Consistent with the employer data of Waters, stereotypes about African Americans were significantly more negative than positive. In contrast, the ratio of positive to negative traits listed about black immigrants was approximately equal. However, Thomas (2004) also found that all three groups of students were able to generate both more positive and more negative stereotypes about African Americans than they could for black immigrants (see table 7.1). White participants in particular were often vague about the latter target group, and more than one-third of them listed no attributes at all. Further, inspection of the content of white's stereotypes about black

Table 7.1   Stereotypes of Black Immigrants and Black Americans
(Percentage Who Mention Each Attribute)

	Black Immigrants	Black Americans

Black Immigrants	Hardworking (52%)
	Good-looking (29%)
	Educated, intelligent,
	  motivated (24%)
	Unintelligent,
	  undereducated (19%)
	Hard to understand (14%)
		Athletic (67%)
		Criminal (48%)
		Good dancer, musical (43%)
		Lazy (43%)
		Unintelligent,
		  undereducated (38%)
		Creative, artistic (24%)

Black Americans	Hardworking (52%)
	Poor (29%)
	Pride in culture (24%)
	Unintelligent,
	  undereducated (24%)
	Family-oriented (19%)
	Dangerous (19%)
		Unintelligent,
		  undereducated (67%)
		Athletic (62%)
		Lazy (62%)
		Good dancer, musical (52%)
		Dangerous (52%)
		Family-oriented (33%)

White Americans	Lazy (21%)
	Hardworking (18%)
	Intelligent, educated (12%)
	Unintelligent,
	  undereducated (12%)
		Criminal (58%)
		Athletic (55%)
		Unintelligent,
		  undereducated (52%)
		Poor (39%)
		Good dancer, musical (36%)
		Motivated (21%)

Source: Adapted from Thomas (2004) data.
Note: Only categories used by more than 10 percent of respondents are included.

immigrants showed little consistency: antonyms were endorsed with equal frequency (for example, lazy and hardworking, intelligent and unintelligent) and no single attribute was agreed upon by even 25 percent of her white sample. Black participants, both native-born and immigrant, were more consistent in their depictions of black immigrants: more than half of each group listed hardworking as a group characteristic, compared to only 18 percent of white participants who mentioned this trait. These latter findings suggest that black immigrants themselves may have a more positive view of their group than whites in the host community do.

Additional data support this suggestion. We asked college students at a public university in New York to judge the favorability of stereotypes of various ethnic immigrant groups, as they perceived people in general to believe. We used what is termed a feeling thermometer to obtain these

Figure 7.2   Favorability Ratings of Immigrant Groups

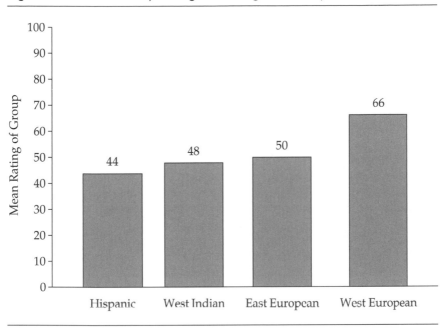

Source: Author's compilation.

ratings, that is, a measure on which people are asked to indicate warmth or positivity toward a group on a thermometer scale that ranges from 0 to 100. As figure 7.2 shows, in general respondents believed that the images of West European immigrants were the most favorable, with East Europeans, West Indians, and Hispanics all rating lower. Because the sample of respondents was so ethnically diverse, as is typical of New York City public colleges, we were able to look at these data more closely in terms of who was doing the rating. Of particular interest is the difference between the views of West Indian respondents and those of white students toward each of the groups. As figure 7.3 shows, for the most part the views of the two groups were not very different—except in the case of the views of West Indians. In this instance, West Indian respondents believed that people in general held very positive views of West Indian immigrants, virtually indistinguishable from those toward Western European immigrants and decidedly more positive than those toward Eastern European and Latino immigrant groups. White respondents, in contrast, saw West Indian

Figure 7.3   Comparison of West Indian Respondents with White U.S.-Born Respondents

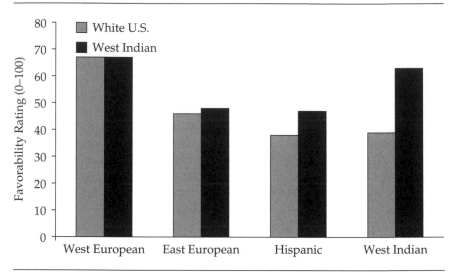

Source: Author's data.

immigrants as no different from the Hispanic groups, with both rated far lower than white immigrants.

Not only do West Indians view their own group more positively in an absolute sense, but they also often share the negative images about African Americans that are held by the society as a whole, as the data in table 7.1 indicate. Waters (1999a) described comments made by black immigrant workers about their African American coworkers in her employment study. As one worker said: "The majority of the black Americans—what I say is, either they're lazy or they don't like to work. . . . They don't—the majority of them, like, they don't have a plan about what they need with their life. I think this welfare system encourages it" (1999a, 217). Vickerman (1999) heard similar comments in his interviews with Jamaican immigrants, but he suggested that these negative evaluations of African Americans by Caribbean immigrants are most typical in the early years of immigration and shift as the immigrants become more familiar with the system and structure of their new country (as I will discuss more fully later in this chapter).

Clearly variations exist in the views that West Indian immigrants encounter when they come to the United States or to other predominantly white countries. Sometimes they benefit from what are seen to be their advantages and even inherent superiority over the resident African American population. Yet at the end of the day, black immigrants are still subject to the negative biases and discriminatory practices that face native-born African Americans, where black is less than white in the judgmental calculus. How then does the West Indian immigrant negotiate his or her life in a context that is often unfavorable? This is the key question for those of us who want to understand the dynamics of immigration, characterized not by a single point of transition but rather by an ongoing process of negotiation, adaptation and choice.

DEFINING A WEST INDIAN IDENTITY

Although most certainly an ongoing process, identity negotiation depends on and can be characterized in terms of the elements elaborated in chapter 5. Here I take that framework and apply it to West Indian immigrants. In focusing on some of those elements—categorization, content and meaning, evaluation, and social embeddedness—the fullness as well as the variations of West Indian identity become more evident.

Categorization

The first element in that framework—categorization—is a key issue for West Indian immigrants. Because of the slave trade of the United States, a black population predated immigration. Accordingly, West Indians who came to the United States in the early part of the twentieth century encountered an established black population, just as immigrants who arrive at the beginning of the twenty-first century do now. For the black immigrant, then, the question has always been how to define oneself in the new context—as a West Indian or as a more generic American black?

Before pursuing this question further, we should recognize that the category West Indian itself is a social construction, one not initially used by immigrants themselves, but instead promoted by those in the United States (and in other destinations as well). As a woman interviewed by Mary Waters (1999a) said, "Before I came here I used to be Jamaican. But now I'm West Indian" (57). Developing the contextual point, a Barbadian immigrant in New York City told Sherri-Ann Butterfield (2004): "I actually don't use 'West Indian' that much . . . in describing myself unless I am talking to someone who is white or black folk not from New York, cuz I know that they probably won't understand what 'Basian' [Barbadian] means" (301).

Not only is West Indian a term that homogenizes citizens from many different countries in the Caribbean (just as the label Hispanic shifts the emphasis from heterogeneity to a single category), but it also carries some ambiguity as to exactly what countries are included in the category

(Vickerman 1999; Foner 2001b). Foner (2001b) suggests that West Indian refers to people from the English-speaking countries of the Caribbean, including Guyana and Belize, thus tying its origin to British colonial history. Other authors include people from countries formerly colonized by the French and the Dutch as well, thus including, for example, Haiti and St. Martin, but exclude Spanish-speaking countries such as Cuba and the Dominican Republic on the assumption that people from those countries are more culturally similar to Central and South Americans (Vickerman 1999). What this debate makes quite clear is that categorization is far from a simple and automatic process. It is constructed, it is subjective, and the boundaries of any category can change over time. In this chapter, I use the term West Indian primarily in the sense that Foner (2001b) advocates, referring to Caribbean immigrants for whom English is a primary language in their country of origin. I will also use the term Afro-Caribbean when language is not a critical feature of the group being discussed.

Afro-Caribbean immigrants seem to differ in their likelihood of using country of origin as a basis of self-categorization. This variation in itself underlines the importance of considering social-historical context in even the most basic analysis of ethnic and national identity. Waters (1999a) reported that immigrants from Jamaica and Haiti were more likely to refer to their country of origin than were immigrants from other countries. Probably not coincidentally, these two countries are the leading sources for Caribbean immigration to the United States. Immigrants from Trinidad and Barbados, Waters reported, were more apt to either say they were West Indian or Afro-American.[4] Guyanese immigrants also were more likely to say Afro-American. In these latter cases, the more varied ethnic composition of their countries (including, in some cases, a substantial population of East Indian origin) is likely to be a critical influence, making race a more salient marker than it is in Jamaica or Haiti (Waters 1999a). Their smaller representation in the United States may be another reason for their willingness to take on a more generic label of membership, allowing them a larger group with whom to identify and share experience. From a cognitive perspective, this preference would be consistent with Brewer's (1991) optimal distinctiveness model, which suggests that people seek a level of group identification that mutually satisfies needs for difference and inclusion. From a more political and strategic perspective, uniting with similar others when one's own numbers are small creates a larger and potentially more effective group presence.

Beyond these differences between countries, the major categorization issue for West Indian immigrants to the United States is the tension between retaining a Caribbean-based identity versus shifting to a more generic identity as an African American. The question is not a new one, but the patterns of resolution may have shifted over time. Milton Vickerman (2001) believes that "West Indians who migrated to the United States before the 1960s generally resolved this tension by casting their lot with African Americans. Whether or not they wished to do so, they had little choice in the matter: Jim Crow segregation was monolithic" (246).

A character in Paule Marshall's wonderful novel about a young Barbadian immigrant coming of age in Brooklyn in the 1930s and 1940s describes exactly this choice. Speaking at a meeting of The Association of Barbadian Homeowners and Businessmen, one of the older male characters in the novel points to the association's banner and begins to speak to the members:

"They need changing," he was shouting. "You need to strike out the word Barbadian and put Negro. That's my proposal. We got to stop thinking about just Bajan. We ain't home no more. It don matter if we don know a person mother or his mother mother. Our doors got to be open to every colored person that qualify." (Marshall 1959/1981, 222)

Yet there were others, both in that novel and at the time, who maintained a strong identity as a West Indian (or as more specific ethnic-national group such as Bajan), a point that Milton Vickerman acknowledged as well (2001, 256, fn. 11). As he observed, "the intensity of their ethnic identity was the source of the reputed conflict between West Indian immigrants and African Americans" (2001, 256). Kenneth Clark, the renowned social psychologist whose work contributed to Brown v. Board of Education and who was himself an immigrant from the Panama Canal Zone, recalled conflicts between American blacks and Caribbean blacks at the local church in New York City when he was a child. A dissenting group of West Indians, including Clark's mother, split from the original church and helped to found St. Luke's Episcopal Church with an exclusively West Indian congregation (Clark 1976). Then as now, categorization was a choice for the person to make, even though the society at large might find a single category of black (or Negro) sufficient.

Vickerman (2001) suggests that it is easier for more recent West Indian immigrants to maintain their ethnic identity. One reason he offers is a claim that blatant racism has decreased in the United States, allowing West Indians to assert their unique cultural roots. On the other hand, one might suggest that it is the continued presence of racism that encourages West Indians to make this distinction. Malcolm Gladwell expressed this latter viewpoint:

The success of West Indians is not proof that discrimination against American blacks does not exist. Rather, it is the means by which discrimination against

American blacks is given one last, vicious twist: I am not so shallow as to despise you for the color of your skin, because I have found people of your color that I like. Now I can despise you for who you are. (1996, 79)

To me a more convincing reason for the shift that Vickerman described, to the extent that there really is such a shift, is the increasing numbers of West Indian immigrants who live in large urban centers such as New York and Toronto. With this critical mass, immigrants can become embedded in a community of shared values and practices and thereby maintain their identity of origin more easily, a point to which I will return shortly.

In the contemporary context, Mary Waters (1994, 1999a, 2001) has done the classic work on questions of immigrant self-definition in a series of interviews with West Indian and Haitian adolescents in New York City, as well as among samples of immigrant teachers and food service workers. In this work, she has found that categorization is neither simple nor static. Identities that may be framed initially in terms of one's country of origin (for example, Trinidad, Jamaica) frequently undergo shifts with increasing residency in the United States. In her 1994 report on first- and second-generation adolescents, Waters identified three distinct categories of ethnic identification. The first she described as a black American identity, characteristic of 42 percent of her sample of eighty-three teenagers. These youngsters chose an identity based on race, and in so doing included themselves within a category of native-born African American blacks. The second category, comprising 30 percent of her sample, consisted of those whose identity was based on their ethnic group. These distinguished themselves sharply from African American blacks and described a unique West Indian identity, one often characterized as superior in some respects to African American. Many in this group had developed specific ways to express their West Indian origins to others, including maintaining or even developing a Caribbean accent. The third category, representing 28 percent of Waters's respondents, was described in terms of a general immigrant attitude. Often more recent arrivals to the United States, members of this third group did not yet see any pressure to choose between identities or to hyphenate their origin (for example, Jamaican-American). Instead they retained their primary identification with the country of origin and in many cases anticipated returning to that country.

In Waters's data, these options were associated with a number of demographic and environmental variables. Students in the second group, for example, whose identification was based on ethnicity and country of origin, were more likely to have a middle-class background, as reflected both in better residential neighborhoods and higher quality of schools. Waters

(1994) also found that second-generation students (that is, those born in the United States) were more likely to identify as Americans than to claim identities based on ethnicity or immigration status, suggesting a time-linked process of incorporation.

This same pattern for increasing identification as an African American with time in the United States was found by Deaux et al. (2005). In a study that included equal numbers of first- and second-generation West Indian students, the former were significantly more likely to identify themselves in terms of their Caribbean heritage than second-generation students were. However, despite the statistical difference on a 5-point scale of identification in which 1 was "definitely West Indian" and 5 was "definitely African American," these results also showed that the majority of all of the students were more closely aligned with a West Indian identity than with an African American identity. The mean scores for first generation and second generation were 1.8 and 2.6, respectively, indicating that both groups placed themselves on the West Indian side of the midpoint (3) of this scale. Looking at the sample overall, we found that 63 percent of the college students rated themselves either definitely or primarily West Indian, 25 percent saw themselves equally identified with both (recalling our discussion of dual identification in chapter 5), and only 12 percent claimed to be primarily or definitely African American.

Why the difference between the patterns of identification found in this study versus those in the Waters (1994) data? I suspect that the factors of social class and education that emerged in the Waters study are relevant here. Our sample was college rather than high school students, and thus probably represents a selection of those first- and second-generation immigrants who are more motivated, better prepared, and financially more able to attend college (even a public college at which tuition is considerably lower than it would be at the typical private institution). It is this type of student, coming from a relatively higher socioeconomic status and somewhat better educational system, who was, in the Waters study, more likely to maintain an ethnic identification with the Caribbean.

The question of whether an immigrant from the Caribbean identifies as African American or West Indian, whether generically or country-specific, implies that the categories are mutually exclusive. As a geographical distinction, this partitioning seems relatively straightforward—although even here, consideration of transnationalism suggests more complexity. When considered in more psychological terms, it is less obvious that ethnic identification is an either-or issue for black immigrants. Thus Butterfield (2004) argues that having both a racial and an ethnic identity is central to the lives of West Indian immigrants. And indeed, some of her respondents describe vividly how they chose which identity to advance, depending on the circumstances. As stated by a person recalling her high school years, she "was . . . black by day and . . . West Indian by night" (298).

This ability to maintain more than one ethnic identity recalls the discussions in chapters 5 and 6 about multiplicity and identity negotiation. To understand this distinction more fully in the context of Afro-Caribbean immigration, however, one must look beyond the labels and to the meanings associated with the categories.

Content and Meaning

The dominant issue for almost all Afro-Caribbean immigrants when they arrive in the United States, or in Canada or in England, is the meaning of race (Bobb 2001; Foner 2001; Vickerman 1999; Waters 1999a). Vickerman quotes the words of a Caribbean woman who emigrated to America: "I had to come all the way to Canada to discover I was black!" (1999, 24). Similarly, a woman from Union Island (St. Vincent and the Grenadines) interviewed by Vilna Bobb commented: "Racism? We never knew what the word was" (2001, 217). Numerous analyses of Caribbean societies note that race is conceptualized very differently there compared to the United States (Rogers 2001; Vickerman 1999; Waters 1999a). In most of the countries of the Caribbean, blacks are the majority population. Color can therefore be taken for granted, rather than being the distinctive marker that it is in the United States—and even more so in Canada and England, which have both had significant Afro-Caribbean immigration while having very small resident black populations. Focusing specifically on Jamaica, Vickerman described a society in which "daily interactions . . . are largely independent of race"; where "race has taken on the aspect of a background variable—important, but largely distant" (1999, 36). Jamaican policy has taken this issue further by explicitly endorsing a policy, exemplified in the national motto of "Out of Many, One People," which essentially treats race as a non-issue (Vickerman 1999).

Class is a sharper base of distinction in some Caribbean countries than is color. As a general rule, Bobb suggested that when a society has more whites than blacks, "the influence of racial discrimination may be easier to see than the influence of class"; in black-majority societies, however, "the influence of class may seem greater than race" (2001, 223). Contrasts between the Caribbean and the American experiences seem to bear this out, though there are subtleties here as well. Within some Caribbean countries, for example, lighter-skinned blacks are reported to be favored over darker-skinned blacks (Waters 1999a). In Jamaica, Vickerman (1999) observed that although members of the upper class were prone to deny the relevance of race in Jamaican society, poorer individuals frequently showed a race consciousness.

In the United States (a society in which there are more whites than blacks), though increasing diversity makes these labels harder to hold onto, racial consciousness and treatment based on race is part of the experience of all African Americans regardless of class. American society is generally insensitive to the nuances and gradations that exist in countries in which blacks predominate. Instead, blacks are treated as a homogeneous and a more consistently stigmatized group. For American society, "one drop of blood" has long served as a sufficient basis of categorization for many, and as a justification for the differential treatment that has followed that labeling process.

I deal more with the process of negotiation on this new racialized turf later in this chapter. For the moment, however, let me concentrate on the issues of content and meaning that distinguish African American from Afro-Caribbean. In contrasting the experiences, Waters listed four key areas of cultural and historical difference: the relative number of Europeans and Africans in the societies; the rules and practices that define racial status; the harshness of the slave system; and the conditions of emancipation, and in particular the earlier independence of the United States and the continued colonialism in the Caribbean (1999a, 25). Because of these differences, race takes on very different meanings in defining one's ethnicity. For African Americans, well-steeped in the culture of racism, it is common to do so with reference to structural factors. In the United States, race is experienced much more directly in everyday interpersonal interaction, becoming very much the foreground rather than the background of experience (Feagin and Sikes 1994; Smith 2000). For Afro-Caribbeans, by contrast, the ideological framework is more mixed, equally likely to emphasize the importance of individual effort (Rogers 2001). As one of Rogers's respondents said, "We are concerned about racism. But basically we don't walk around with a chip on our shoulders like African Americans" (178).

Collective memories of the two groups differ as well. For African Americans, the history of slavery is part of the racial group consciousness, more recent in time and more vivid in cultural representations. For the Afro-Caribbean, however, slavery seems further back in time and was not bridged by the kind of Jim Crow policies that existed for so long in the United States (Rogers 2001). "Not that I have a problem with African Americans, it's just that they have a history . . . legacy . . . that I don't have and vice versa," explained one of Butterfield's respondents (2004, 301). At issue here is not only the perceived relevance of the legacy but also the basic knowledge that immigrants have of African American history. Another respondent in the Butterfield study recalled a high school experience in which the only three black students in the class were Caribbean immigrants who could not respond to the teacher's request to talk about the black experience. "What the hell is the black experience?" this respondent asked, rhetorically, in her interview. "I am thirty years old, and I still don't know what that is, so why was I supposed to know when I was fifteen?" (2004, 298).

Many immigrants from the Caribbean make efforts to distinguish themselves from the African American population, creating two distinctive identity constellations. Being African American is seen as route to downward mobility and African Americans are characterized as having inferior work habits, the wrong priorities, and less motivation to do well (Vickerman 1999; Waters 1999a). "I would say . . . that they are lazy and we from the West Indies work very hard," one of Vickerman's interviewees said (1999, 143). Or, in the words of one of Waters's respondents: "The blacks here should have more of life—they don't try to promote themselves" (1999a, 65). In her analysis of worker interviews, Waters observed that "the West Indians were much more attuned to minute differences between themselves and black Americans and were apt to chronicle differences between the groups and to point to West Indian superiority in even more arenas than the whites did" (1999a, 123). Yet Vickerman (1999) suggested that these negative comparisons are primarily true for those who have just recently immigrated. With time, he believed, West Indian immigrants come to see more commonality than difference, in large part because they experience similar kinds of discriminatory experiences.

The territory of identification is unquestionably complex, and the choice among labels such as black, African American, and West Indian is more than simple terminology. For many immigrants from the Caribbean, combinations of terms or dual identifications allow them to capture a broad range of meaning while at the same making critical distinctions for themselves. In research by Perkins (2006), for example, a first-generation Haitian immigrant explained the term African American in the following way: "Usually I think of the first part of the term as cultural roots and the latter part of the term as your citizenship." With regard to the use of African American versus black, Butterfield (2004) argued that the former refers to a specific cultural and ethnic group, and the latter more generally to a multitude of ethnicities linked by skin color. Like Philogène (1999), she argued that the two terms "are not interchangeable . . . but ones that have specific references and legacies" (Butterfield 2004, 307).

Evaluation

As the previous discussion suggests, differences in content associated with a West Indian versus African American identity are not value free. Rather, the content often carries transparent evaluative implications, attaching explicit positive or negative value to a group label.

It is critical here to distinguish between the private and the public components of personal regard. In terms of how one feels about his or her ethnic identification, we typically find little difference between groups, whichever identification they claim for themselves. A person who describes her or himself as an African American, for example, sees the same degree of positive value in that label that a person who characterizes him or herself as a West Indian or Trinidadian sees in those labels. In terms of the public component of evaluation, in contrast, the two types of identity are clearly not equivalent, as the earlier analysis of stereotypes indicated.

On specific measures of positive versus negative evaluation, the data in figure 7.2 show that people generally rated Caribbean immigrants equivalent to black Americans in favorability. Nonetheless, as figure 7.3 indicates, West Indian immigrants themselves believed that their group is regarded much more favorably, crediting it with a favorability rating of better than 60 compared with the 49 that black Americans received. Consistent with these findings, West Indian immigrants in the Deaux et al. (2005) study were asked to characterize the views that people in general hold of both African Americans and of West Indians, using an adjective rating scale that included six positive attributes (such as hardworking, smart, and friendly) and six negative attributes (including poor, lazy, and criminal). As figure 7.4 shows, both first- and second-generation students believed that people hold more favorable impressions of West Indians than of African Americans. Interestingly, however, the perceived advantage of West Indians in the public eye diminished, though did not disappear, for second-generation students. Thus, with more time in the United States and presumably more opportunity to see West Indians subjected to the same kinds of negative biases and discrimination that native-born African Americans experience, second-generation immigrants revised their estimates of popular opinion. At this stage, differences in the cultural stereotypes are still thought to exist, though not as pronounced as earlier. Might we expect that by the third generation (or perhaps even later in the lives of these second-generation students) that the perceived advantage of being a West Indian would decrease even further?

The difference in the pattern of findings for private and public evaluation, showing little variation for private regard but considerable change over time and group for public regard, attests to the importance of keeping these two aspects of evaluation separate. Moreover, our data allow us to look specifically at how the two forms relate to one another. Theories that assume the internalization or reflected mirroring of other's opinions would predict that public and private regard would be highly correlated. In support of this prediction, we have found positive correlations between the two measures among first-generation West Indian immigrants in two

Figure 7.4   Perceived Favorability of Cultural Stereotypes

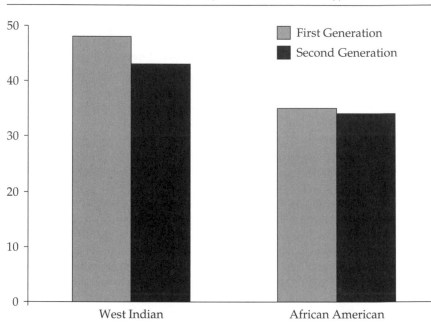

Source: Deaux et al. (2005).
Note: Possible range is 12 to 72, with higher scores indicating greater favorability.

studies—+.31 in Deaux et al. (2005) and +.52 in Wiley, Perkins, and Deaux (2006). Dramatically, however, the association between the two measures is not significant in second-generation immigrants (+.11 and −.09 in the two studies, respectively). It is interesting to consider this pattern of findings in conjunction with work by Jennifer Crocker et al. (1994), in which positive associations between the same two measures were found among white and Asian samples, but no association was found in the African American sample.

We thus must recognize that though private and public views of one's group may correspond for some groups at some times, self-regard is not inevitably determined by what others think of one's group. When one's group is devalued by society, as is often the case for black immigrants, the strategically protective choice is to decouple the private from the public, maintaining positive evaluation in the former despite devaluations from the latter. For the Afro-Caribbean immigrant, this decoupling process becomes a critical part of identity negotiation.

Social Embeddedness and Behavioral Involvement

Ethnic identity is maintained and solidified by practices carried out in everyday contexts. As described in chapter 5, social identities need, or at least benefit from, supportive environments in which one's identity is shared with others. For ethnic communities in general, and for West Indians in this analysis, residential concentration is one way in which social links develop. Throughout the country, many ethnic enclaves can be identified. Within some communities, the 2000 census data suggest an increase in residential concentration, particularly among the newly arriving immigrant groups. Within the greater New York City area, West Indians are the most highly segregated of the eight ethnic groups that Kasinitz, Mollenkopf, and Waters (2002) studied, though second-generation immigrants are less concentrated than the first. A consequence of residential segregation, Bobb suggested, is "pockets of within-group support that also separate and isolate groups from the larger society" (2001, 227). These social networks both increase the social embeddedness of one's ethnic identity and at the same time protect or buffer black immigrants from some of the racial discrimination that they would face outside the protective zone. Residential segregation increases the likelihood that schools, churches, and other neighborhood institutions will provide ethnic-consistent networks of participation. Typically, these neighborhoods and churches represent Afro-Caribbean immigrants generally, rather than a particular nation. Thus they contribute to developing a more pan-ethnic identity as a West Indian rather than maintaining the specific national identity of origin.

In the contemporary reality of Brooklyn, New York, the annual West Indian–American festival is a vibrant example of how a West Indian identity can be actively expressed. Each year over Labor Day weekend this festival, which includes four or five days of music, dance, and ceremony, culminates in a huge parade celebrated by more than a million participants and observers. Under the umbrella of Caribbean heritage, ties to specific countries are also reinforced, so that St. Lucians can distinguish themselves from Jamaicans or other island nationalities (Chan 2003). As optimal distinctiveness theory would predict (Brewer 1991), the overwhelming numbers of West Indians push individuals to reassert claims on more distinctive identities, such as their specific countries of origin represent. This process does not, I think, represent any significant rejection of one identity in favor of another, but rather is a more temporal alternation or shift in emphasis or label. The meanings associated with the two labels may not differ substantially, but the surrounding context can influence the immediate choice—to be West Indian when the majority of people in one's environment have other origins or to identify with a specific country when relating to home.

For many West Indians, connections to the country of origin remain strong and offer another kind of social embeddedness for ethnic identity. Exemplifying the concept of transnationalism, West Indian immigrants often move back and forth between their country of origin and the United States (Basch 2001; Foner 2001b; Waters 1999a). Dual citizenship is often possible, and a number of Caribbean countries have developed policies and practices that encourage the maintenance of a national identity of origin, such as allowing voting in the country's elections and even changing the date of Carnival to a time of year more conducive to migrant return (Basch 2001). To the extent that these ties to the towns and countries of origin remain strong, a pan-ethnic West Indian identity may be less important than a more focused identification with country.

These transnational practices are not new, as several scholars remind us (Foner 1997; Watkins-Owens 2001). Letters, money, and goods have long traveled back to the families of immigrants who remained in the home country, just as many immigrants throughout the past century made plans to return to their home country when education and economic needs were satisfied. What is new, however, as described in chapter 6, are the technological advances that make communication and travel much easier. Regular telephone contact and frequent flights to the Caribbean allow immigrants to remain embedded in their home country at the same time that they establish new networks in the United States.

The links that West Indian immigrants maintain with their country of origin are typically based on personal networks rather than formal organizations (Foner 2001b). As Linda Basch put it, "Kin are often the central pegs of migrant transnational social fields" (2001, 126). Contrasting West Indian immigrants with the Mexican immigrant communities that Robert Smith (1998) studied, Foner sees little evidence of the kind of community organizations in the West Indies that Smith described in Mexico, and she knows of no village-based West Indian associations in New York City. Waters (1999a) also found little evidence of involvement in home-country politics that characterized some other immigrant groups, such as Dominicans. The embeddedness of West Indian immigrants appears to be primarily with the family, though with a family that may be widely dispersed, including relatives in Canada or Great Britain. These extended family ties preserve a more specific country identification—but one that may be less nationalistic than that of immigrants from some other countries.[5]

Not all immigrants from the West Indies have these family contacts. Indeed, the extent to which West Indian immigrants continue to have close family members in their home country is probably a strong predictor of the degree to which a West Indian identification continues to be strong and transnational patterns evolve. Contrast two Jamaican woman of the same age, both immigrants, whom Vickerman interviewed. The first said, "most of my family is still there," and continued to be in close contact by telephone and by travel. The second described assorted family members who had moved to Canada, Trinidad, and New York, and said, "So, like, no one is left in Jamaica" (2002, 356). She had virtually no direct contact with Jamaica.

Thus, as in all aspects of identification, it is important to recognize the distinctions among individuals and to resist easy assumptions of homogeneity within immigrant groups. Further, as Milton Vickerman (2002) noted, patterns of transnational involvement vary depending on historical and political circumstances. Political crises in the country of origin may elicit much more active contact than a more placid, predictable political climate does. More at the level of the individual, Vickerman also suggested that stage in the life cycle is relevant to predictions of transnational involvement. Children who accompany their parents back to the Caribbean in their childhood may give up the practice when they are on their own, either involved in other arenas or unwilling to pay for the air fare from their own resources. Later in life, some of these same people may feel an urge to regain their roots. Yet here too there are wide variations. Even within a single family, one spouse may want to move back to the homeland, whereas the other may be firmly entrenched in the United States or other country of residence, a pattern I have observed on more than one occasion.

For the Afro-Caribbean immigrant who identifies as African American, social embeddedness and behavioral involvement take different forms. Adoption of an American black identity can be indicated by music preferences, subgroup membership, linguistic patterns, or style of dress. Waters (1999a) described a cult of materialism that is associated with the American identity, evidenced in the desire for expensive sneakers or fashionable jewelry. This desire to obtain and display the "big and fancy" things signals an identity orientation quite different from a West Indian loyalty. Variations such as these, expressing identity affiliations with one or another group, serve as markers for the identity negotiation processes in which all immigrants engage.

NEGOTIATING IDENTITY AND RACE

The conditions and demands that immigrants from the Caribbean confront when they come to the United States are in many respects similar to those of other immigrant groups. They connect with families, friends, or friends of friends. They need to find places to live and schools to attend. They look for work in an unfamiliar labor market. Unlike many immigrants, immigrants from Caribbean countries formerly under British rule come with

English as their first language, making some of the transitions to job and school significantly easier, in comparative terms. But most immigrants from the Caribbean also come with black skin, a marker that places them squarely in the context of American racism.

As virtually every student of West Indian immigration has observed, this contact with racism is a defining feature of the context with which immigrants must contend (Bobb 2001; Foner 1985; Gladwell 1996; Rogers 2001; Vickerman 1999; Waters 1999a). The novelist Elizabeth Nunez poignantly described the first encounter of a young Trinidadian girl with the unfeeling prejudices of a Midwestern family:

> Then, after that evening, I would never again be able to return to a childish innocence in which evil existed only in books or in places far remote from where I was. . . . It would be a journey that would end in my beginning, that would return me to the purity and source of a racial past I had not yet acknowledged, and would link me irreversibly to black America. (1998, 120)

Waters (1999a) characterized West Indian immigrants' understanding of race in three ways: first, their lack of an oppositional identity, second, expectations of structural racism, and, third, low expectations of interpersonal racism. With regard to the first, Waters pointed to the nature of West Indian societies in which, as I have noted, black-white is not the primary dimension of comparison. In contrast, the black-white color line continues to shape the American psyche, evident in all aspects of the society (Ogbu 1978; Sidanius and Pratto 1999). For the immigrant, initial responses to this distinction often include a sense that the distinction does not apply to them. As foreigners, or what Ogbu has termed voluntary immigrants, they see themselves in a different category, not bound to be judged in terms of the simplistic black-white dichotomy.

Waters's second and third points make an important distinction with regard to anticipated racism. For the most part, Waters suggested, West Indian immigrants expect some forms of structural racism—the awareness of a society in which whites hold the majority of the positions of power and in which blacks are more likely to be found in the lower echelons of the society. This awareness is easily accessed from the media, whether in television, movies, or newspaper accounts of Washington politics. Further, structural racism in the United States is not wholly at variance from what many West Indians have experienced at home. There, though race is far less prominent, the history of colonialism still lingers in the greater likelihood of whites or light-skinned blacks to be in the top positions of the society. As Waters (1999a) noted, race does not determine socioeconomic position in the countries of the Caribbean, but it is often correlated with it.

In contrast, Waters wrote that "almost everyone we spoke to was unprepared for the degree of interpersonal racism they encountered in the United States—the overarching concern with race in every encounter, the constant role race plays in everyday life, and the subtle experiences that are tinged with racial suspicions and overtones" (1999a, 153). Whether in looking for housing, seeking a job, hailing a cab, or interacting with people in stores and on the street, West Indians encounter discriminatory treatment in a way that they have not experienced before. In some instances the treatment is blatant and strident. Bobb quoted an interview with an immigrant from St. Vincent who had experienced the ugly face of American racism: "So when coming to American, and they were calling you 'black,' [saying] 'West Indians come from a tree,' 'You're a monkey,'. . . . You work in a hospital and they would spit on you and tell you don't touch them and tell you to take your black so and so away from them" (2001, 218). For men in particular, Butterfield suggested, racism can mean bodily harm. As one Jamaican man told her, "that is what separates us from the women. I know that they go through some things, but I don't think that they have a daily sense that their lives are in danger like we do" (2004, 305–6). Some forms of discrimination are more subtle, such as the cab that doesn't stop, the department store clerk who is suddenly too busy, or the coworker who never joins a table for lunch. Yet, even in this more ambiguous form, the racism is usually recognized for what it is.

Interviews with West Indian immigrants suggest several strategies for dealing with the prejudice and discrimination that they experience (Bobb 2001; Vickerman 1999). Bobb saw two principal means of dealing with racism in the first-generation immigrants that she interviewed—either ignoring the problems or avoiding the problems. Ignoring racism, in her categorization, includes denial that the acts of discrimination are even troublesome. Alternatively, a person may accept discrimination as something that is part of the culture, to be endured but not to be distracted by. Avoidance, for Bobb, represents a more active choice to not put oneself in situations in which prejudice can be anticipated. As one woman told her, "It doesn't bother me because I don't invite them to my house" (2001, 221). Other respondents talked of avoiding white businesses or seeking neighborhoods where whites did not live. In the extreme, however, this strategy of avoidance often precipitated a return to the Caribbean, suggesting that avoidance is difficult to maintain in a society so thoroughly penetrated by racism.

Vickerman (1999) postulated a more differentiated set of coping strategies, which takes into account the active or passive nature of both the actions directed toward the immigrant and his or her reaction to that action. Reactions to discriminatory treatment will vary, Vickerman suggested, depending on whether the treatment itself is overt, such as a physical attack or direct insult, or if it is more subtle, such as refusing to give service or denying promotions or housing. In both cases, however, immigrants often react with active forms of coping. "West Indians, in general, have gained a reputation for being outspoken in the face of discrimination," he claimed, citing several examples both from his own interviews and from published accounts of earlier West Indian immigration (99). In the face of overt discriminatory treatment, the immigrant might confront the agent of discrimination, challenging the accusations or protesting biased decisions. The strength of this reaction will vary, however, depending on characteristics of the target. A threat by the police, for example, is likely to evoke a more subdued reply, which Vickerman termed a "pragmatic" response—though such a reaction is not necessarily effective, as recent well-publicized and tragic incidents in New York of immigrants being killed by police who were operating under false and biased assumptions have shown.

When actions from the target are more subtle or institutionalized, such as being slow to give service, passing one over for promotion, or avoiding overtures of friendship, assertive strategies take a somewhat different form. In these cases, the active strategy involves some initiated action on the part of the immigrant, raising issues or interjecting oneself into a situation where one was being ignored. Thus the worker who is being ignored by his white colleagues can suggest a shared coffee break, or the worker who has not been promoted can raise the issue with her employer. Such strategies of course offer no guarantee that the outcome will be reversed; short-term attempts at assertion may evolve into longer-term states of resignation.

Resignation represents a more passive strategy, resembling the forms of ignoring affronts and racist practices that Bobb (2001) heard from some of her interviewees. The strategy here is also one of caution, avoiding areas in which one suspects trouble will occur, seeking out places where other West Indians will be, and defining one's territory in racial terms that will allow some feeling of safety and security.

No single strategy necessarily prevails, and Vickerman's fourfold schema (of active or passive actions by the agent and active or passive reactions by the immigrant) should not be taken as a personality typology. Immigrants will negotiate their lives depending on the contexts and circumstances they encounter. Relationships in one domain, such as work, may be quite different from relationships in another domain, such as church, even if both are racially integrated settings. Strategies will also evolve over time, and in fact Vickerman speculated that perhaps all the coping strategies he described are short-term remedies, used in the early stages of an immigrant's experience in the United States but replaced by a more long-term sense of racial consciousness.

In this developing racial consciousness, the West Indian immigrant comes to expect that interpersonal discrimination will occur—not only does racism structure the economic and political system, but it also inescapably permeates day-to-day experience. Further, as Vickerman (1999) contended, racial consciousness involves an increased sense of pessimism with regard to the possibilities of change toward a truly color-blind society. "Not in my lifetime" becomes the operating assumption.

Generation is one of the markers of this shift in expectations. As Waters observed:

> The first generation is likely to believe that while racism exists in the United States, it can be overcome or circumvented through hard work, perseverance, and the right values and attitudes. The second generation experiences racism and discrimination constantly and develops perceptions of the overwhelming influence of race on their lives and life chances that differ from their parents' views. (1999a, 309)

According to Vilna Bobb and Averill Clarke (2001), both first- and second-generation West Indian immigrants believe in the value of education as a means to advancement. Yet for the second generation, these authors argued, education is considered a necessary but not necessarily a sufficient tool. Unlike their parents, who believe that education guarantees successful outcomes, second-generation immigrants are more fully aware of the ways in which racism can affect them personally. This is not to say that first-generation immigrants are not aware of racism. Experiences with it are almost immediately part of the West Indian experience, and the kinds of coping mechanisms that Bobb and Vickerman have described are adopted quickly in order to deal with it. In my own studies, using a measure of sensitivity to race-based discrimination developed by Mendoza-Denton and his colleagues (2002), we have found no differences between first- and second-generation black immigrants in their expectations and concerns about discrimination. However, the realization that one cannot easily escape pervasive discrimination on the basis of one's own merits develops more slowly. Further, second-generation immigrants are likely to tune in to some of the more subtle aspects of the American educational status, one in which different colleges have different levels of resources and different statuses and where, as a consequence, degrees from different schools have different amounts of cachet.

In discussing the differences between first- and second-generation West Indian immigrants, Bobb and Clarke (2001) pointed to three factors. First, they suggest that the first generation continue to use country of origin as a reference point, keeping themselves at some distance from the racism of the United States. Second, first-generation immigrants are more likely to remain within ethnic enclaves and West Indian networks, thus avoiding many potentially unpleasant encounters and restricting their social comparisons. Finally, Bobb and Clarke suggested that first-generation West Indian immigrants can use their foreignness as a marker, leading others to see them as distinctive from and presumably more favorable than U.S.-born African Americans. This latter feature in particular suggests the kinds of psychological work in which immigrants necessarily engage, shaping both self-representations and self-presentations in ways that can be both protective and facilitating.

GENERATIONAL CHANGE AND STEREOTYPE THREAT

Discussions of difference between first- and second-generation Afro-Caribbean immigrants often suggest that these two groups have distinctive orientations, based on their particular experiences and encounters with racism in the society. The psychological underpinnings of these suggested distinctions have not previously been explored. Yet if the explanation for group differences in, for example, educational outcomes or employment patterns is to be interpreted in terms of coping strategies and self-representations, then it is necessary to explore these psychological processes more fully. Elements of identity, as discussed, are important not just as a way of characterizing and differentiating immigrants from one another, but also for how they are linked to other choices and behaviors of the individual immigrant.

As a social psychologist, my goal is to understand, at the level of individual process, what happens that leads to differences between first- and second-generation West Indians. What does it mean to use foreignness as a marker and does it work? Can we demonstrate, in convincing ways, that something different is operating for these two generations? And, most important for the study I will describe, can differences between generations be found, not just in comparisons of parents and their children, but as well between cohorts of the same age who nonetheless differ in immigration status, some having come to the United States with their family and others born in the United States to parents who emigrated years before? We have found that psychological issues of ethnic identification are critically involved in the answers to these questions. Phenomena already analyzed solely in terms of the demographic marker of generation (that is, place of birth and time of arrival) can be more fully understood if psychological processes are taken into account.

As we have seen, many discussions of West Indian immigrants stress the negative impact of encounters with racism in the United States—not just structural racism, which defines the position of one's group in the prevailing hierarchy, but also interpersonal racism, which has an impact on everyday encounters. The degree to which an awareness of discrimination, both understood at the group level and experienced at the individual level, is taken as relevant to oneself—particularly in areas considered important to oneself—is an important predictor of how one reacts to situations in which the identity category is seen as relevant. Awareness of the stereotypes of others can affect one's performance, as the increasing mass of work on stereotype threat has shown. As discussed in chapter 4, an ever-increasing body of research compellingly shows that when negative stereotypes about a group's abilities and potential are "in the air," they can undermine the performance of members of that group. Particularly relevant to present concerns are studies of stereotype threat that compare the performance of African American students to that of white students (Steele and Aronson 1995). Here the data show that when the negative stereotype of black intellectual ability is made salient, by characterizing the test as diagnostic versus nondiagnostic, African American students perform more poorly on an achievement task than whites do. By contrast, when ethnicity is not salient, the two groups perform at equivalent levels, after adjusting for SAT scores.

Drawing on these studies, we wanted to know whether some of the differences between first- and second-generation West Indians that have been observed in educational and occupational outcome data and suggested in ethnographic studies might be at least partially explained by a greater susceptibility to stereotype threat on the part of the second generation (Deaux et al. 2005). With more time in the United States, second-generation black immigrants will have had more exposure to the negative stereotypes about black intellectual capability, and those stereotypes might be more likely to be salient when they are engaged in intellectual tasks—particularly if they have begun to identify as African American.

In exploring this possibility, we started with a comparison between first- and second-generation immigrants, a typical point of reference for sociologists and demographers. In addition, however, we wanted to look at more psychological processes that might be at work—specifically, at the ethnic identification of the immigrants as it varied from maintaining a connection with the country of origin or shifted to identifying more with American blacks. It seemed reasonable to hypothesize that those immigrants who identify as African Americans would be more likely to see stereotypes about African Americans as relevant than immigrants who continue to identify with their country of origin. Accordingly, we predicted that the generational differences between first- and second-generation West Indian immigrants are associated, at least in part, with differential susceptibility to stereotype threat effects. Specifically, we predicted that first-generation West Indian immigrants are protected from or insensitive to stereotype threat, and that they will thus not show a performance decrement when stereotypes are salient, that is, when a test is described as diagnostic of ability. In contrast, we predicted that second-generation West Indian immigrants will show the same pattern of stereotype threat effects typically evidenced in African American respondents, that is, decrements in performance when a test is labeled diagnostic as opposed to nondiagnostic. In statistical terms, we predicted a significant interaction between stereotype threat condition and generation.

A parallel set of predictions was made in terms of subjective ethnic identification. Specifically, we hypothesized that identification as an African American makes the West Indian immigrant susceptible to stereotype threat effects. In contrast, those who continue to define themselves primarily in terms of their ethnic-national origin should be protected from the effects of stereotype threat. Again, the prediction is for an interaction effect, in this case between stereotype threat condition and ethnic identification (West Indian versus African American).

The participants in our study were all students in the City University of New York, a system that includes more than twenty colleges and universities. Earlier we had obtained questionnaire data from 270 students of West Indian background. Of these, 145 were first generation, and had on the average come to the United States when they were fourteen years old. The other 125 were second generation, and had been born in the United States to parents who had immigrated from countries in the Caribbean. From this larger sample, we recruited seventy-five students, equally balanced between first and second generation and representing a range of ethnic identification, from strongly West Indian to strongly African American. On the whole, however, these students were more likely to identify as West Indian, as indicated earlier.

The procedures for studies of stereotype threat effects are really quite simple. What is striking is how strong the effects of a simple instructional set can be on performance. In our study, the experimenters read one of two sets of instructions aloud to participants as they waited to begin the test, which was a set of twenty-seven questions taken from a GRE English examination preparation book. In one case, which was the condition in which stereotype threat was made salient, the instructions stressed that the test was a diagnostic assessment of the student's verbal abilities and limi-

Figure 7.5   Performance of West Indian Immigrants in Stereotype
              Threat Study

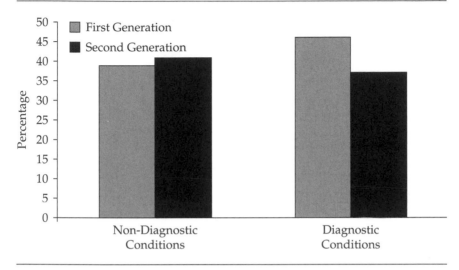

Source: Deaux et al. (2005).

tations. In the other case, the test was described as an exercise in test development, evaluating the test rather than individual ability. The only difference between the test-taking conditions for the two groups of students was
thus the emphasis. Numerous studies of the stereotype threat phenomenon have shown that if a test is described as diagnostic, then the awareness
of negative stereotypes about one's group will come into play. In contrast,
if the test is seen to be irrelevant to one's ability, then those same stereotypes are apparently not salient.

In these studies, the impact of stereotype threat is indicated by the student's performance on the test, specifically the percentage of questions that
are answered correctly. How did the West Indian students do under these
two different conditions? Figure 7.5 shows the results of our study. Although
neither generation nor stereotype threat condition on its own made a difference, the two-way interaction between generation and diagnostic condition on performance was significant in an analysis of variance test (F (1,67)
= 4.59, p = .036). When the test was nondiagnostic, there was no difference
between the first- and second-generation students. When it stressed academic ability, however, and presumably made stereotypes salient, second-
generation students showed a significant decrease in performance compared
to the first-generation students.

How is this generational difference related to the ethnic identification of the students? Perhaps not surprisingly, the two variables are related (r = .43, p < .001 in this sample), and thus we cannot completely separate them, particularly in a sample of this size. However, we did conduct a separate analysis, now dividing participants on the basis of their ethnic identification rather than of their generational status. As noted earlier, ethnic identification scores in our sample were skewed toward identification as West Indian. Accordingly, in the analysis we divided the sample on the basis of stronger or weaker West Indian identification, such that those who said they were either definitely or mostly West Indian were contrasted with those who said they were either definitely or mostly African American or that they endorsed the two labels equally.

Results of this analysis showed the anticipated pattern, although the interaction was not as strong as the previous analysis (F (1,65) = 2.50, p = .12). Students whose ethnic identification had shifted toward African American showed more evidence of a stereotype threat effect, performing worse (38 percent correct) when the test was labeled diagnostic than when it was not (42 percent). In contrast, students who identified strongly as West Indians performed better when the test was diagnostic (44 percent correct) than when it was not (39 percent). This pattern supports the hypothesis that students more closely identified with African American will be more susceptible to the effects of stereotype threat. Further, we can speculate that if the two groups of students were more sharply differentiated on the basis of ethnic identity—that is, if we had a group of students as polarized in adopting an African American identity as the students claiming a West Indian identity—then the observed effects would have been even stronger.

Recent work by Teceta Thomas (2003) has also indicated differences in the ways that first- and second-generation West Indian immigrants respond to challenges. In her work, students were placed in an experimental situation in which the likelihood that a judge would be discriminatory toward them was varied. In comparison to groups of second-generation black immigrants and native-born African Americans, first-generation immigrants had especially high expectations of their success when they learned that they would be judged by someone who was highly likely to be prejudiced against minorities.[6]

Findings such as these help elucidate the tensions and misunderstandings between first-generation parents and second-generation students that Butterfield (2004) reported. The parents believed that the schools were fair playing fields, grounds where their children could achieve as much as they were capable of doing, in large part because their ethnic background made them "different" and should make them proud of themselves. The children, in contrast, tried "to convince their parents that they were not actually better than their peers" (2004, 298). The parents were holding on to a positive West Indian identity that they expected their children to maintain as well, whereas the children were identifying with their African American classmates—and as a result, making themselves candidates for the negative consequences of stereotype threat.

It is important to stress that in the studies described in this section, generation does not mean age differences. In each study, comparisons were made between students of the same age and in the same academic setting. What differed was not their age, but the social context in which they had grown up—in the case of second-generation students, being in the United States from birth, and in the first generation, having come to the United States later, typically in their early teen or pre-teen years. We still have a great deal to learn about the nature of these contexts and what experiences are critical for psychological development. What is certain, however, is that immigration for Afro-Caribbeans and other black immigrants is a dynamic and ongoing process that cannot be captured by demographic labels alone.

ON SPECIFICITY AND GENERALITY

In detailing the West Indian case, I've tried to show how all the parts of the model in figure 7.1 come into play—the historical circumstances, the current attitudinal climate, the situational demands, and the concerns and negotiations of the immigrants. The dynamic interplay of these factors takes a unique shape for each immigrant group. For West Indians, a critical element of this dynamic is the historical and present manifestations of racism in the United States—and, though not covered in any detail, in most of the other Anglo countries that have been destinations for Caribbean immigration. Yet even here, although negative attitudes toward black immigrants are to a large extent common across the countries, some differences in experience result because of the different demographics and history of the United States versus, for example, Britain, as Foner has described (2005).

Being black in the United States structures a set of immediate experiences as well as more long-term opportunities that influence the ways in which immigrants will negotiate their paths in the new territory. Even more specifically, being a black male has different consequences than being a black female (Foner 2005). Being a black immigrant influences social comparison processes, offering the native-born African American as a seemingly natural point of reference—a reference point used by others as well. Further, as the work on stereotype threat has shown, alternative categories and meanings available in the cultural "air" need to be dealt with in some fashion, determining a relationship between self and other that will define the terms of engagement.

Another relatively unique aspect of the West Indian case is the proximity of the country of origin combined with, in the case of those emigrating from former British colonies, a facility with the official language of the English-speaking host country. Compared to Asia, for example, communication and travel to one's country of origin are easier, as is maintaining a sense of dual citizenship or transnational reality. Additionally, in contrast to the Mexican immigrants who are even closer geographically to the United States, English as a first language is a tremendous advantage to the West Indians. Although their Caribbean accents will mark them as nonnatives, the marker can also allow West Indians to benefit from a relatively positive stereotype.

For groups other than Afro-Caribbeans, the basic framework of figure 7.1 is equally applicable, although each level of analysis will differ according to the group in question. Attitudes and stereotypes exist for most immigrant groups, for example, though the specifics differ, and white immigrant groups generally benefit from the differences. Identity negotiation is a process that can be charted in all immigrant groups, but the options and the motivations for different identity choices will also differ. In our own data, for example, we find very different patterns when we look at groups of Asian, Latino, or white immigrants, compared to the black immigrant results described here.

It is also important to stress that neither ethnic group nor generation should be considered in essentialist terms. Although we may find differences between generations or among ethnic groups—as we do, in so many of our studies—these differences should not lead to conclusions about the nature of the groups per se. It is instead imperative that the context of experience be in the foreground of any analysis, pressing us to look at all of the factors in a particular setting that affect the immigrant experience and shape the choices the immigrant makes. These considerations are essential to any future analyses, whether research or policy is the focus.

Chapter Eight | Envisioning an Agenda for a Social Psychology of Immigration

In the opening chapter, I recalled Oscar Handlin's classic work *The Uprooted*—an account of the immigrant experience that focused on the immigrants. Although his perspective was a welcome shift from discussions that looked only at the impact of immigrants on the societies they entered, the picture he painted was bleak. Handlin focused his analysis on first-generation immigrants, typically those who came from villages in Europe and moved to the cities of the eastern United States. "Always, the start was in the village," he began (1951, 8), tracing a course from the agricultural fields of their homeland to the cold and unsupportive climate of American cities. In this new world, Handlin contended, "the attributes the immigrants held in high esteem were not those that brought success in America" (80), where pressures toward competition and achievement outweighed the value of community. "In this world the notion of improvement is delusive," he continued: "the free structure of American life permitted them with few restraints to go their own way, but under the shadow of a consciousness that they would never belong" (285). Only in a brief look toward the second generation in the closing chapter of the book did Handlin find what reflects a ray of hope, as he gave the following words to a son of an immigrant: "We will justify their pitiable struggle for dignity and meaning by extending it in our lives toward an end they had not the opportunity to envision" (273).

Until recently, psychological analyses of immigration began with a gloomy set of assumptions as well. The central topic was acculturative stress, described as "one of the most obvious and frequently reported consequences of acculturation" (Berry 1990, 224) and characterized by some combination of social disintegration and personal distress. Clinical

203

frameworks were most often brought to bear, and the mental health of the individual immigrant served as the key outcome of interest.

Negative outcomes are surely one part of the story. Yet as I hope has become apparent throughout the preceding chapters, a full account of the psychology of immigration reveals much more complexity, more variability and more agency on the part of the immigrants themselves. The situations that immigrants confront vary widely, from each other and from the context that Handlin described. Countries themselves, and the United States in particular, are far more diverse, the result of decades of steadily increasing immigrant flows. Ethnic enclaves, family networks, and greater familiarity with the country prior to movement give the immigrant more access to resources. Possibilities for collective action are more apparent, in some instances, than they were in earlier analyses. Further, the dynamics of individual identity negotiation show the multiple ways in which immigrants can combine old and new, nationality and ethnicity, in distinctive forms that can contribute to cultural competence and psychological growth. Development and innovation move to the foreground in this approach, and acculturative stress is just one of many possible outcomes.

From this broader perspective, the work of social psychologists can both relate and contribute to the work in other fields of immigration research, offering a way to connect social structure to individual functioning and helping chart the ongoing and evolving patterns of immigrant life. The critical mediating role played by social psychological processes allows us to fill in gaps, providing accounts of how it is to be an immigrant.

THE FRAMEWORK OF ANALYSIS: A REPRISE

The social psychological model that I first introduced in chapter 1 (see figure 1.1) and used again in chapter 7 for the specific case of Afro-Caribbean immigration offers a working framework for moving forward. Each of the three levels in this model is essential, I believe, to derive a full understanding of the immigrant experience—not simply as a static account of occurrence but as a dynamic and ongoing process that takes many forms and has many ramifications.

The macro level of analysis is most familiar to those who study immigration, including as its exemplars both policy analyses and demographic summaries. Although this information is clearly essential to understanding the patterns of immigration, it is not enough. As Suzanne Model has observed, "census analysis cannot uncover human motives" (2001, 79). Nor can such analyses alone tell us how a society views and evaluates the movement of people and the shaping of policy. Other more sociocultural elements are needed, at this macro level of analyses and at the meso and micro levels.

The social representations that members of a society hold are fundamental. As I discussed in chapter 2, cultural metaphors such as the melting pot or the salad bowl become the ground on which more specific attitudes and stereotypes take shape. Within the United States, the melting pot has a nearly century-long history, a record prolonged in part by the ambiguity and multiple meanings that the concept connotes (Gleason 1964). In other countries, other representations prevail, such as the diversity position of Canada or the "we are all French" position of France.

As the creation of people who are in turn influenced by them, social representations exist as both realities and potentialities, subject to change and re-creation as circumstances change. As just one example, the events of September 11 have lead to some turns in the immigration discourse within the United States, as immigration is linked to terrorists, particularly by those seeking to direct the course of political debate. Thus, President George W. Bush, in his State of the Union address in January 2005, offered the following contrasting images as he described the need for new immigration legislation: "We should not be content with laws that punish hard-working people who want only to provide for their families. . . . It is time for an immigration policy . . . that closes the border to drug dealers and terrorists."

One man does not a social representation make, even if that man is president of a media-saturated country in which messages are often strategically controlled, and it remains to be seen how deeply the imagery of immigrant as potential terrorist will penetrate commonly held representations. What is clear from that quote, however, and documented elsewhere (for example, Bean and Stevens 2003; Mizrahi 2005) is the ambivalence that many people feel toward immigrants—on the one hand, seeing them as exemplars of determination and hard work to make a better life for themselves and their families and, on the other, as a threat to a way of life, to personal security (both economic and now—with the introduction of terror themes—physical as well), and to the common good. This attitudinal ambivalence exists not only at the macro level of representation and policy but at the meso level of social interactions as well. More specifically, social representations take root at the level of social interchange as the product becomes part of the process of daily discourse.

It is perhaps at this mid-level of analysis, the intersection of macro forces and individual cognitions and feelings, that social psychology has the most to offer. Here is where the abstractions of the cultural mind become realized in the actions of individuals and the groups to which they belong. The dynamics of interactions—between immigrant and host, between individual and group, between one group of immigrants and another—constitute the lived process of the immigrant experience, and the experience of all whose lives are in some way connected to the introduction of new members to the larger community.

Previous analyses of immigration have often focused on the direct path between macro and micro, pointing to the societal level events and describing their consequences for the individual. It is only by introducing the mediational processes that characterize the meso level, however, that we can see how such events are incorporated and transformed in the lives of individuals. These meso-level analyses are a way for us to understand the variations in immigrant experience—why some people thrive and others falter, why some assimilate and others remain in immigrant enclaves. Consider the conditions of prejudice and stigmatization (see chapter 4) as just one example. For the immigrant who experiences these conditions, adapting to the new country will require developing some means to deal with outgroup discrimination, either as an individual or as part of a group. The phenomenon of reactive ethnicity that Portes and Rumbaut describe is one example: "Direct experiences of discrimination trigger a reaction away from things American and toward reinforcement of the original immigrant identities" (2001, 187). Here the specific treatment that a person encounters, itself shaped in meso-level terms by particular attitudes and stereotypes and emerging from macro-level contexts of representation and policy, becomes the proximal cause of individual identity work. Without a careful analysis of this level of interpersonal process, it would be difficult to describe the link between general contexts and particularized psychological phenomena.

At the micro level of analysis, where expectations and motivations, attitudes and values, and identity itself reside, the individual immigrant experience becomes most sharply defined. Here is where we need to ask the questions that prompted Handlin more than fifty years ago when he attempted to view immigration through the eyes of those who had made the journey. Gordon (1964) was in many ways prescient in recognizing that the umbrella term of assimilation contained several not necessarily correlated processes, involving both immigrant and host. Even earlier, Park's definition of assimilation (1930) suggested subtle psychological processes at work. In their eras, however, social science did not have the theoretical tools (or the methodological capabilities) to push the analyses further. Our understanding of psychological process is far more sophisticated now than it was then, and we can bring a great many concepts and theoretical frameworks to bear. Understanding the various elements of identification, for example, as well as the possibilities for combinations and alternations, allows us to think about processes of assimilation and incorporation in a much more complicated but at the same time more veridical and representative way. Theories of identity allow us to see how the political concept of nation-state must be taken to the level of psychological functioning in order to explain activity, whether of individual negotiation or of grass-roots movements (see Upegui-Hernandez 2005). Analyses of collective identification create a language whereby the individual actor is understood in terms of a social context, both immediate and distal, that is also subject to development and change.

This model of social psychological analysis is elastic and broadly applicable. Although I have, perhaps inevitably, drawn most heavily on the U.S. context for my references and examples, the framework can be used as a template for immigration analyses at any place and time. At the macro level, it is essential that the conditions in any particular country be specified, because the history, the demographics, the policy, and the prevailing representations will certainly vary across time and place. These conditions in turn shape the possibilities and conditions characterized by the meso level of analysis, which in turn sets a context for micro-level concerns. At these two levels, content and context specificity will surely be observed. At the same time, I believe that we can see some commonalities and regularities at these levels as well, as fundamental features of human experience play out on their particular stages.

PSYCHOLOGY AND POLICY: WHAT CAN WE CONTRIBUTE?

Greater understanding of the psychological aspects of the immigration experience, as well as recognition of the interplay between levels of analyses that the model offers, can provide new points of entry for interpretation and for developing policies related to immigration issues. Numerous examples are possible, but let me just detail a few.

Voter Propositions in California

In California during the 1990s, voters approved two propositions that dealt with the needs and conditions of immigrants (Portes and Rumbaut 2001). Proposition 187 denied some social and health care services to undocumented immigrants and their children; Proposition 227 provided for one-year English immersion classes for immigrant children and abolished remedial classes. In their analysis of the politics of these referenda, Portes and Rumbaut (2001) described what they saw as two distinct ideologies underlying the propositions, one they termed intransigent nativism and the other forceful assimilation. The first they defined as a position that "seeks to stop all or most immigration, send unauthorized immigrants back as quickly as possible, and put immigrants who remain in the United States on notice that they occupy an inferior position, ineligible for the privileges of citizens" (2001, 271). The second they defined as seeking "to mainstream immigrants and their children as far and as swiftly as possible" (271).

Both positions find their roots in material discussed in this book. Intransigent nativism clearly expresses the ideology of social dominance, with its endorsement of status hierarchies and the maintenance of white privilege (see chapter 3). Interestingly, as characterized by Portes and Rumbaut, it also marks a rejection of the dominant representation of a melting pot. With this positioning, adherents of nativism conveniently ignore the long immigration history of the United States, and perhaps their own family histories as well, and instead echo the nativist discourse of the early twentieth century. Such a discourse, to the extent that it becomes widely shared, may signal the emergence of alternative representations with different consequences for policy and practice. As played out in California via the ballot propositions, intransigent nativism may also reflect more specific group stereotypes, in this case specifically attached to Mexican immigrants, both documented and undocumented. Samuel Huntington's recent book (2004) offers another example of this nativist position, using Mexican immigrants as his prime target. The intersection of general attitudes about immigration and these more targeted beliefs about certain kinds of immigrants become the site for discriminatory practice to emerge.

Forceful assimilation has a different attitudinal base. Here general beliefs about desirable strategies of acculturation (see chapters 3 and 6) are combined with implicit theories of identification, specifically a model that rejects the possibility of dual (or multiple) identification in favor of an either-or position (see chapters 5 and 6). From this stance, language immersion programs in the school are considered the most appropriate way to move immigrant children from one identity position to another. At the same time, such programs give the always implicit and often explicit message that the language of the parents is to be disparaged and discarded—a direct assault on what might be considered family values of maintaining culture and tradition. In devaluing the position of the parents in the belief that total assimilation is the only desired end state, a community can weaken ties within families and negate the potential contributions that ethnic communities, acting as recognized and valued collectives, might make to the greater good. Children within the schools can suffer as well, Portes and Rumbaut (2001) suggested, as both expectations and achievement may be dampened by the limited bilingualism that results from immersion programs.

In contrasting the attitudinal base of these two California propositions, I want to make the point that it is important to uncover the ideologies and assumptions that underlie antagonism toward immigrants, as immigrant-related discussions and practices are neither supported by the same belief systems nor driven by the same motivations. Policies are often supported by implicit and unexamined assumptions; by holding these implicit theories up to the scrutiny of empirical assessment, more informed policy can emerge. A more articulated analysis of psychological process should provide a better starting point for any planned interventions, whatever form those interventions might take.

Skill Discounting

Employment and integration into a country's labor force depends on a decision by an employer to hire. The form and basis of these decisions clearly vary, from a general willingness to take anyone who applies to a more formalized and extensive evaluation system. In the former case, legal statutes that require an employer to have documentation of immigrant status are often ignored by employers who want cheap labor and are willing to look the other way when questions of documentation are raised. The extent of this practice in the United States was made vivid by a recent report (Porter 2005) that illegal immigrants are contributing as much as $7 billion per year to the Social Security system, paying in money they will never receive when they leave the labor pool.

At higher job levels, evaluation is often more systematic, relying on some combination of past record and present impression. Considerable work over the years in industrial, organizational, and social psychology has testified to the potential sources of bias in these processes. More recently, concerned specifically with the ability of immigrants to enter the labor force at levels appropriate to their skills, Esses and her colleagues have shown how basic elements such as the site of one's educational degree can negatively affect the outcomes of immigrant applicants (Esses, Dietz, and Bhardwaj 2006). In their Canadian-based studies, these investigators looked first at available data suggesting that employers favored applicants whose educational training was based in Canada. The existence of this differential hiring pattern does not in itself prove unfair discrimination, as it is possible that Canadian education is truly superior to alternative forms, and that potential employees who have experienced that better system have more skills to bring to an employer than do those who have been trained elsewhere.

Through the use of experimental methods, however, it is possible to control for these differences, presenting identical credentials from candidates who differ in their ethnic and immigrant background. Differences that might emerge in such controlled conditions can then be directly linked to assumptions about immigrants and their experiences, rather than to actual differences in skill level. This is exactly the work that Esses and her colleagues have done (Esses, Dietz, and Bhardwaj 2006). In their study, Canadian citizens were asked to evaluate résumés of applicants for a position as a psychometrist, whose job would include the evaluation of neuropsychological tests. Three variations were included in the study: the applicant was described as being born and trained either in Canada, in Britain, or in India. In all cases, however, the candidate was named Anita Singh and was said to be proficient in English, French, and Hindi. Judgments of the candidate were linked to a measure of attitudes toward immigrants that the investigators had assessed earlier. The results of the study were quite clear, showing an interactive effect of a person's general attitudes and the specific evaluative task. For those participants whose attitudes toward immigrants were more positive, the credentials of the candidates were considered to be equivalent, whatever their country of origin. In contrast, participants whose attitudes toward immigrants were less favorable found less to recommend in the credentials of the applicant who went to school in India, even though on paper they were identical to the British-trained and Canadian-trained applicants. Thus, in a classical social psychological demonstration of person-situation interaction, both a personal disposition and a situational "justification" were required for the anti-immigrant prejudice to manifest itself. The immigrant from Britain was not devalued because of her immigration status, and in fact tended to be evaluated more favorably than the Canadian applicant, perhaps reflecting the history of Canada's place in the British Empire.

This experimental demonstration of skill discounting provides important evidence of one channel through which discrimination against immigrants may occur. As an intervention strategy, based on these results, one might want to inform employers of the ways in which subtle evaluation biases work. The geographical origin of credentials, in and of itself, should not be sufficient grounds for devaluation. It is certainly possible that educational institutions can be unequal in the skills that they instill in their graduates. Those differences need to be established, however, rather than assumed and influenced by ethnic prejudice. The contribution of the experimental study is not to prove that discrimination is the sole explanation for differential hiring patterns, but rather to establish the possibility that discrimination occurs and to point to strategies that can reduce and even eliminate that possibility from the work setting.

Stereotype Threat and Academic Performance

In chapter 7, I described a study in which stereotype threat affected the performance of some West Indian immigrants on an academically oriented test. The important message from that study is the critical importance of cultural conditions as they affect individual outcomes. Prior analyses of West Indian immigrants have often sought explanations in some essential characteristic of the West Indian that distinguishes them from native-born African Americans—for example, higher motivation, a greater value placed on education, or some intangibles of British heritage. Yet in our study, first- and second-generation immigrants, whose experience in the United States differed by less than a dozen years, showed significant differences in performance. Second-generation immigrants showed patterns just like those of African Americans in nonimmigrant samples. Thus the explanatory focus needs to be shifted to the experiences that black immigrants have in the United States and the effect that living in that discriminatory context can have on one's identity and experiences.

As the findings on skill discounting also show, employers need to be aware of the possibilities of discrimination in ways that they may not have considered before, and companies need to put policies and practices in place that safeguard against the possibility of discrimination. Being a West Indian may be a positively biasing factor in initial job selection, as Kasinitz (1992) observed, but on-the-job treatment may be more influenced by just being black. Similar to the case of gender, the correction of initial selection bias is only one step in a process that demands vigilance and continued sensitivity to the subtle ways in which bias and prejudice can operate (Fiske et al. 1991; Biernat, Crosby, and Williams 2004).

It seems quite likely that the pattern of findings that we obtained when comparing first- and second-generation West Indian immigrants would also emerge in studies of other groups in other countries. For Turkish children in Germany, for example, or North African children in France, increasing recognition of the negative regard of others toward one's group could be the source of stereotype threat, dissociation of public and private sources of regard, and other conditions that would create generational differences in groups with the same ethnic background. From a policy perspective, these situational sources of influence need to be brought to the forefront of any analysis, overcoming dispositional biases to find the major explanation for a group's outcomes in attributes of the people themselves.

DIRECTIONS FOR RESEARCH

I hope that I have presented a convincing case for the contributions that a social psychological analysis can make. At the same time, it should be clear that the inquiry is still in its early stages. The elements of figure 1.1 offer less a theory and more a general road map or directory of where and how we need to look. Within these broad categories, many more specific questions need to be posed and many more insights are yet to be derived. The detailing of all the possibilities awaits the active involvement of the next generation of researchers. But as a marker of this time and place, let me suggest a few promising areas of investigation.

Social Representations and Attitudes

At the macro level of analysis, social representations of immigration serve as cultural summaries, often vivid in their imagery and far-reaching in their implications. Within the United States, the melting pot has dominated the discourse for almost a century. Yet while the term has persisted, the meanings of that term are less constant. Along with the continuing ambiguity that Gleason (1964) observed more that forty years ago, one senses shifts in the applicability of the term as well as the emergence of other metaphors that speak to different images of immigration. In a recent contentious analysis of American culture, Samuel Huntington (2004) rejected both the melting pot and the tossed salad as appropriate representations, arguing instead for "an Anglo-Protestant tomato soup to which immigration adds celery, croutons, spices, parsley, and other ingredients that enrich and diversify the taste, but which are absorbed into what remains fundamentally tomato soup." I doubt that "tomato soup" will have the cachet or the longevity that the melting pot has shown; nonetheless, its variation on a theme testifies to the attraction of metaphorical representations as expressions of cultural phenomena.

A representational analysis of the meanings associated with these varying images, as evidenced in the media, in political discourse, or in everyday language, could be highly informative, particularly if that analysis were done longitudinally and could capture the ebb and flow of particular associations. Just as the Leo Chavez (2001) analysis of magazine covers revealed trends in the positive and negative images associated with immigrants over thirty-five years of U.S. history (see chapter 3), so could a more detailed representational analysis tell a story of changing norms and values.

An expansion of such an analysis to other nations, where different social representations prevail, would be informative as well. The melting pot as metaphor had its origin in the United States, although many countries in Latin America, for example, have a concept of mestizaje that refers to race blending (Telles 2004). Other countries hold on to other images, consistent with their immigration practices and policies, that could be more or less durable and more or less accepted. Despite the technical difficulties of equating sources across countries for a solid comparative analysis, within-country analyses could surely prove illuminating of the images that guide and underlie a country's immigration policies.

At the more specific level of attitudes, a wealth of survey data is available from the frequent national polling studies. Beyond the general information about a population's stance on key issues (for example, should immigration be increased, decreased, or remain the same), many intriguing questions about people's attitudes need to be addressed. Ambivalence, for example, is almost always found when multiple aspects of immigration are explored, yet the sources of that ambivalence and the consequences for behavior are not at all understood. What are the presumably different sources of the positive and negative beliefs that a person can hold simultaneously? What determines whether a positive or a negative belief takes precedence when action is required? Or does the combination of positive and negative lead to unique patterns of behavior, unpredictable by either single position in itself? Here is an area in which some of the fundamental work by social psychologists on attitude structure and attitude change could be brought to bear.

Much more work is also needed to analyze differences in the perceptions of various immigrant groups. With the influx of immigrants from so many different parts of the world (and the variations in these patterns across different receiving countries), how do native-born residents distinguish among immigrants from particular countries, viewing some more positively and others more negatively? In posing this question, it will be important to consider not only the characteristics of the group, but also those historical and structural factors that frame and define a group's experience in the new country. Attributions made to essential characteristics of a group may well be influenced by factors outside the group, and the interplay of group and context needs to be examined.

Intergroup Processes

The analysis of intergroup processes is another area rich with potential. In using this general term, I am really thinking of two levels of analysis: one, as expressed in personal interactions between members of different immigrant groups, and the second as expressed in either cooperative or competitive interactions between one immigrant group and another or an immigrant group and a native group.

Demographic studies of residential segregation provide one basis for estimating the likelihood of interactions between members of different immigrant groups, and rates of intermarriage provide one window on the extent of interaction. In addition to these standard demographic markers that provide information on general outcomes, much could be learned from more detailed analyses of social networks that would chart, at the individual level, the nature of a person's social world. To what extent do networks reach beyond the geographical boundaries of neighborhood? Are there systematic patterns of extension as a function of age, generation, or ethnicity? Can the movement away from ethnic enclaves be foreshadowed by the pattern of an individual's social network? How much does participation in nonethnic settings at work or school contribute to an extended network, and do the domains of work and family overlap or remain separate? Knowing how permeable or constraining those boundaries are would be useful for many endeavors.

People relate to other people in a variety of ways—as friends and allies, as sources of social comparison, and as opponents or competitors for limited resources or symbolic advantage. With few exceptions (for example, Pettigrew et al. 2005) this territory remains uncharted with respect to the immigrant experience. Within the literature on intergroup relations, increasing evidence points to the importance of friendship patterns as a mediator of intergroup attitudes (Pettigrew and Tropp 2000, 2005). That is, having a positive personal relationship with a member of another group is likely to result in more positive attitudes toward that group as a whole. Although these studies have typically focused on groups with some history of animosity, one could also imagine using the paradigm to study relations between two groups with less history but with the potential for conflict, as immigrant groups in similar economic and occupational circumstances might be.

Even when contacts between groups are minimal, a person may use the members of other groups as a source of social comparison, judging his or her own successful incorporation into the new society as measured against the success of another. To the extent that these comparisons are negative, relative deprivation is likely (Tropp and Wright 1999). If the attributions are group-based—for example, a belief that discrimination against one's own group is impeding progress when outcomes are compared to those experienced by members of another more favored group of immigrants—then collective action may well be pursued. In contrast, an unfavorable comparison made at an individual level, perhaps even within one's own group, would situate the deprivation differently and lead to other, more individually directed consequences.

Relationships between groups, as opposed to members of the groups, are another area of interest and potential payoff. Studies of pan-ethnic organizations are one way to think about some of these issues, analyzing processes and outcomes in organizations that define their mission in terms broader than a single ethnic group. In recent years, numerous instances of pan-ethnic organizations have emerged in both the Asian and the Latino communities (Itzigsohn 2005; Okamoto 2005). The success of these organizations depends on the degree to which members of the group can identify with the superordinate structure while, in many instances, continuing to maintain an identification with the original ethnic group. Studies within social psychology (for example, Gaertner et al. 1993; Greenwood 2005) are beginning to explore the conditions of unification (as well as dissension) and pan-ethnic organizations seem a natural locus for further analysis of the processes.

Collective Identity and Its Consequences

In chapters 5 and 6 I emphasized the importance of collective identification as a central feature of the immigrant experience; in an earlier section of this chapter I commented on the relevance of conceptions of identity for ideological beliefs about assimilation. These beliefs about what kind of identity structures are possible and how people can or cannot combine different identities are fundamental to the immigration debate, and the assumption that identity necessarily must be singular or monolithic is often a key point in the argument. Although frequently endorsed, this one-dimensional assumption is not supported by the data that are emerging. Rather, it appears that people can successfully maintain identification with both a country of origin and a country of residence, and that transnational behaviors consistent with this dual identification are feasible as well (Itzigsohn and Giorguli-Saucedo 2005). Although the outlines of this position are becoming increasingly clear, the analysis of identity still calls for a much more careful parsing of identity elements, allowing us to say exactly how identities are combined and which elements are more or less malleable, more or less compatible, and more or less independent of one another. The elements described in chapter 5 represent one point of departure for this analysis, but are surely a starting point rather than a resolution of all the issues involved in multiple identification.

The dynamics of identity negotiation, as opposed to the structural definition of identity, is a topic that also demands more careful thought and exploration. Just as arrival in a new country is simply one step on a path, rather than a definitive state of transition, so do the psychological workings of identification need a more extended time frame. Some forms of ethnic and national identification may persist for a lifetime; others may become remnants of memory rather than active instigators of action. The ebb and flow of identification patterns, as they are influenced by circumstances and events, present a challenge for all who would seek to understand the immigrant experience.

Further, far more work is needed to understand how the collective identifications of individuals are channeled into activity at both the individual and group level. Recent work on the determinants of collective action suggests that identification plays an important role (Deaux et al. 2006; Stürmer and Simon 2004). Thus, although traditional theories of social movement stress a calculation of costs and benefits, more recent analyses are providing convincing evidence that the push of one's identification with the group—the immigrant's ethnic affiliation in this case—also plays a significant role in the likelihood that someone will engage in collective action on behalf of the group. As in other areas of investigation (see Downey, Eccles, and Chatman 2006), identity is proving to be a critical mediator in our understanding of links between belief and action.

FINAL THOUGHTS

At all levels of analysis and in all domains of experience, we need to know more about what it means to be an immigrant. The psychological design, as constructed by both individuals and groups, and the social fabric in which those designs take form are interrelated in ways that are only slowly being appreciated and explored for their fullest implications. Social psychology brings one perspective to this task, and one that I believe has much to offer. But the social psychological elements of explanation can only be one of many voices that speak to the immigrant experience. Its insights and truths will necessarily be interwoven with and dependent on the lessons of historians, economists, political scientists, anthropologists, sociologists, and other social scientists who chart the broad context in which individual and social action is carried out. At the same time, analysis focused on the functioning person within these environments is critical to a full articulation of the functions and processes assumed by more global analyses.

Immigration is a major issue on the agenda of the twenty-first century throughout the world. Not only does immigration change individual lives, but it also necessitates a reconfiguration of all aspects of a society, from the unit of family to the constitution of the state. Not all countries will come to the same resolution of the challenges that immigration poses for a nation. In every country, however, the immigrant experience will be a domain that must be examined and a story that must be told.

Notes |

CHAPTER 2

1. Handlin begins the first chapter of *The Uprooted* with the following statement: "Once I thought to write a history of the immigrants in America. Then I discovered that the immigrants were American history" (1951, 3).

2. A perhaps unintended consequence of the more restrictive immigrant policy was the emergence of the illegal immigrant, a category that had not been necessary in earlier periods of open immigration. Thus, it is not surprising that the establishment of the U.S. Border Patrol dates to 1924 as well (Isbister 1996).

3. For a more detailed analysis of structural forces that both promote immigration and attract immigrants, see Massey (1999).

4. As far as I know, none of the plane hijackers had immigrant status in the United States, but their entry to the United States, via tourist or student visas, was in some cases handled by the U.S. Immigration Service.

5. At the same time, although a majority (57 percent) of those questioned believed that melting pot policies had made the country stronger at the beginning of the twentieth century, respondents were more likely to see the current effects less favorably (27 percent stronger, 44 percent weaker, 23 percent no effect, and 6 percent undecided).

6. It is somewhat ironic that Hayward was herself an American. Thus, just as a British citizen gave the melting pot to the United States, so a citizen of the United States is credited with creating the Canadian metaphor.

7. These percentages have increased in both countries since the Bourhis and Marshall analysis, which was based on 1990 and 1991 Census figures for the United States and Canada, respectively. Current estimates are approximately 31 percent for the United States (Bean et al. 2004) and more than 13 percent for Canada (Esses, personal communication), showing the increase but maintaining the original point that Bourhis and Marshall made.

CHAPTER 3

1. LePen's victory was made possible by a badly split Socialist party opposition. As a result, the 17 percent vote that LePen gained (similar in fact to what he had garnered in the previous election) placed him second in a crowded field.
2. Perhaps somewhat surprisingly, a 1995 Princeton Survey Research Associates poll showed that 44 percent of the respondents rated immigration from African countries as about right, while only 33 percent said it was too many (Lapinski et al. 1997). Interpretation of these attitudes would require, however, knowing how many African immigrants the respondents thought were currently entering the United States. It also seems likely that the majority of Americans have very little exposure to immigrants from Africa and so would not perceive the group to be problematic.
3. In data collected in 1989 and reported by Sidanius and Pratto in 1999, Arabs were also included in the ratings and were generally rated slightly higher than blacks and Latinos, but markedly lower than Asians.
4. Color-based hierarchies are not unique to the United States. For a comprehensive analysis of the significance of skin color in Brazil, a country often claimed to be color-blind, see Edward Telles (2004).
5. In chapter 6, I deal with the actual behaviors involved in assimilating and the alternatives. Here I focus only on the attitudes toward these processes, by members of both host and immigrant groups.
6. Bourhis et al. (1997) make two modifications: they change the definition of cultural adaptation from an emphasis on maintaining relationships to the criterion of "adopting the cultural identity of the host community"; and they subdivide the marginalization cell into anomie (emphasizing marginalization as cultural alienation from both host and origin) and individualism (defined as a preference for definition as an individual rather than as a member of any group).

CHAPTER 4

1. It is now widely believed that the second author on this book was actually W. I. Thomas, who was unable to publish under his own name for several years because of a sex-related scandal.
2. This period of investigation, it should be noted, stops just after the liberalization of U.S. immigration policy and the resultant change in demographic patterns of immigration.
3. Another fourth-generation study of national stereotypes is that of Madon et al. (2001). Because they used a slightly different methodology and sample than the original Katz and Braly study, I am not using them as a basis of comparison here.
4. The 1951 Gilbert data showed a considerably higher number of 15.3. That figure seems somewhat out of line with the other three data points, suggesting

that special circumstances, either of the testing conditions or the historical context, contributed to an anomalous data point.

5. Groups included in this set were Belgians, Dutch, English, French, Germans, Greeks, Hungarians, Irish, Italians, Norwegians, Poles, Portuguese, Russians, Scots, Spaniards, Swedes, Swiss, Turks, and Welsh.

6. It was not until 1988 that the U.S. government officially apologized for the actions of this period and gave reparation awards of $20,000 to each living survivor of the camps (Nieves 2001).

7. In at least one recent case in New York City, workers in this situation successfully filed a lawsuit alleging discrimination and received a cash settlement for lost wages.

CHAPTER 5

1. Within the social science literature, both *social identity* and *collective identity* are used to refer to membership in social categories. Although debates about the relative advantage of one or the other term exist (see Ashmore, Deaux, and McLaughlin-Volpe 2004), I will use them as interchangeable equivalents in this book.

2. The exact wording of the census inquiry was as follows: "Print the ancestry group with which the person identifies. Ancestry (or origin or descent) may be viewed as the nationality group, the lineage, or the country in which the person or the person's parents were born before their arrival in the United States. Persons who are of more than one origin and who cannot identify with a single group should print their multiple ancestry" (Waters 1990).

3. Verkuyten (2005) suggests that this form of hyphenation is more problematic in Europe, where a term such as Turkish-German carries ethnic meaning in both halves of the term, as well as a nationality referent.

4. Berry is not the first to offer a four-category model of cultural adaptation. Indeed, Rudmin (2003) traces the general concept back to Plato and identifies nearly seventy theoretical formulations that are similar in form to the Berry model. Common to many of these models is the assumption that there is some static resolution of the two attitudinal orientations, which is at least implicitly often taken as a personality typology.

5. Berry does not assume that each orientation must be either/or, although he has typically represented his model in this 2×2 format. Theoretically, however, the orientations are dimensions on which degree of endorsement can vary.

6. These investigators used the following vignette: "I am a bicultural who keeps American and Chinese cultures separate and feels conflicted about these two cultures. I am mostly just a Chinese who lives in America (versus a Chinese-American), and I feel as someone who is caught between two cultures." Respondents indicated their agreement with this characterization on a 5-point scale,

ranging from 1 (definitely not true) to 5 (definitely true). On average, respondents scored at approximately the midpoint (Benet-Martínez and Haritatos 2002), which could indicate either moderation or ambivalence.

CHAPTER 6

1. Considerable sociological work relevant to questions of ethnic enclaves and opportunity structures is available (for more detail on these topics, see Hirschman, Kasinitz, and DeWind 1999; Massey 1998).
2. These authors also relied on expressions of intentionality, in this case, statements by the respondents that they intended to emigrate soon or eventually. However, they also followed up with exploration of available databases and found that almost all of those who had said that they intended to emigrate had done so within the following four years.
3. I am speaking here of the experience of all those who initially come to a new country, not simply those who apply for legal immigration status. As Massey and Malone (2002) have reported, two-thirds of those who receive a visa for permanent residence in the United States have been in the country previously, through a variety of pathways (for example, student and exchange visits, refugees, or illegal border crossings).
4. As Claudio Lomnitz observes in his witty and incisive *Boston Review* critique, "Huntington is very concerned by the fact that Mexicans actually *value* their Spanish language, that they *care* about what happens back in Mexico, and that they cede to the unpatriotic impulse of sending money to their families across the border rather than investing it here (the way American corporations do)" ("American Soup: Are We All Anglo-Protestants?" February/March 2005, pp. 38–39, emphasis in original).
5. Within the City University of New York system, approximately half of the students are either first- or second-generation immigrants from all parts of the world.
6. To ensure that cell sizes were adequate for some of our analyses, we combined black and Latino samples. Comparison of these two groups showed them to be substantially the same on most measures, thus justifying the combination.
7. The most common country of origin of the white immigrants in our sample was Russia, followed by Poland and other countries of the former Soviet Union. Black and Latino immigrants were primarily from the Caribbean, especially Jamaica and the Dominican Republic.
8. A subsequent data set, comparing first- to second-generation immigrants, suggests that this assumption may not prove true for some white immigrants, who experience discrimination (for example, on the basis of religion or language) and do not move as readily into the white majority as they had perhaps anticipated.

9. This study considers only stated beliefs about the desirability of collective action and not actual behavior. Further research is needed to determine the degree to which these orientations result in concrete actions on behalf of one's group.

CHAPTER 7

1. Since 1990, immigration from Africa to the United States has increased sharply as well, to a level now surpassing the numbers estimated during the middle passage years of slavery (Roberts 2005). The experiences of immigrants who come from English-speaking countries in Africa may well be similar to those of West Indian immigrants; to date, however, little research has been done on this newly emerging group.
2. The group label itself differs between the two countries. Within the United States, West Indian is the most common usage, whereas in Britain, that label is viewed as politically incorrect, recalling the colonial era, and the terms African Caribbean or Afro-Caribbean are preferred (Foner 2005).
3. Although data relevant to hiring suggest a West Indian advantage over native-born African Americans, the broader picture of employment practices and experience may be less differentiated. As Kasinitz (1992) observed, though "being West Indian has a great deal to do with what jobs people get, it is often being black that structures the dynamics of the job situation" (108–9).
4. A counterexample is reported by Butterfield (2004) in the statement of a twenty-three-year-old immigrant from Barbados who said, "I consider myself to be a black Basian. I have to say 'black' because there are a lot of different races in Barbados . . . and I have to say 'Basian' because there are so many different kinds of black people in New York, and while we share a phenotype, that's all we got going on in common. Just ask my boy from Ghana" (301).
5. In a more intensive consideration of the role of family structure in ethnic and racial identification within the Caribbean (Trinidad and Tobago, and Guyana in her analysis), Abraham (2001) argued that colonial and postcolonial policies that defined and privileged "respectable family structure" contributed to the centrality of family in the discourse of race and ethnic relations.
6. Thomas's immigrant sample included people from both the Caribbean and from Africa. Her sample was too small, however, to explore possible differences between these two groups of immigrants.

References

Abraham, Sara. 2001. "The Shifting Sources of Racial Definition in Trinidad and Tobago, and Guyana: A Research Agenda." *Ethnic and Racial Studies* 24(6): 979–97.

Abric, Jean-Claude. 2001. "A Structural Approach to Social Representations." In *Representations of the Social,* edited by Kay Deaux and Gina Philogène. Oxford: Blackwell Publishing.

Adler, Rachel H. 2005. "From 'The Burg' to 'El Barrio': Ethnic Transition in a Trenton, N.J. Neighborhood." Paper presented at conference at Russell Sage Foundation, Immigration to the U.S.: New Sources and Destinations. New York (February 2005).

Alarcón, Rafael. 2000. "Skilled Immigrants and Cerebreros: Foreign-born Engineers and Scientists in the High-Technology Industry of Silicon Valley." In *Immigration Research for a New Century: Multidisciplinary Perspectives,* edited by Nancy Foner, Rubén Rumbaut, and Steven J. Gold. New York: Russell Sage Foundation.

Alba, Richard. 1985. *Italian Americans: Into the Twilight of Ethnicity.* Englewood Cliffs, N.J.: Prentice-Hall.

———. 1990. *Ethnic Identity: The Transformation of White America.* New Haven, Conn.: Yale University Press.

———. 1999. "Immigration and the American Realities of Assimilation and Multiculturalism." *Sociological Forum* 14(1): 3–25.

Alba, Richard, and Victor Nee. 1999. "Rethinking Assimilation Theory for a New Era of Immigration." In *The Handbook of International Migration: The American Experience,* edited by Charles Hirschman, Philip Kasinitz, and Josh DeWind. New York: Russell Sage Foundation.

———. 2003. *Remaking the American Mainstream: Assimilation and Contemporary Immigration.* Cambridge, Mass.: Harvard University Press.

Ali, Mohammed Naseehu. 2004. "My Name is Not Cool Anymore." *The New York Times,* November 24, section 14, p. 6.

Allen, Irving Lewis. 1983. *The Language of Ethnic Conflict: Social Organization and Lexical Culture.* New York: Columbia University Press.

Anderson, Benedict. 1983. *Imagined Communities: Reflections on the Origin and Spread of Nationalism*. London: Verso.

Arboleya, Jesús. 1996. *Havana-Miami: The U.S.-Cuba Migration Conflict*. Melbourne, Australia: Ocean Press.

Aronson, Joshua, Michael J. Lustina, Catherine Good, Kelli Keough, Claude M. Steele, and Joseph Brown. 1999. "When White Men Can't Do Math: Necessary and Sufficient Factors in Stereotype Threat." *Journal of Experimental Social Psychology* 35(1): 29–46.

Ashmore, Richard D., Kay Deaux, and Tracy McLaughlin-Volpe. 2004. "An Organizing Framework for Collective Identity: Articulation and Significance of Multidimensionality." *Psychological Bulletin* 130(1): 80–114.

Ayres, B. Drummond, Jr. 2001. "Political Briefing: Terrorism Issue at Play in Two Races." *New York Times*, October 21, IA, p. 30.

Basch, Linda. 2001. "Transnational Social Relations and the Politics of National Identity: An Eastern Caribbean Case Study." In *Islands in the City: West Indian Migration to New York*, edited by Nancy Foner. Berkeley: University of California Press.

Bean, Frank D., Jennifer Lee, Jeanne Batalova, and Mark Leach. 2004. "Immigration and fading color lines in America." New York and Washington: Russell Sage Foundation and Population Reference Bureau.

Bean, Frank D., and Gillian Stevens. 2003. *America's Newcomers and the Dynamics of Diversity*. New York: Russell Sage Foundation.

Benet-Martínez, Verónica, and Jana Haritatos. 2002. "Bicultural Identity Integration (BII): Components, Dynamics, and Psychosocial Correlates." Unpublished paper. University of Michigan, Ann Arbor.

Benet-Martínez, Verónica, Janxin Leu, Fiona Lee, and Michael W. Morris. 2002. "Negotiating Biculturalism: Cultural Frame Switching in Biculturals with Oppositional versus Compatible Cultural Identities." *Journal of Cross-Cultural Psychology* 33(5): 492–516.

Berger, Joseph. 2004. "The Many Channels that Say Home; Wave of Foreign TV Becomes an 'Emotional Outlet' for Immigrants." *The New York Times*, February 23, 2004, p. B1, 3.

Berlin, Isaiah. 2001. "Notes on Prejudice." *The New York Review of Books*, October 18, 2001, 12.

Bernstein, Richard. 2004. "Letter from Europe: A Continent Watching Anxiously over the Melting Pot." *The New York Times*, December 5, 2004.

Berry, John W. 1980. "Social and cultural change." In *Handbook of Cross-Cultural Psychology: Vol. 5. Social Psychology*, edited by Harry C. Triandis and Richard Brislin. Boston, Mass.: Allyn & Bacon.

———. 1984. "Multicultural Policy in Canada: A Social Psychological Analysis." *Canadian Journal of Behavioural Science* 16(4): 353–70.

———. 1990. "Psychology of Acculturation." In *Cross-Cultural Perspectives: Nebraska Symposium on Motivation*, vol. 37, edited by John J. Berman. Lincoln: University of Nebraska Press.

————. 1992. "Acculturation and Adaptation in a New Society." *International Migration Review* 30: 69–85.

————. 1997. "Immigration, Acculturation, and Adaptation." *Applied Psychology: an International Review* 46(1): 5–34.

————. 2001. "A Psychology of Immigration." *Journal of Social Issues* 57(3): 615–31.

Berry, John W., and Uichol Kim. 1988. "Acculturation and Mental Health." In *Health and Cross-Cultural Psychology,* edited by Pierre R. Dasen, John W. Berry, and Norman Sartorius. London: Sage Publications.

Berry, John W., Uichol Kim, Thomas Minde, and Doris Mok. 1987. "Comparative Studies of Acculturative Stress." *International Migration Review* 21(3): 491–511.

Berry, John W., Uichol Kim, S. Power, M. Young, and M. Bujaki. 1989. "Acculturation Attitudes in Plural Societies." *Applied Psychology: An International Review* 38(2): 185–206.

Berry, John W., and David L. Sam. 1997. "Acculturation and Adaptation." In *Handbook of Cross-Cultural Psychology,* edited by John W. Berry, Marshall H. Segall, and Cigdem Kagitcibasi. Boston: Allyn & Bacon.

Biernat, Monica, Faye Crosby, and Joan Williams, eds. 2004. *The Maternal Wall: Research and Policy Perspectives on Discrimination against Mothers.* Oxford: Blackwell Publishing.

Bikmen, Nida. 2005. "History, Memory and Identity: Remembering the Homeland in Exile." Unpublished Ph.D. diss. Graduate Center of the City University of New York.

Bobb, Vilna F. Bashi. 2001. "Neither Ignorance nor Bliss: Race, Racism, and the West Indian Immigrant Experience." In *Migration, Transnationalism, and Race in a Changing New York,* edited by Héctor R. Cordero-Guzmán, Robert C. Smith, and Ramón Grosfoguel. Philadelphia: Temple University Press.

Bobb, Vilna F. Bashi, and Averill Y. Clarke. 2001. "Experiencing Success: Structuring the Perception of Opportunities for West Indians." In *Islands in the City: West Indian Migration to New York,* edited by Nancy Foner. Berkeley: University of California Press.

Bobo, Lawrence D., and Devon Johnson. 2000. "Racial Attitudes in a Prismatic Metropolis: Mapping Identity, Stereotypes, Competition, and Views of Affirmative Action." In *Prismatic Metropolis: Inequality in Los Angeles,* edited by Lawrence D. Bobo, Melvin L. Oliver, James H. Johnson Jr., and Abel Valenzuela Jr. New York: Russell Sage Foundation.

Bobo, Lawrence D., and Michael P. Massagli. 2001. "Stereotyping and Urban Inequality." In *Urban Inequality: Evidence from Four Cities,* edited by Alice O'Connor, Chris Tilly, and Lawrence D. Bobo. New York: Russell Sage Foundation.

Boneva, Bonka S., and Irene Hanson Frieze. 2001. "Toward a Concept of a Migrant Personality." *Journal of Social Issues* 57(3): 477–91.

Bourhis, Richard Y., and David F. Marshall. 1999. "The United States and Canada." In *Handbook of Language and Ethnic Identity,* edited by Joshua A Fishman. New York: Oxford University Press.

Bourhis, Richard Y., Lena Celine Moise, Stephanie Perreault, and Sacha Senecal. 1997. "Towards an Interactive Acculturation Model: A Social Psychological Approach." *International Journal of Psychology* 32(6): 369–86.

Bourhis, Richard Y., Annie Montreuil, and Genevieve Barrette. 1999. "Testing the Interactive Acculturation Model in Quèbec." Poster presented at SPSSI conference on immigrants and immigration. Toronto (August 12–15, 1999).

Breakwell, Glynis M., and David V. Canter. 1993. *Empirical Approaches to Social Representations.* Oxford: Clarendon Press.

Breton, Raymond, Wsevolod W. Isajiw, Warren E. Kalbach, and Jeffrey G. Reitz. 1990. *Ethnic Identity and Equality: Varieties of Experience in a Canadian City.* Toronto: University of Toronto Press.

Brewer, Marilynn B. 1991. "The Social Self: On Being the Same and Different at the Same Time." *Personality and Social Psychology Bulletin* 17(5): 475–82.

Brubaker, Rogers. 1992. *Citizenship and Nationhood in France and Germany.* Cambridge, Mass.: Harvard University Press.

Brubaker, Rogers, and Frederick Cooper. 2000. "Beyond 'Identity.' " *Theory and Society* 29(1): 1–47.

Bryan, Jennifer L. 2005. "Constructing 'the True Islam' in Hostile Times: The Impact of 9/11 on Arab Muslims in Jersey City." In *Wounded City: The Social Impact of 9/11,* edited by Nancy Foner. New York: Russell Sage Foundation.

Butterfield, Sherri-Ann P. 2004. "We're Just 'Black': The Racial and Ethnic Identities of Second-Generation West Indians in New York." In *Becoming New Yorkers: Ethnographies of the New Second Generation,* edited by Philip Kasinitz, John H. Mollenkopf, and Mary C. Waters. New York: Russell Sage Foundation.

Campbell, Donald T. 1967. "Stereotypes and the Perception of Group Differences." *American Psychologist* 22(10): 817–29.

Carter, Susan B., and Richard Sutch. 1999. "Historical Perspectives on the Economic Consequences of Immigration into the United States." In *The Handbook of International Migration: The American Experience,* edited by Charles Hirschman, Philip Kasinitz, and Josh DeWind. New York: Russell Sage Foundation.

Casas, J. Manuel, Joseph G. Ponterotto, and Michael Sweeney. 1987. "Stereotyping the Stereotyper: A Mexican American Perspective." *Journal of Cross-Cultural Psychology* 18(1): 45–57.

Chan, Erin. 2003. "At Parade, St. Lucians Raise Loud, Joyful Voice for Small Country." *The New York Times,* September 2, 2003, p. B5, 2.

Chavez, Leo R. 2001. *Covering Immigration: Popular Images and the Politics of the Nation.* Berkeley: University of California Press.

Chiswick, Barry R. 1979. "The Economic Progress of Immigrants: Some Apparently Universal Patterns." In *Contemporary Economic Problems,* edited by William Fellner. Washington, D.C.: American Enterprise Institute.

Choy, Catherinie Ceniza. 2000. " 'Exported to Care': A Transnational History of Filipino Nurse Migration to the United States." In *Immigration Research for a New*

Century: Multidisciplinary Perspectives, edited by Nancy Foner, Rubén Rumbaut, and Steven J. Gold. New York: Russell Sage Foundation.

Chryssochoou, Xenia. 2000. "Memberships in a Superordinate Level: Re-thinking European Union as a Multi-national Society." *Journal of Community & Applied Social Psychology* 10(5): 403–20.

Clark, Kenneth B. 1976. "The Reminiscences of Kenneth Bancroft Clark: oral history 1976." Interviews conducted by Ed Edwin. Columbia University Libraries, New York City.

Comas-Díaz, Lillian. 2001. "Hispanics, Latinos, or Americanos: The Evolution of Identity." *Cultural Diversity and Ethnic Minority Psychology* 7(2): 115–20.

Congressional Digest. 1965. "Congress and U.S. Immigration Policy." *Congressional Digest* 44(5)(May): 160.

Cooley, C. H. 1902. *Human Nature and the Social Order.* New York: Charles Scribner's Sons.

Cornell, Stephen, and Douglas Hartmann. 1998. *Ethnicity and Race: Making Identities in a Changing World.* Thousand Oaks, Calif.: Pine Forge Press.

Coser, Lewis A. 1992. "Introduction: Maurice Halbwachs 1877–1945." In *Maurice Halbwachs: On Collective Memory,* edited by Lewis A. Coser. Chicago: University of Chicago Press.

Crenshaw, Kimberlè. 1995. "Mapping the Margins: Intersectionality, Identity Politics, and Violence Against Women of Color." In *Critical Race Theory,* edited by Kimberlè Crenshaw, Neil Gotanda, Gary Peller, and Kendall Thomas. New York: Free Press.

Crocker, Jennifer, Riia Luhtanen, Bruce Blaine, and Stephanie Broadnax. 1994. "Collective Self-esteem and Psychological Well-Being among White, Black, and Asian College Students." *Personality and Social Psychology Bulletin* 20(5): 503–13.

Crocker, Jennifer, and Brenda Major. 1989. "Social Stigma and Self-Esteem." *Psychological Review* 96: 608–30.

Crocker, Jennifer, Brenda Major, and Claude Steele. 1998. "Social Stigma." In *Handbook of Social Psychology,* 4th ed., vol. 2, edited by Daniel Gilbert, Susan T. Fiske, and Gardner Lindzey. Boston: McGraw-Hill.

Crosby, Faye. 2004. *Affirmative Action Is Dead; Long Live Affirmative Action.* New Haven, Conn.: Yale University Press.

Crosby, Faye, Aarti Iyer, Susan Clayton, and Roberta A. Downing. 2003. "Affirmative Action: Psychological Data and the Policy Debates." *American Psychologist* 58(2): 93–115.

Cross, William E., Jr. 1991. *Shades of Black: Diversity in African-American Identity.* Philadelphia: Temple University Press.

Cuddy, Amy J. C., Susan T. Fiske, and Peter Glick. 2004. "Behaviors from Intergroup Affect and Stereotypes: The BIAS map." Unpublished manuscript. Princeton University.

Day, Richard J. F. 2000. *Multiculturalism and the History of Canadian Diversity*. Toronto: University of Toronto Press.

Deaux, Kay. 1996. "Social Identification." In *Social Psychology: Handbook of Basic Principles*, edited by E. Tory Higgins and Arie W. Kruglanski. New York: Guilford Press.

———. 2004. "Immigration and the Color Line." In *Racial Identity in Context: The Legacy of Kenneth B. Clark*, edited by Gina Philogène. Washington, D.C.: American Psychological Association.

Deaux, Kay, and Kathleen A. Ethier. 1998. "Negotiating Social Identity." In *Prejudice: The Target's Perspective*, edited by Janet Swim and Charles Stangor. New York: Academic Press.

Deaux, Kay, Alwyn Gilkes, Nida Bikmen, Ana Ventumeac, Yvanne Joseph, Yasser Payne, and Claude Steele. 2005. "Becoming American: Stereotype Threat Effects in Black Immigrant Groups." Manuscript under review.

Deaux, Kay, and Daniela Martin. 2003. "Interpersonal Networks and Social Categories: Specifying Levels of Context in Identity Processes." *Social Psychology Quarterly* 66(2): 101–17.

Deaux, Kay, and Gina Philogène. 2001. *Representations of the Social: Bridging Theoretical Traditions*. Oxford: Blackwell Publishing.

Deaux, Kay, Anne Reid, Daniela Martin, and Nida Bikmen. 2006. "Ideologies of Diversity and Inequality: Predicting Collective Action in Groups Varying in Ethnicity and Immigrant Status." *Political Psychology* 27(1): 123–46.

Deaux, Kay, Anne Reid, Kim Mizrahi, and Kathleen A. Ethier. 1995. "Parameters of Social Identity." *Journal of Personality and Social Psychology* 68(2): 280–91.

Deaux, Kay, Claude Steele, Jennifer Eberhardt, Mary Waters, and Ewart Thomas. 1999. *Ethnic Identification and Stereotype Threat: The Case of West Indians*. Proposal submitted to Russell Sage Foundation, September.

DeFreitas, Gregory. 1992. "Economic Effects of Recent Immigration to the United States." In *Immigration and Ethnicity: American Society "Melting Pot" or "Salad Bowl?"* edited by Michael D'Innocenzo and Josef P. Sirefman. Westport, Conn.: Greenwood Press.

DeLaet, Debra L. 2000. *U.S. Immigration Policy in an Age of Rights*. Westport, Conn.: Praeger

Diamond, Jeff. 1998. "African-American Attitudes towards United States Immigration Policy." *International Migration Review* 32(2): 451–70.

Diaz, Rosemary, Dana Martin, and Kay Deaux. 1999. "Latina Gender and Ethnicity: Self-Descriptions of Multiple Social Identities." Unpublished paper. New York: CUNY Graduate Center.

Doise, Willem. 2001. "Human Rights Studied as Normative Social Representations." In *Representations of the Social: Bridging Theoretical Traditions*, edited by Kay Deaux and Gina Philogène. Oxford: Blackwell Publishing.

Doosje, Bertjan, and Nyla Branscombe. 2003. "Attributions for the Negative Historical Actions of a Group." *European Journal of Social Psychology* 33(2): 235–48.

Dovidio, John F., Jack C. Brigham, Blair T. Johnson, and Sam L. Gaertner. 1996. "Stereotyping, Prejudice, and Discrimination: Another Look." In *Stereotypes and Stereotyping*, edited by Neil C. Macrae, Charles Stangor, and Miles Hewstone. New York: Guilford.

Dovidio, John F., and Victoria M. Esses. 2001. "Immigrants and Immigration: Advancing the Psychological Perspective." *Journal of Social Issues* 57(3): 375–87.

Dovidio, John F., and Sam L. Gaertner. 1993. "Stereotypes and Evaluative Intergroup Bias." In *Affect, Cognition, and Stereotyping,* edited by Diane M. Mackie and David L. Hamilton. San Diego, Calif.: Academic Press.

Downey, Geraldine, Jacquelynne S. Eccles, and Celina M. Chatman, eds. 2006. *Navigating the Future: Social Identity, Coping, and Life Tasks.* New York: Russell Sage Foundation.

Dublin, Thomas. 1993. *Immigrant Voices: New Lives in America, 1773–1986.* Urbana: University of Illinois Press.

Du Bois, W. E. B. 1903/1976. *The Souls of Black Folk.* New York: Alfred A. Knopf.

Eagly, Alice H., and Mary E. Kite. 1987. "Are Stereotypes of Nationalities Applied to Both Women and Men?" *Journal of Personality and Social Psychology* 53(3): 451–62.

Eberhardt, Jennifer, and Kay Deaux. 2000. Unpublished data.

Edmonston, Barry, and Jeffrey S. Passel. 1994. "Ethnic Demography: U.S. Immigration and Ethnic Variations." In *Immigration and Ethnicity: The Integration of America's Newest Arrivals,* edited by Barry Edmonston and Jeffrey S. Passel. Washington, D.C.: Urban Institute.

Elliott, Andrea. 2004. "Study Finds City's Muslims Growing Closer Since 9/11." *The New York Times,* October 5.

Espenshade, Thomas J., and Katherine Hempstead. 1996. "Contemporary American Attitudes toward U.S. Immigration." *International Migration Review* 30(2): 535–70.

Espiritu, Yen Le, and Thom Tran. 2003. " 'Viet Nam, Nuo'c Toi' (Vietnam, My Country): Vietnamese Americans and Transnationalism." In *The Changing Face of Home: The Transnational Lives of the Second Generation,* edited by Peggy Levitt and Mary C. Waters. New York: Russell Sage Foundation.

Esses, Victoria M., Joerg Dietz, and Arjun Bhardwaj. 2006. "The Role of Prejudice in the Discounting of Immigrant Skills." In *Cultural Psychology of Immigration,* edited by Ram Mahalingam. Mahwah, N.J.: Lawrence Erlbaum.

Esses, Victoria M., John F. Dovidio, and Gordon Hodson. 2002. "Public Attitudes Toward Immigration in the United States and Canadian Response to the September 11, 2001, 'Attack on America.' " *Analyses of Social Issues and Public Policy* 2(1): 69–85.

Esses, Victoria M., John F. Dovidio, Lynne M. Jackson, and Tamara L. Armstrong. 2001. "The Immigration Dilemma: The Role of Perceived Group Competition, Ethnic Prejudice, and National Identity." *Journal of Social Issues* 57(3): 389–412.

Esses, Victoria M., Lynne M. Jackson, and Tamara L. Armstrong. 1998. "Intergroup Competition and Attitudes Toward Immigrants and Immigration: An Instrumental Model of Group Conflict." *Journal of Social Issues* 54(4): 699–724.

Esses, Victoria M., Lynne M. Jackson, Jeffery M. Nolan, and Tamara L. Armstrong. 1999. "Economic Threat and Attitudes Towards Immigrants." In *Immigrant Canada: Demographic, Economic, and Social Challenges,* edited by Shiva S. Halli and Leo Driedger. Toronto: University of Toronto Press.

Ethier, Kathleen, and Kay Deaux. 1990. "Hispanics in Ivy: Assessing Identity and Perceived Threat." *Sex Roles* 22(7/8): 427–40.

———. 1994. "Negotiating Social Identity when Contexts Change: Maintaining Identification and Responding to Threat." *Journal of Personality and Social Psychology* 67(2): 243–51.

Fairchild, Henry Pratt. 1926. *The Melting-pot Mistake.* Boston, Mass.: Little, Brown.

Falomir-Pichastor, Juan Manuel, Daniel Muñoz-Rojas, Federica Invernizzi, and Gabriel Mugny. 2004. "Perceived In-group Threat as a Factor Moderating the Influence of In-group Norms on Discrimination against Foreigners." *European Journal of Social Psychology* 34(2): 135–53.

Feagin, Joe R., and Melvin P. Sikes. 1994. *Living with Racism: The Black Middle-Class Experience.* Boston, Mass.: Beacon Press.

Fears, Darryl. 2003. "Latinos or Hispanics? A Debate about Identity." *Washington Post,* August 25, 2003, p. A01.

Fenby, Jonathan. 1998. *France on the Brink.* New York: Arcade Publishing.

Fennelly, Katherine. 2004. "Prejudice toward Immigrants in the Midwest." Unpublished paper. Hubert H. Humphrey Institute of Public Affairs, University of Minnesota.

Fernandez, Ronald. 2000. *America's Banquet of Cultures: Harnessing Ethnicity, Race, and Immigration in the Twenty-first Century.* Westport, Conn.: Praeger.

Fiske, Susan T. 1998. "Stereotyping, Prejudice, and Discrimination." In *The Handbook of Social Psychology,* vol. II, 4th ed., edited by Daniel T. Gilbert, Susan T. Fiske, and Gardner Lindzey. Boston, Mass.: McGraw-Hill.

———. 2004. *Social Beings: A Core Motives Approach to Social Psychology.* New York: John Wiley & Sons.

Fiske, Susan T., Donald N. Bersoff, Eugene Borgida, Kay Deaux, and Madeline E. Heilman. 1991. "Social Science Research on Trial: Use of Sex Stereotyping Research on Price Waterhouse v. Hopkins." *American Psychologist* 46(10): 1049–1060.

Fiske, Susan T., Amy J. C. Cuddy, Peter Glick, and Jun Xu. 2002. "A Model of (Often Mixed) Stereotype Content: Competence and Warmth Respectively Follow from Perceived Status and Competition." *Journal of Personality and Social Psychology* 82(6): 878–902.

Fleming, Charles, and John Carreyrou. 2003. "In France, Policy on Muslims Comes to Head on Scarves." *The Wall Street Journal,* June 26, 2003, p. A1, 10.

Foner, Nancy. 1979. "West Indians in New York City and London: A Comparative Analysis." *International Migration Review* 13(2): 284–97.

———. 1985. "Race and Color: Jamaican Migrants in London and New York City." *International Migration Review* 19(4): 708–27.

———. 1997. "The Immigrant Family: Cultural Legacies and Cultural Changes." *International Migration Review* 31(4): 961–74.

———. 1998a. "Towards a Comparative Perspective on Caribbean Migration." In *Caribbean Migration: Globalised Identities,* edited by Mary Chamberlain. London: Routledge.

———. 1998b. "West Indian Identity in the Diaspora: Comparative and Historical Perspectives." *Latin American Perspectives* 100(25): 173–88.

———. 2000. *From Ellis Island to JFK: New York's Two Great Waves of Immigration.* New Haven and New York: Yale University Press and Russell Sage Foundation.

———. 2001a. "Comparative Perspectives on Immigrants in New York–Across Time and Space." Paper presented at conference, Host Societies and the Reception of Immigrants: Institutions, Markets, and Policies. Cambridge, Mass. (May 2001).

———. 2001b. "Introduction. West Indian Migration to New York: An Overview." In *Islands in the City: West Indian Migration to New York,* edited by Nancy Foner. Berkeley: University of California Press.

———. 2005. *In a New Land: A Comparative View of Immigration.* New York: New York University Press.

Foster, Kate. 1926. *Our Canadian Mosaic.* Toronto: YWCA.

Foster, Kenneth. 2004. "Relation of Well-being, Attitudinal and Behavioral Correlates of Three Types of Black identity: Assimilated, Afrocentric, Multicultural." Ph.D. diss., City University of New York Graduate Center.

Frederickson, George M. 1999. "Models of American Ethnic Relations: A Historical Perspective." In *Cultural Divides: Understanding and Overcoming Group Conflict,* edited by Deborah A. Prentice and Dale T. Miller. New York: Russell Sage Foundation.

Friedberg, Rachel M., and Jennifer Hunt. 1999. "Immigration and the Receiving Economy." In *The Handbook of International Migration: The American Experience,* edited by Charles Hirschman, Philip Kasinitz, and Josh DeWind. New York: Russell Sage Foundation.

Fuligni, Andrew J. 1998. "The Adjustment of Children From Immigrant Families." *Current Directions in Psychological Science* 7(4): 99–103.

Fuligni, Andrew J., Vivian Tseng, and May Lam. 1999. "Attitudes Towards Family Obligations among American Adolescents with Asian, Latin American, and European Backgrounds." *Child Development* 70(4): 1030–44.

Gaertner, Sam L., John F. Dovidio, P. A. Anastasio, B. A. Bachman, and M. C. Rust. 1993. "The Common Ingroup Identity Model: Recategorization and the Reduction of Intergroup Bias." In *European Review of Social Psychology,* vol. 4, edited by Wolfgang Stroebe and Miles Hewstone. Chichester, UK: John Wiley & Sons.

Galeano, Eduardo. 1991. *The Book of Embraces.* New York: W. W. Norton.

Gans, Herbert J. 1973. "Introduction." In *Ethnic Identity and Assimilation: The Polish Community*, edited by Neil Sandberg. New York: Praeger.

———. 1979. "Symbolic Ethnicity: The Future of Ethnic Groups and Cultures in America." *Ethnic and Racial Studies* 2(1): 1–20.

———. 1992. "Comment: Ethnic Invention and Acculturation, a Bumpy-line Approach." *Journal of American Ethnic History* 12(1): 43–52.

———. 1994. "Symbolic Ethnicity and Symbolic Religiosity: Towards a Comparison of Ethnic and Religious Acculturation." *Ethnic and Racial Studies* 17(4): 577–92.

Gibson, James L. 2004. *Overcoming Apartheid: Can Truth Reconcile a Divided Nation?* New York: Russell Sage Foundation.

Gibson, James L., and Amanda Gouws. 2000. "Social Identities and Political Intolerance: Linkages Within the South African Mass Public." *American Journal of Political Science* 44(2): 278–92.

Gilbert, G. M. 1951. "Stereotype Persistence and Change Among College Students." *Journal of Personality and Social Psychology* 46(2): 245–54.

Giles, Howard. 1970. "Evaluative Reactions to Accents." *Educational Review* 22(2): 211–27.

———. 1977. *Language, Ethnicity and Intergroup Relations*. London: Academic Press.

Giles, Howard, and Peter F. Powesland. 1975. *Speech Style and Social Evaluation*. New York: Academic Press.

Gilkes, Alwyn D. 2004. *Among Thistles and Thorns: West Indian Diaspora Immigrants in New York City and Toronto*. Ph.D. diss., City University of New York Graduate Center.

Gladwell, Malcolm. 1996. "Black Like Them." *The New Yorker*, April 29, 1996, p. 74–81.

Glazer, Nathan, and Daniel P. Moynihan. 1964. *Beyond the Melting Pot*. Cambridge, Mass.: MIT Press and Harvard University Press.

Gleason, Philip. 1964. "The Melting Pot: Symbol of Fusion or Confusion?" *American Quarterly* 16(1): 20–46.

———. 1983. "Identifying Identity: A Semantic History." *The Journal of American History* 69(4): 910–31.

Glick, Peter, and Susan T. Fiske. 1996. "The Ambivalent Sexism Inventory: Differentiating Hostile and Benevolent Sexism." *Journal of Personality and Social Psychology* 70(3): 491–512.

———. 2001. "Ambivalent Sexism." In *Advances in Experimental Social Psychology*, edited by Mark P. Zanna. Thousand Oaks, Calif.: Academic Press.

Golash-Boza, Tanya. 2005. "Assessing the Advantages of Bilingualism for the Children of Immigrants." *International Migration Review* 39 (3):721–53.

Gordon, Linda W. 2005. "Trends in the Gender Ratio of Immigrants to the United States." *International Migration Review* 39(4): 796–818.

Gordon, Milton M. 1964. *Assimilation in American Life*. New York: Oxford University Press.

Grant, Madison. 1921. *The Passing of the Great Race*, 4th revised ed. New York: Charles Scribner's Sons.

Greeley, Andrew M. 1974. *Ethnicity in the United States: A Preliminary Reconnaissance*. New York: John Wiley & Sons.

Greenhouse, Steven. 2005. "Two Restaurants to Pay Workers $164,000." *The New York Times*, January 12, p. B3.

Greenwood, Ronni Michelle. 2005. Ph.D. diss., Graduate Center of the City University of New York.

Gumperz, J. J. 1982. *Language and Social Identity*. Cambridge: Cambridge University Press.

Gurin, Patricia, Aida Hurtado, and Timothy Peng. 1994. "Group Contacts and Ethnicity in the Social Identities of Mexicanos and Chicanos." *Personality and Social Psychology Bulletin* 20(5): 521–32.

Gurin, Patricia, and Aloen Townsend. 1986. "Properties of Gender Identity and their Implications for Gender Consciousness." *British Journal of Social Psychology* 25(2): 139–48.

Halbwachs, Maurice. 1992. *On Collective Memory*, edited by Lewis A. Coser. Chicago: University of Chicago Press.

Handlin, Oscar. 1951. *The Uprooted: The Epic Story of the Great Migrations that Made the American People*. Boston: Little, Brown.

Harris Survey. 1993. "The Melting Pot." September.

Harwood, Edwin. 1983. "Alienation: American Attitudes Toward Immigration." *Public Opinion* 6(3): 49–51.

———. 1986. "American Public Opinion and U.S. Immigration Policy." *The Annals of the American Academy of Political and Social Science* 487(September): 201–12.

Hayward, Veronica. 1922. *Romantic Canada*. Toronto: Macmillan.

Healy, Patrick. 2004. "Public Lives: Looking at Immigration from Both Sides." *The New York Times*, January 13, p. B2, 3.

Henry, Jacques M., and Carl L. Bankston III. 2001. "Ethnic Self-identification and Symbolic Stereotyping: the Portrayal of Louisiana Cajuns." *Ethnic and Racial Studies* 24(6): 1020–45.

Herskovits, Melville J. 1935. "Social History of the Negro." In *A Handbook of Social Psychology*, vol. 1, edited by Carl Murchison. New York: Russell & Russell.

Hing, Bill Ong. 1998. "Asian Immigrants: Social Forces Unleashed After 1965." In *The Immigration Reader* edited by David Jacobson. Malden, Mass.: Blackwell Publishing.

Hirsch, Jennifer S. 2000. "En el Norte la Mujer Manda: Gender, Generation, and Geography in a Mexican Transnational Community." In *Immigration Research for a New Century: Multidisciplinary Perspectives*, edited by Nancy Foner, Rubén Rumbaut, and Steven J. Gold. New York: Russell Sage Foundation.

Hirschman, Charles. 1983. "America's Melting Pot Reconsidered." *Annual Review of Sociology* 9: 397–423.

———. 1999. "Theories of International Migration. A Preliminary Reconnaissance of Ideal Types." In *The Handbook of International Migration: The American Experi-*

ence, edited by Charles Hirschman, Philip Kasinitz, and Josh DeWind. New York: Russell Sage Foundation.

Hirschman, Charles, Philip Kasinitz, and Josh DeWind. 1999. *The Handbook of International Migration: The American Experience.* New York: Russell Sage Foundation.

Hochschild, Jennifer L. 1995. *Facing Up to the American Dream.* Princeton, N.J.: Princeton University Press.

Hoffman, Eva. 1989. *Lost in Translation.* New York: Penguin Books.

———. 1999. "The New Nomads." In *Letters of Transit: Reflections on Exile, Identity, Language, and Loss,* edited by André Aciman. New York: The New Press.

Hondagneu-Sotelo, Pierrette. 2003. *Gender and U.S. Immigration: Contemporary Trends.* Berkeley: University of California Press.

Hong, Ying-yi, Michael W. Morris, Chi-yue Chiu, and Verónica Benet-Martínez. 2000. "Multicultural Minds: A Dynamic Constructivist Approach to Culture and Cognition." *American Psychologist* 55(7): 709–20.

Hong, Ying-yi, Glen I. Roisman, and Jing Chen. 2006. "A Model of Cultural Attachment: A New Approach for Studying Bicultural Experience." In *Acculturation and Parent-Child Relationships: Measurement and Development,* edited by M. H. Bornstein and L. R. Cote. Mahwah, N.J.: Lawrence Erlbaum.

Horenczyk, Gabriel. 1996. "Migrant Identities in Conflict: Acculturation Attitudes and Perceived Acculturation Ideologies." In *Changing European Identities,* edited by Glynis M. Breakwell and Evantha Lyons. Oxford: Butterworth Heinemann.

Horowitz, Donald L. 1998. "Immigration and Group Relations in France and America." In *The Immigration Reader: America in a Multidisciplinary Perspective,* edited by David Jacobson. Malden, Mass.: Blackwell Publishing.

Huddy, Leonie, and Simo Virtanen. 1995. "Subgroup Differentiation and Subgroup Bias Among Latinos as a Function of Familiarity and Positive Distinctiveness." *Journal of Personality and Social Psychology* 68(1): 97–108.

Huntington, Samuel P. 2004. *Who Are We? The Challenges to America's National Identity.* New York: Simon & Schuster.

Hurh, Won Moo, and Kwang Chung Kim. 1984. *Korean Immigrants in North America: A Structural Analysis of Ethnic Confinement and Adhesive Adaptation.* Madison, N.J.: Fairleigh Dickinson University Press.

Ignatiev, Noel. 1995. *How the Irish Became White.* New York: Routledge.

Isbister, John. 1996. *The Immigration Debate: Remaking America.* West Hartford, Conn.: Kumarian Press.

Itzigsohn, José. "The Multiple Meanings of Latino/a Panethnicity." Paper presented to the CUNY Graduate Center Immigration Series Lectures. New York (April 4, 2005).

Itzigsohn, José, and Silvia Giorguli-Saucedo. 2005. "Incorporation, Transnationalism, and Gender: Immigrant Incorporation and Transnational Participation as Gendered Process." *International Migration Review* 39(4): 895–920.

Jackson, James S., Kendrick T. Brown, and Daria C. Kirby. 1998. "International Perspectives on Prejudice and Racism." In *Confronting Racism: The Problem and the*

Response, edited by Jennifer L. Eberhardt and Susan T. Fiske. Thousand Oaks, Calif.: Sage Publications.

Jackson, James S., Kendrick T. Brown, Tony N. Brown, and Bryant Marks. 2001. "Contemporary Immigration Policy Orientation Among Dominant-group Members in Western Europe." *Journal of Social Issues* 57(3): 431–56.

Jacobson, Matthew Frye. 1998. *Whiteness of a Different Color: European Immigrants and the Alchemy of Race.* Cambridge, Mass.: Harvard University Press.

Jain, Neelu, and Benjamin Forest. 2004. "From Religion to Ethnicity: The Identity of Immigrant and Second Generation Indian Jains in the United States." *National Identities* 6(3): 277–97.

Javier, F. 2004. "This City is a Monster." *The New York Times,* November 21, p. CY6.

Jencks, Christopher. 2001. "Who Should Get In?" *New York Review of Books,* November 29, 2001, 57–63.

Jodelet, Denise. 1991. *Madness and Social Representations.* London: Harvester Wheatsheaf.

Johnson, James H., Jr., Walter C. Farrell, Jr., and Chandra Guinn. 1997. "Immigration Reform and the Browning of America: Tensions, Conflicts and Community Instability in Metropolitan Los Angeles." *International Migration Review* 31(4): 1055–95.

Joppke, Christian. 1998. "Multiculturalism and Immigration: A Comparison of the United States, Germany, and Great Britain." In *The Immigration Reader: America in a Multidisciplinary Perspective,* edited by David Jacobson. Malden, Mass.: Blackwell Publishing.

Jost, John T., and Mahzarin R. Banaji. 1994. "The Role of Stereotyping in System-Justification and the Production of False Consciousness." *British Journal of Social Psychology* 33(1): 1–27.

Jost, John T., Diana Burgess, and Cristina O. Mosso. 2001. "Conflicts of Legitimation Among Self, Group and System: The Integrative Potential of System Justification Theory." In *The Psychology of Legitimacy,* edited by John T. Jost and Brenda Major. New York: Cambridge University Press.

Jung, Courtney. 2000. *Then I Was Black: South African Political Identities in Transition.* New Haven, Conn.: Yale University Press.

Kalmign, Matthijs. 1996. "The Socioeconomic Assimilation of Caribbean American Blacks." *Social Forces* 74(3): 911–30.

Karlins, Marvin, Thomas L. Coffman, and Gary Walters. 1969. "On the Fading of Social Stereotypes: Studies in Three Generations of College Students." *Journal of Personality and Social Psychology* 13(1): 1–16.

Kasinitz, Philip. 1992. *Caribbean New York: Black Immigrants and the Politics of Race.* Ithaca, N.Y.: Cornell University Press.

———. 2001. "Invisible No More? West Indian Americans in the Social Scientific Imagination." In *Islands in the City: West Indian Migration to New York,* edited by Nancy Foner. Berkeley: University of California Press.

Kasinitz, Philip, John Mollenkopf, and Mary C. Waters. 2002. "Becoming American/ Becoming New Yorkers: Immigrant Incorporation in a Majority Minority City." *International Migration Review* 36(4): 1020–36.

Kasinitz, Philip, John Mollenkopf, Mary C. Waters, and Jennifer Holdaway. 2005. " 'I Will NEVER Deliver Chinese Food!' The Second Generation Goes to Work." Paper presented to the CUNY Graduate Center Immigration Series Lectures. New York (February 17, 2005).

Kasinitz, Philip, and Jan Rosenberg. 1996. "Missing the Connection: Social Isolation and Employment on the Brooklyn Waterfront." *Social Problems* 43(2): 180–96.

Katz, Daniel, and Kenneth Braly. 1933. "Racial Stereotypes of One Hundred College Students." *Journal of Abnormal and Social Psychology* 28: 280–90.

Kaushal, Neeraj, Robert Kaestner, and Cordelia Reimers. 2004. "Backlash: Effects of 9/11 on Muslims and Arabs living in the U.S." Unpublished paper. Columbia University.

Kennedy, John Fitzgerald. 1964. *A Nation of Immigrants.* New York: Harper & Row.

Kevles, Daniel J. 1985. *In the Name of Eugenics: Genetics and the Uses of Human Heredity.* New York: Alfred A. Knopf.

Kibria, Nazli. 2002. "Of Blood, Belonging, and Homeland Trips: Transnationalism and Identity Among Second-Generation Chinese and Korean Americans." In *The Changing Face of Home: The Transnational Lives of the Second Generation,* edited by Peggy Levitt and Mary C. Waters. New York: Russell Sage Foundation.

Kleugel, James R., and Eliot R. Smith. 1986. *Beliefs About Inequality: Americans' Views About What is Right and What Ought to Be.* New York: Aldine de Gruyter.

Knarr, Jack. 2004. "Palmer Makes Push for Immigrants." *The Trentonian,* December 23, 2004, p. 3.

Kosic, Ankica, Arie W. Kruglanski, Antonio Pierro, and Lucia Mannetti. 2004. "The Social Cognition of Immigrants' Acculturation: Effects of the Need for Closure and the Reference Group at Entry." *Journal of Personality and Social Psychology* 86(6): 796–813.

Kruglanski, Arie W. 1989. *Lay Epistemics and Human Knowledge: Cognitive and Motivational Bases.* New York: Plenum.

Kurien, Prema. 1999. "Gendered Ethnicity: Creating a Hindu Indian Identity in the United States." *American Behavioral Scientist* 42(4): 648–70.

LaFromboise, Teresa, Hardin L. K. Coleman, and Jenifer Gerton. 1993. "Psychological Impact of Biculturalism: Evidence and theory." *Psychological Bulletin* 114(3): 395–412.

LaLonde, Richard N., and James E. Cameron. 1993. "An Intergroup Perspective on Immigrant Acculturation with a Focus on Collective Strategies." *International Journal of Psychology* 28(1): 57–74.

Lambert, Bruce. 2000. "40 Percent in New York Born Abroad." *New York Times,* July 24, 2000, p. B1, 5.

Lapinski, John S., Pia Peltola, Greg Shaw, and Alan Yang. 1997. "Trends: Immigrants and Immigration." *Public Opinion Quarterly* 61(2): 356–83.

Leslie, Lisa M., Vanessa S. Constantine, Susan T. Fiske, Yarrow Duncan, and Mahzarin Banaji. 2005. "The Princeton Quartet: Public versus Private Stereotype Change." Unpublished paper. Princeton University.

Levine, Robert A., and Donald T. Campbell. 1972. *Ethnocentrism: Theories of Conflict, Ethnic Attitudes, and Group Behavior.* New York: John Wiley & Sons.

Levitt, Peggy, and Mary C. Waters. 2002. "Introduction." In *The Changing Face of Home: The Transnational Lives of the Second Generation,* edited by Peggy Levitt and Mary C. Waters. New York: Russell Sage Foundation.

Levy, Andrea. 2004. *Small Island.* New York: Picador.

Liebkind, Karmela. 1996a. "Acculturation and Stress: Vietnamese Refugees in Finland." *Journal of Cross-Cultural Psychology* 27(2): 161–80.

———. 1996b. "Vietnamese Refugees in Finland: Changing Cultural Identity." In *Changing European Identities,* edited by Glynis M. Breakwell and Evantha Lyons. Oxford: Butterworth Heinemann.

Liebkind, Karmela, Inga Jasinskaja-Lahti, Gabriel Horenczyk, and Paul Schmitz. 2002. "The Interactive Nature of Acculturation: Perceived Discrimination, Acculturation Attitudes and Stress Among Young Ethnic Repatriates in Finland, Israel and Germany." Paper presented at General Meeting of the European Association of Experimental Social Psychology. San Sebastian (June 2002).

Lin, Monica H., Virginia S. Y. Kwan, Anna Cheung, and Susan Fiske. 2005. "Stereotype Content Model Explains Prejudice for an Envied Outgroup: Scale of Anti-Asian American Stereotypes." *Personality and Social Psychology Bulletin* 31(1): 34–47.

Loewen, James W. 1971. *The Mississippi Chinese: Between Black and White.* Cambridge, Mass.: Harvard University Press.

López, David E. 1999. "Social and Linguistic Aspects of Assimilation Today." In *The Handbook of International Migration: The American Experience,* edited by Charles Hirschman, Philip Kasinitz, and Josh DeWind. New York: Russell Sage Foundation.

Luhtanen, Riia, and Jennifer Crocker. 1992. "A Collective Self-esteem Scale: Self-evaluation of One's Social Identity." *Personality and Social Psychology Bulletin* 18(3): 302–18.

Lyons, Evantha. 1996. "Coping with Social Change: Processes of Social Memory in the Reconstruction of Identities." In *Changing European Identities,* edited by Glynis M. Breakwell and Evantha Lyons. Oxford: Butterworth Heinemann.

Madon, Stephanie, Max Guyll, Kathy Aboufadel, Eulices Monteil, Alison Smith, Polly Palumbo, and Lee Jussim. 2001. "Ethnic and National Stereotypes: The Princeton Trilogy Revisited and Revised." *Personality and Social Psychology Bulletin* 27(8): 996–1010.

Markus, Hazel Rose, and Shinobu Kitayama. 1991. "Culture and the Self: Implications for Cognition, Emotion, and Motivation." *Psychological Review* 98(2): 224–53.

Markus, Hazel Rose, Claude M. Steele, and Dorothy M. Steele. 2001. "Colorblindness as a Barrier to Inclusion: Assimilation and Nonimmigrant Minorities." *Daedalus* 129(4): 233–59.

Marrow, Helen. 2003. "To Be or Not to Be (Hispanic or Latino): Brazilian Racial and Ethnic Identity in the United States." *Ethnicities* 3(4): 427–64.

Marshall, Paule. 1959/1981. *Brown Girl, Brownstones*. New York: Feminist Press.

Massey, Douglas S. 1985. "Ethnic Residential Segregation: A Theoretical Synthesis and Empirical Review." *Sociology and Social Research* 69(3): 315–50.

———. 1993. "Latinos, Poverty, and the Underclass: A New Agenda for Research." *Hispanic Journal of Behavioral Sciences* 15(4): 449–75.

———. 1995. "The New Immigration and Ethnicity in the United States." *Population and Development Review* 21(3): 631–52.

———. 1998. *Worlds in Motion: Understanding International Migration at the End of the Millennium*. New York: Oxford University Press.

———. 1999. "Why Does Immigration Occur? A Theoretical Synthesis." In *The Handbook of International Migration: The American Experience*, edited by Charles Hirschman, Philip Kasinitz, and Josh DeWind. New York: Russell Sage Foundation.

Massey, Douglas S., and Nancy A. Denton. 1993. *American Apartheid: Segregation and the Making of the Underclass*. Cambridge, Mass.: Harvard University Press.

Massey, Douglas S., Jorge Durand, and Nolan J. Malone. 2002. *Beyond Smoke and Mirrors: Mexican Immigration in an Era of Economic Integration*. New York: Russell Sage Foundation.

Massey, Douglas S., and Nolan Malone. 2002. "Pathways to Legal Immigration." *Population Research and Policy Review* 21(6): 473–504.

McCharen, Jennifer. 2004. Unpublished paper. Sarah Lawrence College.

McLellan, Janet, and Anthony H. Richmond. 1994. "Multiculturalism in Crisis: A Postmodern Perspective on Canada." *Ethnic and Racial Studies* 17(4): 662–83.

Meiklejohn, Susan Turner. 2004. "Creating Community in Sunnyside: Understanding Affiliative Ties between Immigrants and Their Neighbors in a Highly Multi-ethnic Neighborhood." Proposal to Russell Sage Foundation, August 15, 2004.

Mendoza-Denton, Rodolfo, Geraldine Downey, Valerie J. Purdie, Angelina Davis, and Janina Pietrzak. 2002. "Sensitivity to Status-based Rejection: Implications for African American students' College Experience." *Journal of Personality and Social Psychology* 83(4): 896–918.

Meyers, Eytan. 2004. *International Immigration Policy: A Theoretical and Comparative Analysis*. New York: Palgrave Macmillan.

Mizrahi, Kim. 2005. *Americans' Attitudes Toward Immigration and Immigrants*. Ph. D. diss. CUNY Graduate Center.

Model, Suzanne. 1995. "West Indian Prosperity: Fact or Fiction?" *Social Problems* 42(4): 535–53.

———. 2001. "Where New York's West Indians Work." In *Islands in the City: West Indian Migration to New York,* edited by Nancy Foner. Berkeley: University of California Press.

Morawska, Ewa. 2003. "Disciplinary Agendas and Analytic Strategies of Research on Immigration and Transnationalism: Challenges of Interdisciplinary Knowledge." *International Migration Review* 37(3): 611–40.

———. 2004. "Exploring Diversity in Immigrant Assimilation and Transnationalism: Poles and Russian Jews in Philadelphia." *International Migration Review* 38(4): 1372–1412.

Moscovici, Serge. 1976. *La Psychonalyse Son Image et Son Public,* 2nd ed. Paris: Presses Universitaires de France.

———. 1988. "Notes Toward a Description of Social Representations." *European Journal of Social Psychology* 18(3): 211–50.

Mukherjee, Bharati. 1999. "Imagining Homelands." In *Letters of Transit: Reflections on Exile, Identity, Language, and Loss,* edited by André Aciman. New York: The New Press.

Mullen, Brian. 1991. "Group Composition, Salience, and Cognitive Representations: The Phenomenology of Being in a Group." *Journal of Experimental Social Psychology* 27(4): 297–323.

———. 2001. "Ethnophaulisms for Ethnic Immigrant Groups." *Journal of Social Issues* 57(3): 457–75.

Murchison, Carl, ed. 1935. *A Handbook of Social Psychology,* vol. 1. New York: Russell & Russell.

Murphy, Eleanor J., and Ramaswami Mahalingam. 2003. "Perceived Congruence Between Expectations and Outcomes: Implications for Mental Health Among Caribbean Immigrants." Unpublished paper. University of Michigan, Ann Arbor.

Navarro, Mireya. 2003. "Going Beyond Black and White, Hispanics in Census Pick 'Other.' " *The New York Times,* November 9, p. 1, 2.

Nesdale, Drew, and Anita S. Mak. 2000. "Immigrant Acculturation Attitudes and Host Country Identification." *Journal of Community and Applied Social Psychology* 10(6): 483–95.

Nieves, Evelyn. 2001. "Past Recalled for Japanese-Americans." *The New York Times,* September 28, 2001, p. A26, 4.

Nisbett, Richard. 2003. *The Geography of Thought: How Asians and Westerners Think Differently . . . and Why.* New York: Simon & Schuster.

No, Sun, and Ying-yi Hong. 2004. "Negotiating Bicultural Identity: Contrast and Assimilation Effects in Cultural Frame Switching." Poster presented at the 2004 annual meeting of the Society for Personality and Social Psychology. Austin, Texas (January, 2004).

Nugent, Walter. 1992. *Crossings: The Great Transatlantic Migrations, 1870–1914.* Bloomington: Indiana University Press.

Nunez, Elizabeth. 1998. *Beyond the Limbo Silence.* New York: Ballantine Books.

O'Brien, Gerald. 2003. "Indigestible Food, Conquering Hordes, and Waste Materials: Metaphors of Immigrants and the Early Immigration Restriction Debate in the United States." *Metaphor and Symbol* 18(1): 33–47.

Ogbu, John. 1978. *Minority Education and Caste: The American System in Cross-cultural Perspective.* New York: Academic Press.

Okamoto, Dina. 2005. "Panethnicity in Asian Organizations." Paper presented to the CUNY Graduate Center Immigration Series Lectures. New York (April 4, 2005).

Olick, Jeffrey K., and Joyce Robbins. 1998. "Social Memory Studies: From 'Collective Memory' to the Historical Sociology of Mnemonic Practices." *Annual Review of Sociology* 24(1): 105–40.

Park, Robert E. 1928. "Human Migration and the Marginal Man." *American Journal of Sociology* 33(6): 881–93.

———. 1930. "Assimilation, social." In *Encyclopedia of the Social Sciences*, vol. 2, edited by Edwin R. A. Seligman and Alvin Johnson. New York: Macmillan.

Park, Robert E., and Ernest W. Burgess. 1921/1969. *Introduction to the Science of Sociology.* Chicago: University of Chicago Press.

Park, Robert E., and Herbert A. Miller. 1921. *Old World Traits Transplanted.* New York: Harper Bros.

Pérez, Lisandro. 1996. "The Households of Children of Immigrants in South Florida: An Exploratory Study of Extended Family Arrangements." In *The New Second Generation*, edited by Alejandro Portes. New York: Russell Sage Foundation.

Perkins, Krystal. 2006. "Diasporic Representations of African American: Exploring the Contours of Identity." Unpublished paper. Graduate Center of the City University of New York.

Perlez, Jane. 2002. "Deep Fears Behind Australia's Immigration Policy." *The New York Times*, May 8, 2002, p. A3, 1.

Pessar, Patricia R. 1999. "The Role of Gender, Households, and Social Networks in the Migration Process: A Review and Appraisal." In *The Handbook of International Migration: The American Experience*, edited by Charles Hirschman, Philip Kasinitz, and Josh DeWind. New York: Russell Sage Foundation.

———. 2003. "Engendering Migration Studies: The Case of New Immigrants in the United States." In *Gender and U.S. Immigration: Contemporary Trends*, edited by Pierrette Hondagneu-Sotelo. Berkeley: University of California Press.

Pettigrew, Thomas F. 1997. "Personality and Social Structure: Social Psychological Contributions." In *Handbook of Personality Psychology*, edited by Robert Hogan, John Johnson, and Stephen Briggs. New York: Academic Press.

———. 1998. "Reactions Toward the New Minorities of Western Europe." *Annual Review of Sociology* 24: 77–103.

Pettigrew, Thomas F., and Roel W. Meertens. 1995. "Subtle and Blatant Prejudice in Western Europe." *European Journal of Social Psychology* 25(1): 57–75.

Pettigrew, Thomas F., and Linda R. Tropp. 2000. "Does Intergroup Contact Reduce Prejudice? Recent Meta-analytic Findings." In *Reducing Prejudice and Discrimination,* edited by Stuart Oskamp. Mahwah, N.J.: Lawrence Erlbaum.

———. 2005. "A Meta-Analytic Test of Intergroup Contact Theory." *Psychological Science* 16(12): 951–1023.

Pettigrew, Thomas F., Ulrich Wagner, Oliver Christ, and Jost Stellmacher. 2005. "Direct and Indirect Intergroup Contact Effects on Prejudice." Unpublished paper. University of California, Santa Cruz.

Phalet, Karen, and Edwin Poppe. 1997. "Competence and Morality Dimensions of National and Ethnic Stereotypes: A Study in Six Eastern-European Countries." *European Journal of Social Psychology* 27(6): 703–23.

Philogène, Gina. 1999. *From Black to African American: A New Social Representation.* Westport, Conn.: Greenwood-Praeger.

Phinney, Jean S., and Linda L. Alipuria. Forthcoming. "Multiple Social Categorization and Identity Among Multiracial, Multiethnic, and Multicultural Individuals: Processes and Implications." In *Multiple Social Categorization: Processes, Models and Applications,* edited by R. J. Crisp and Miles Hewstone. Hove, E. Sussex: Psychology Press (Taylor & Francis).

Phinney, Jean S., and Mona Devich-Navarro. 1997. "Variations in Bicultural Identification Among African American and Mexican American Adolescents." *Journal of Research on Adolescence* 7(1): 3–32.

Pinel, Elizabeth C. 1999. "Stigma Consciousness: The Psychological Legacy of Social Stereotypes." *Journal of Personality and Social Psychology* 76(1): 114–28.

Piontkowski, Ursula, Arnd Florack, Paul Hoelker, and Peter Obdrzalek. 2000. "Predicting Acculturation Attitudes of Dominant and Non-dominant groups." *International Journal of Intercultural Relations* 24(1): 1–26

Poppe, Edwin, and Hub Linssen. 1999. "In-group Favoritism and the Reflection of Realistic Dimensions of Difference between National States in Central and Eastern European Nationality Stereotypes." *British Journal of Social Psychology* 38(1): 85–102.

Porter, Eduardo. 2005. "Illegal Immigrants Are Bolstering Social Security with Billions." *The New York Times,* April 5, 2005, p. A1, C7.

Portes, Alejandro, ed. 1996. *The New Second Generation.* New York: Russell Sage Foundation.

———. 1998. "From South of the Border: Hispanic Minorities in the United States." In *The Immigration Reader,* edited by David Jacobson. Malden, Mass.: Blackwell Publishing.

Portes, Alejandro, and Rubén G. Rumbaut. 1996. *Immigrant America.* Berkeley: University of California Press.

———. 2001. *Legacies: The Story of the Immigrant Second Generation.* Berkeley and New York: University of California Press and Russell Sage Foundation.

Portes, Alejandro, and Richard Schauffler. 1996. "Language and the Second Generation: Bilingualism Yesterday and Today." In *The New Second Generation,* edited by Alejandro Portes. New York: Russell Sage Foundation.

Portes, Alejandro, and Min Zhou. 1993. "The New Second Generation: Segmented Assimilation and Its Variants among Post-1965 Immigrant Youth." *Annals of the American Academy of Political and Social Science* 530(1): 74–96.

Postmes, Tom, and Nyla Branscombe. 2002. "Influence of Long-Term Racial Environmental Composition on Subjective Well-Being in African Americans." *Journal of Personality and Social Psychology* 83(3): 735–51.

Pratto, Felicia, and Anthony F. Lemieux. 2001. "The Psychological Ambiguity of Immigration and Its Implications for Promoting Immigration Policy." *Journal of Social Issues* 57(3): 413–30.

Rahman, Anika. 2001. "Fear in the Open City." *New York Times,* September 19, 2001, p. A27, 2.

Raijman, Rebeca, and Marta Tienda. 1999. "Immigrants' Socioeconomic Progress Post-1965: Forging Mobility or Survival?" In *The Handbook of International Migration: The American Experience,* edited by Charles Hirschman, Philip Kasinitz, and Josh DeWind. New York: Russell Sage Foundation.

Reicher, Stephen, and Nick Hopkins. 2001. *Self and Nation: Categorization, Contestation and Mobilization.* London: Sage Publications.

Reid, I. D. A. 1939. *The Negro Immigrant: His Background, Characteristics and Social Adjustment, 1899–1937.* New York: Columbia University Press.

Reitz, Jeffrey G. 2001. "Immigrant Success in the Knowledge Economy: Institutional Change and the Immigrant Experience in Canada, 1970–1995." *Journal of Social Issues* 57(3): 579–613.

Reitz, Jeffrey G., and Raymond Breton. 1994. *The Illusion of Difference: Realities of Ethnicity in Canada and the United States.* Ottawa: C. D. Howe Institute.

Roback, Abraham A. 1944. *A Dictionary of International Slurs.* Cambridge, Mass.: Sci-Art Publishers.

Roberts, Sam. 2005. "More Africans Enter U.S. Than in Days of Slavery." *The New York Times,* February 21, 2005, p. A1, B4.

Roccas, Sonia, Gabriel Horenczyk, and Shalom H. Schwartz. 2000. "Acculturation Discrepancies and Well-Being: The Moderating Role of Conformity." *European Journal of Social Psychology* 30(3): 323–34.

Rodriguez, Gregory. 2001. "Identify Yourself." *The New York Times,* September 23.

Rodriguez, Richard. 1982. *Hunger of Memory.* New York: Bantam Books.

Rogers, Reuel. 2001. " 'Black Like Who?' Afro-Caribbean Immigrants, African Americans, and the Politics of Group Identity." In *Islands in the City: West Indian Migration to New York,* edited by Nancy Foner. Berkeley: University of California Press.

Rosenbloom, Susan Rakosi, and Niobe Way. 2004. "Experiences of Discrimination among African American, Asian American, and Latino Adolescents in an Urban High School." *Youth & Society* 35(4): 420–51.

Rosenzweig, Roy, and David Thelen. 1998. *The Presence of the Past: Popular Uses of History in American Life.* New York: Columbia University Press.

Rudmin, Floyd W. 2003. "Critical History of the Acculturation Psychology of Assimilation, Separation, Integration, and Marginalization." *Review of General Psychology* 7(1): 3–37.

Ruiz-Navarro, Patricia. 2004. "Mexican Immigrants' Activism across Borders: Transforming Nations, Transforming Institutions." Presented at meeting of the Society for the Psychological Study of Social Issues, Washington, D.C. (June 2004).

———. 2005. "Guadalupaño Identity: Religious Practices and Discourses of Mexican Immigrants." Unpublished paper. City University of New York Graduate Center.

Rumbaut, Rubén G. 1976. "The One-and-a-half Generation: Crisis, Commitment, Identity." In *The Dispossessed: An Anatomy of Exile,* edited by Peter I. Rose. Amherst: University of Massachusetts Press.

———. 1999. "Assimilation and its Discontents: Ironies and Paradoxes." In *The Handbook of International Migration: The American Experience,* edited by Charles Hirschman, Philip Kasinitz, and Josh DeWind. New York: Russell Sage Foundation.

———. 2002. "Severed or Sustained Attachments? Language, Identity, and Imagined Communities in the Post-Immigrant Generation." In *The Changing Face of Home: The Transnational Lives of the Second Generation,* edited by Peggy Levitt and Mary C. Waters. New York: Russell Sage Foundation.

———. 2003. "Conceptual and Methodological Problems in the Study of the 'Immigrant Second Generation' in the United States." Paper prepared for the conference on Conceptual and Methodological Developments in the Study of International Migration. Princeton University (May 23–24, 2003).

———. 2004. "Ages, Life Stages, and Generational Cohorts: Decomposing the Immigrant First and Second Generations in the United States." *International Migration Review* 38(3): 1160–1205.

Rumbaut, Rubén G., and Alejandro Portes, eds. 2001. *Ethnicities: Children of Immigrants in America.* Berkeley and Los Angeles: University of California Press.

Rusk, Dean. 1965. "Testimony before the Subcommittee on Immigration and Naturalization of the Committee on the Judiciary, U.S. Senate, February 24, 1965." *Congressional Digest* 44(5)(May): 142–46.

Saenz, Rogelio. 2004. "Latinos and the Changing Face of America." *The American People: Census 2000.* New York and Washington: Russell Sage Foundation and Population Reference Bureau.

Sanchez, George J. 2000. "Race and Immigration History." In *Immigration Research for a New Century,* edited by Nancy Foner, Rubén G. Rumbaut, and Stephen J. Gold. New York: Russell Sage Foundation.

Sandberg, Neil. 1973. *Ethnic Identity and Assimilation: The Polish Community.* New York: Praeger.

Schaller, Mark, Lucian Gideon Conway III, and Tracy L. Tanchuk. 2002. "Selective Pressures on the Once and Future Contents of Ethnic Stereotypes: Effects of the Communicability of Traits." *Journal of Personality and Social Psychology* 82(6): 861–77.

Schermerhorn, Richard A. 1978. *Comparative Ethnic Relations: A Framework for Theory and Research*. Chicago: University of Chicago Press.

Schlesinger, Arthur M. 1959. "America's Influence: Our Ten Contributions to Civilization." *Atlantic Monthly* 203 (March).

Sears, David O., Jack Citrin, Sharmaine V. Cheleden, and Colette van Laar. 1999. "Cultural Diversity and Multicultural Politics: Is Ethnic Balkanization Psychologically Inevitable?" In *Cultural Divides: Understanding and Overcoming Group Conflict*, edited by Deborah A. Prentice and Dale T. Miller. New York: Russell Sage Foundation.

Sears, David O., Mingying Fu, P. J. Henry, and Kerra Bui. 2003. "The Origins and Persistence of Ethnic Identity Among the 'New Immigrant' Groups." *Social Psychology Quarterly* 66(4): 419–37.

Sellers, Robert M., Stephanie A. J. Rowley, Tabbye M. Chavous, Nicole J. Shelton, and Mia A. Smith. 1997. "Multidimensional Inventory of Black Identity: A Preliminary Investigation of Reliability and Construct Validity." *Journal of Personality and Social Psychology* 73(4): 805–18.

Sellers, Robert M., Mia A. Smith, Nicole J. Shelton, Stephanie A. J. Rowley, and Tabbye M. Chavous. 1998. "Multidimensional Model of Racial Identity: A Reconceptualization of African American Racial Identity." *Personality and Social Psychology Review* 2(1): 18–39.

Shalamova, Shifra. 2004. "The Train with Stops around the World." *New York Times*, November 21, 2004, section 14, p. 10.

Shanahan, Suzanne, and Susan Olzak. 2002. "Immigration and Conflict in the United States." In *Mass Migration to the United States*, edited by Pyong Gap Min. Walnut Creek, Calif.: Alta Mira Press.

Shorris, Earl. 1992. *Latinos: A Biography of a People*. New York: W. W. Norton.

Shweder, Richard A., Martha Minow, and Hazel Rose Markus. 2000. "The End of Tolerance: Engaging Cultural Differences." *Daedalus* 129(4): v–ix.

Sidanius, Jim, and Felicia Pratto. 1999. *Social Dominance: An Intergroup Theory of Social Hierarchy and Oppression*. Cambridge: Cambridge University Press.

Sigelman, Lee, and Steven A. Tuch. 1997. "Metastereotypes: Blacks' Perceptions of Whites' Stereotypes of Blacks." *Public Opinion Quarterly* 61(1): 87–101.

Simon, Rita J. 1985. *Public Opinion and the Immigrant: Print Media Coverage, 1880–1980*. Lexington, Mass.: Lexington Books.

———. 1987. "Immigration and American Attitudes." *Public Opinion* 10(2): 47–50.

Singer, Audrey. 2004. "The Rise of New Immigrant Gateways." Paper presented at The Brookings Institution conference, The Living Cities Census Series. Washington, D.C. (February 2004).

———. 2005. "Breaking Ground: Examining the Causes of Immigrant Growth in New Metropolitan Destinations." Paper presented at Russell Sage Foundation conference, Immigration to the United States: New Sources and Destinations. New York (February 3–4, 2005).

Sládková, Jana. 2005. "Narratives of Migration in Copán Ruinas, Honduras." Paper presented at International Society for Cultural and Activity Research. Seville, Spain (September 2, 2005).

Smith, Allison G., Abigail J. Stewart, and David G. Winter. 2004. "Close Encounters with the Midwest: Forming Identity in a Bicultural Context." *Political Psychology* 2(4): 611–41.

Smith, Craig S. 2005. "France Faces a Colonial Legacy: What Makes Someone French?" *The New York Times,* November 11, 2005, p. A1.

Smith, Robert C. 1998. "Transnational Localities: Community, Technology, and the Politics of Membership Within the Context of Mexico and U.S. Migration." In *Transnationalism From Below,* edited by Michael Peter Smith and Luis Eduardo Guarnizo. New Brunswick, N.J.: Transaction Publishers.

Smith, Tom W. 2000. *Taking America's Pulse II.* New York: National Conference for Community and Justice.

Statistics Canada. 1999. 1996 Public Use Microdata File on Individuals: User Documentation. Ottawa: Statistics Canada.

Steele, Claude M. 1997. "A Threat in the Air: How Stereotypes Shape Intellectual Identity and Performance." *American Psychologist* 52(6): 613–29.

Steele, Claude M., and Joshua Aronson. 1995. "Stereotype Threat and the Intellectual Test Performance of African-Americans." *Journal of Personality and Social Psychology* 69(5): 797–811.

Steele, Claude M., Steven J. Spencer, and Joshua Aronson. 2002. "Contending with Group Image: The Psychology of Stereotype and Social Identity Threat." *Advances in Experimental Social Psychology* 34: 379–440.

Stephan, Walter G., Oscar Ybarra, Carmen Martinez Martinez, Joseph Schwarzwals, and Michal Tur-Kaspa. 1998. "Prejudice Towards Immigrants in Spain and Israel: An Integrated Threat Theory Analysis." *Journal of Cross-Cultural Psychology* 29(4): 559–76.

Stoller, Elanor Palo. 1996. "Sauna, Sisu and Sibelius: Ethnic Identity among Finnish Americans." *Sociological Quarterly* 37(1): 145–77.

Stürmer, Stefan, and Bernd Simon. 2004. "Collective Action: Towards a Dual-Pathway Model." In *European Review of Social Psychology,* vol. 15, edited by Wolfgang Stroebe and Miles Hewstone. East Sussex, UK: Psychology Press.

Suárez-Orozco, Marcelo M. 2002. "Everything You Ever Wanted to Know About Assimilation but Were Afraid to Ask." In *Engaging Cultural Differences: The Multicultural Challenge in Liberal Democracies,* edited by Richard A. Shweder, Martha Minow, and Hazel Rose Markus. New York: Russell Sage Foundation.

Suárez-Orozco, Carolo, and Marcelo M. Suárez-Orozco. 1995. *Transformations: Immigration, Family Life, and Achievement Motivation Among Latino Adolescents*. Stanford, Calif.: Stanford University Press.

———. 2001. *Children of Immigration*. Cambridge, Mass.: Harvard University Press.

Swarns, Rachel L. 2004. "African-American Becomes a Term for Debate." *The New York Times*, August 29, 2004, p. A1, 20.

Tajfel, Henri. 1981. *Human Groups and Social Categories: Studies in Social Psychology*. Cambridge: Cambridge University Press.

Tartakovsky, Eugene, and Shalom H. Schwartz. 2001. "Motivation for Emigration, Values, Well-Being, and Identification Among Young Russian Jews." *International Journal of Psychology* 36(2): 88–99.

Telles, Edward E. 2004. *Race in Another America: The Significance of Skin Color in Brazil*. Princeton, N.J.: Princeton University Press.

Thomas, Teceta E. R. 2003. "Black Americans and Black Immigrants: The Influence of Ethnic Identification on Perceptions of Race, Prejudice, and Individual Success in American Society." Unpublished paper. Stanford University.

———. 2004. "The Meaning of Blackness: Stereotypes About Immigrant and American Blacks." Unpublished paper. City University of New York Graduate Center.

Thomas, William I., and Florian Znaniecki. 1918/1920. *The Polish Peasant in Europe and America*, 5 vols. Chicago: University of Chicago Press.

Thompson, Paul, and Elaine Bauer. 2003. "Evolving Jamaican Migrant Identities: Contrasts between Britain, Canada and the USA." *Community, Work & Family* 6(1): 89–102.

Thornton, Michael C., and Yuko Mizuno. 1999. "Economic Well-Being and Black Adult Feelings toward Immigrants and Whites, 1984." *Journal of Black Studies* 30(1): 15–44.

Timotijevic, Lada, and Glynis M. Breakwell. 2000. "Migration and Threat to Identity." *Journal of Community & Applied Social Psychology* 10(5): 355–72.

Toribio, Almeida Jacqueline. 2004. "Linguistic Displays of Identity Among Dominicans in National and Diasporic Settings." In *English and Ethnicity*, edited by Catherine Evans Davis and Janina Brutt-Griffler. New York: Palgrave Macmillan.

Tropp, Linda R., and Stephen C. Wright. 1999. "Ingroup Identification and Relative Deprivation: An Examination Across Multiple Social Comparisons." *European Journal of Social Psychology* 29(5/6): 707–24.

Turner, John C. 1999. "Some Current Issues in Research on Social Identity and Self-Categorization Theories." In *Social Identity: Context, Commitment, Content*, edited by Naomi Ellemers, Russell Spears, and Bertjan Doosje. Oxford: Blackwell Publishing.

Turner, John C., Michael A. Hogg, Penelope J. Oakes, Stephen D. Reicher, and Margaret S. Wetherell. 1987. *Rediscovering the Social Group: A Self-Categorization Theory*. Oxford: Blackwell Publishing.

Udelson, Joseph H. 1990. *Dreamer of the Ghetto: The Life and Works of Israel Zangwill.* Tuscaloosa: University of Alabama Press.

United Nations Secretariat. 2004. *A Social Perspective on International Migration: Background Note Prepared by the Secretariat.* Prepared for 42nd session of the Commission for Social Development, New York (February 4–13, 2004).

Upegui-Hernandez, Debora. 2005. "Transnationalism: A Challenge for the Psychological Study of Migration." Unpublished paper. City University of New York Graduate Center.

U.S. Census Bureau. 2000. Census 2000 Gateway. Available at: www.census.gov/main/www/cen2000.html.

———. 2001. *Profile of the Foreign-Born Population in the United States: 2000.* December. Washington: U.S. Department of Commerce.

Vandiver, Beverly J., William E. Cross Jr., Frank C. Worrell, and Peony E. Fhagen-Smith. 2002. "Validating the Cross Racial Identity Scale." *Journal of Counseling Psychology* 49(1): 71–85.

Van Oudenhoven, Jan Pieter, Karen S. Prins, and Bram P. Buunk. 1998. "Attitudes of Minority and Majority Members towards Adaptation of Immigrants." *European Journal of Social Psychology* 28(6): 995–1013.

Verkuyten, Maykel. 2005. *The Social Psychology of Ethnic Identity.* New York: Psychology Press.

Verkuyten, Maykel, and Angela de Wolf. 2002a. "Being, Feeling and Doing: Discourses and Ethnic Self-Definitions Among Minority Group Members." *Culture & Psychology* 8(4): 371–99.

———. 2002b. "Ethnic Minority Identity and Group Context: Self-Descriptions, Acculturation Attitudes and Group Evaluations in an Intra- and Intergroup Situation." *European Journal of Social Psychology* 32(6): 781–800.

Vickerman, Milton. 1999. *Crosscurrents: West Indian Immigrants and Race.* New York: Oxford University Press.

———. 2001. "Tweaking a Monolith: The West Indian Immigrant Encounter with 'Blackness.' " In *Islands in the City: West Indian Migration to New York,* edited by Nancy Foner. Berkeley: University of California Press.

———. 2002. "Second-Generation West Indian Transnationalism." In *The Changing Face of Home: The Transnational Lives of the Second Generation,* edited by Peggy Levitt and Mary C. Waters. New York: Russell Sage Foundation.

Waldinger, Roger. 2001. "Up from Poverty? 'Race,' Immigration, and the Fates of Low-Skilled Workers." In *Strangers at the Gates: New Immigrants in Urban America,* edited by Roger Waldinger. Berkeley: University of California Press.

Waldinger, Roger, and Claudia Der-Martirosian. 2001. "The Immigrant Niche: Pervasive, Persistent, Diverse." In *Strangers at the Gates: New Immigrants in Urban America,* edited by Roger Waldinger. Berkeley: University of California Press.

Waldinger, Roger, and Greta Gilbertson. 1994. "Immigrants' Progress: Ethnic and Gender Differences among U.S. Immigrants in the 1980s." *Sociological Perspectives* 37(3): 431–44.

Waldinger, Roger, and Jennifer Lee. 2001. "New Immigrants in Urban America." In *Strangers at the Gates: New Immigrants in Urban* America, edited by Roger Waldinger. Berkeley: University of California Press.

Waters, Mary C. 1990. *Ethnic Options: Choosing Identities in America.* Berkeley: University of California Press.

———. 1994. "Ethnic and Racial Identities of Second-Generation Black Immigrants in New York City." *International Migration Review* 28(4): 795–820.

———. 1999a. *Black Identities: West Indian Immigrant Dreams and American Realities.* Cambridge, Mass., and New York: Harvard University Press and Russell Sage Foundation.

———. 1999b. "West Indians and African Americans at Work: Structural Differences and Cultural Stereotypes." In *Immigration and Opportunity,* edited by Frank Bean and Stephanie Bell-Rose. New York: Russell Sage Foundation.

———. 2001. "Growing Up West Indian and African American: Gender and Class Differences in the Second Generation." In *Islands in the City: West Indian Migration to New York,* edited by Nancy Foner. Berkeley: University of California Press.

Watkins-Owens, Irma. 2001. "Early-Twentieth-Century Caribbean Women: Migration and Social Networks in New York City." In *Islands in the City: West Indian Migration to New York,* edited by Nancy Foner. Berkeley: University of California Press.

Weber, Max. 1921/1968. *Economy and Society: An Outline of Interpretive Sociology,* edited by Guenther Roth and Claus Wittich, translated by Ephraim Fischoff. New York: Bedminster Press.

Wiley, Shaun M. 2005. " 'Proving Yourself in Both Worlds': A Study of Bicultural Identification with Mexican and Dominican Immigrants." Unpublished paper. City University of New York Graduate Center.

Wiley, Shaun, Krystal Perkins, and Kay Deaux. 2006. "Through the Looking Glass: Ethnic and Generational Patterns of Immigrant Identity." Unpublished paper. City University of New York.

Wilson, Kenneth, and Alejandro Portes. 1980. "Immigrant Enclaves: An Analysis of the Labor Market Experiences of Cubans in Miami." *American Journal of Sociology* 86(2): 295–319.

Winnicott, Donald W. 1971. *Playing and Reality.* Middlesex, UK: Penguin Books.

Woodsworth, J. S. 1909/1972. *Strangers within Our Gates.* Toronto: University of Toronto Press.

Yankelovich Partners. 1993. Survey for *Time* magazine, September 8–9, 1993.

Yu, Henry. 2001. *Thinking Orientals: Migration, Contact, and Exoticism in Modern America.* Oxford: Oxford University Press.

Xie, Yu and Kimberly A. Goyette. 2004. *The American People Census 2000. A Demographic Portrait of Asian Americans.* New York and Washington: Russell Sage Foundation and Population Reference Bureau.

Zagefka, Hanna, and Rupert Brown. 2002. "The Relationship Between Accultura-tion Strategies, Relative Fit and Intergroup Relations: Immigrant-Majority Rela-tions in Germany." *European Journal of Social Psychology* 32(2): 171–88.

Zangwill, Israel. 1909/1994. *The Melting Pot: Drama in Four Acts.* New York: Ayer Co.

Zárate, Michael A., Berenice Garcia, Azenett A. Garza, and Robert T. Hitlan. 2004. "Cultural Threat and Perceived Realistic Group Conflict as Dual Predictors of Prejudice." *Journal of Experimental Social Psychology* 40(1): 99–105.

Zhou, Min. 1999. "Segmented Assimilation: Issues, Controversies, and Recent Research on the New Second Generation." In *The Handbook of International Migra-tion: The American Experience,* edited by Charles Hirschman, Philip Kasinitz, and Josh DeWind. New York: Russell Sage Foundation.

Zhou, Min, and Carl L. Bankston III. 1998. *Growing Up American: How Vietnamese Children Adapt to Life in the United States.* New York: Russell Sage Foundation.

Zick, Andreas, Ulrich Wagner, Rolf van Dick, and Thomas Petzel. 2001. "Accultur-ation and Prejudice in Germany: Majority and Minority Perspectives." *Journal of Social Issues* 57(3): 541–57.

Index

Boldface numbers refer to figures and tables.